Stories

WITHIN

Stories

Stories

WITHIN

Stories

FROM THE JEWISH ORAL TRADITION

RETOLD BY

Peninnah Schram

JASON ARONSON INC.

Northvale, New Jersey
Jerusalem

This book was set in 11 pt. ITC Galliard by Alabama Book Composition of Deatsville, AL, and printed and bound by Book-Mart Press, Inc. of North Bergen, NJ.

Copyright © 2000 by Peninnah Schram

10 9 8 7 6 5 4 3 2 1

Library of Congress Cataloging-in-Publication Data

Schram, Peninnah.
    Stories within stories : from the Jewish oral tradition /
retold by Peninnah Schram.
        p.   cm.
    Includes bibliographical references.
    ISBN 0-7657-6142-4
    1. Jews—Folklore.   2. Tales.   3. Frame-stories.   I. Title.
GR98 .S33 2000
398.2'089'924—dc21   99-462236

Printed in the United States of America on acid-free paper. For information and catalog, write to Jason Aronson Inc., 230 Livingston Street, Northvale, NJ 07647-1726, or visit our website: www.aronson.com

To my childhood friend, Katherine Peterson Ameika,
who shares
reminiscences of our hometown,
New London, Connecticut,
and treasured memory stories of our parents

Contents

Foreword by Howard Schwartz   xi

Acknowledgments   xv

Preface   xix

Introduction
Apples of Gold in Frames of Silver   1

1   The King Who Loved Stories   30

2   We Never Lose Old Treasures   32

3   The Emperor's Daughter and the King's Son   36

4   The Gates of Tears   49

5   Which Way Should One Look—Up or Down?   54

6   The Most Peculiar Thing in Life   57

7   Friends in Deed   62

8   The Leopard and the Fox   69

9   A Match Made in Heaven   78

10   The Wedding Gifts   82

11   The Fire That Didn't Warm   88

12   The Princess Who Would Not Speak   91

13   The Luck of Faradj, the Rope Maker   101

14   The Broken Betrothal   106

15   A Story of Consolation   111

16   The Golden Buttons   115

17   100 Grams More or Less   119

18   The King's Daughter and the Choice of Her Heart   125

19   According to the Two Witnesses   132

20   The Camel's Wife   137

21   Two Friends   143

22   The Maggid of Dubno   148

23   The Fulfilled Dream   157

24   The Poor People and Their Shares   161

25   The Yemenite King and His Jewish Advisor   165

26   Money Comes and Money Goes But a Skill Stays
     with You Forever   171

27   There Is No Justice in the World   175

28 Can Fate Be Changed? 179

29 The Prince of the East and the Princess of the West 182

30 Queen Hatam and King Tye 190

31 The Twelve Sons of the Emir 208

32 The Lie That Can Stand on Its Own 212

33 The Exchanged Letters 216

34 The Neighbor in Paradise 225

35 Caliph Harun al-Rashid 230

36 Ungrateful Men 244

37 The Jewish Weaver's Wisdom 249

38 A Remembered Story 252

39 The Wonderful Healing Leaves 257

40 The King's Three Questions 263

41 The Emir, the Jewish Advisor, and the Sheep 267

42 Princess Zohara and Prince Ali 280

43 The Tiger and the Son of the Woodcutter 288

44 The Bequest 291

45 The Queen and the Forty Robbers 301

46 Ashmedai's Magic Flute 306

47   The King, Bahlul, and the Clever Maiden   312

48   What Made Rabbi Yitzhak Change His Behavior   318

49   The Indian King and the Jewish Shepherd   323

50   The Horse That Got Stuck in the Mud   327

     Glossary   331

     Bibliography   335

     Index   341

Foreword

by Howard Schwartz

Everyone knows that the greatest story-within-a-story is *The Arabian Nights*, framed with the story of how Scheherazade saved herself from certain death by telling the king a spellbinding tale each night, leaving the story unfinished till the next night, then telling a new one that also remained incomplete. In this way, she saved herself for a thousand and one nights of delectable tales.

Over the centuries there have been a handful of anthologies of Jewish stories that use one story to serve as a framework for all the rest. The oldest of these collections is *The Book of Jubilees*, from the second century B.C.E., in which an angel reveals the history of the world to Moses from creation till his own time. Another such collection is *The Alphabet of Ben Sira*, from the eighth or ninth century, in which Ben Sira tells twenty-two stories to a king, each illustrating an aphorism. A third example is Ibn Zabara's *Sefer Sha'ashuim* (*The Book of Delight*), a collection of tales from the twelfth century, with Greek, Indian, and Arabic influence, that contains stories and proverbs within the framework of a background story. In addition, there are many examples of individual stories with a frame scattered throughout post-biblical Jewish literature.

Peninnah Schram's *Stories within Stories: From the Jewish Oral Tradition* is a great compendium of such stories, a Jewish Arabian Nights, with fifty tales drawn primarily from oral sources. The preeminent source is the Israel Folktale Archives, founded by Professor Dov Noy of Hebrew

University and housed at the University of Haifa. The IFA is a great treasure house of oral tales that to date has collected 20,000 tales in Israel from immigrants of every Jewish ethnic origin. Many of these immigrants, such as Flora Cohen of Egypt, the teller of "The Prince of the East and the Princess of the West," were themselves remarkable storytellers with considerable repertoires.

In researching and retelling the stories in this collection, Peninnah Schram has delved into the wealth of the archives and recovered dozens of unusual stories, every one an example of a story-within-a-story. At the same time these stories have been drawn from other sources, especially some dazzling hasidic ones, which demonstrate that the telling of this type of tale had taken root in hasidic tradition. Not only are there several tales of the Baal Shem Tov, founder of Hasidism, but there are also tales of other great rebbes, including Levi Yitzhak of Berditshev, the Belzer Rebbe, and Rabbi Nachman of Bratslav.

The tales of the Baal Shem Tov, in particular, often depend on the story-within-a-story structure. The Besht, as he is known, was able to discern the history of a person's soul as well as his future destiny. He makes good use of this knowledge in many tales, such as "The Wedding Gifts" and "A Remembered Story," included here.

The stories of the oral tradition are, by their nature, anonymous. All that is generally known, if anything, is the identity of the most recent teller. One major exception is the stories of Rabbi Nachman of Bratslav. Rabbi Nachman began telling tales to his *hasidim* in the last four years of his life, which were recorded by his loyal scribe, Reb Nathan. These are fascinating, complex tales, especially known for having stories-within-stories, and this collection includes one of the best, "The Emperor's Daughter and the King's Son." But Rabbi Nachman was such a compelling figure himself, that, in addition to the stories he told, there are many stories told about him, including "Which Way Should One Look—Up or Down?"

Perhaps the greatest master of the story-within-a-story was the Maggid of Dubno. The Maggid had a story for every occasion, and he would consistently astonish people by telling the right story at precisely the right moment. His stories are almost always allegories whose meaning cannot be missed. In "The Maggid of Dubno" Peninnah

Schram, who adores the Maggid, has strung together five of these exceptionally clever stories.

Where are these peculiar Jewish stories-within-stories found? They were told both in Ashkenazic (Eastern European) and Sephardic (Middle Eastern) traditions, but they were especially popular among the Sephardim. Why is this? Perhaps because of the proximity of the Arab folk culture, or perhaps because elaborate, imaginative tales are a staple of the Middle East. Certainly, many of the stories collected in this anthology reflect the far flung lands out of which they emerged: Not only Eastern Europe, but also Egypt, Yemen, Morocco, Persia (Iran), Turkey, Tunisia, and, of course, Israel.

Just as *The Arabian Nights* grew out of the Arab cultures living in the Middle East, so, too, was found there a rich Jewish oral tradition. The telling of stories and the migration of tales from one land to another was the rule, and the passing on of these stories a powerful family and cultural tradition.

Stories satisfy us because, in having a beginning, a middle, and an end, they feel complete and demonstrate that the events of our lives can be meaningful. What then is the attraction of a story-within-a-story? Sometimes it is the simple delight of creating a connection between two tales. Or it can be the impulse to create a Chinese puzzle, with one tale inside another; or there may be a desire to create a chain story, linking several tales. But in many of these tales, such as "The Broken Betrothal," the frame story and the story-within-a-story are crucially interrelated, and ultimately the two stories become one. Here the fact that a man and his wife are childless turns out to be directly related to the way she treated her former fiance many years before.

One of the most popular uses of telling a tale within a tale is simply to have an excuse to tell other tales. In many of these stories the frame story is often associated with some kind of a test, as in "The Princess Who Would Not Speak." One suitor after another tries to get the princess to speak three times, but each fails, and consequently loses his life. Finally a clever suitor gets her to speak by telling her a tale and then asking her opinion about it. As this story demonstrates, no one can resist giving his or her opinion, not even a mute princess.

As Peninnah Schram ably demonstrates in her extensive Introduction to this collection, stories-within-stories are found in every possible variety: as folktales, fairy tales, fables, allegories, supernatural tales, mystical tales, and even as jokes. The power of these stories is demonstrated again and again, as in "A Match Made in Heaven," in which the philosopher Moses Mendelssohn tells a young woman a story that quickly convinces her to marry him despite his considerable deformities. What story could be so persuasive? Read it and find out.

Many of these stories will seem familiar. Indeed, variants of them are found throughout the world, in Jewish and non-Jewish traditions. But a good part of the pleasure of enjoying a folktale is to be aware of these other versions, for variants are the mother's milk of folktales, and Peninnah Schram has done an excellent job of identifying them in the fascinating notes that follow the stories.

The task of locating these unusual and often far-flung stories required a fine scholar, and the ability to tell them so that they come alive required a masterful storyteller. Peninnah Schram has succeeded on both counts, and the world of books and of storytelling is richer by far.

Acknowledgments

The idea for this book came about in a circuitous way, as an idea within an idea. About seven years ago, Arthur Kurzweil and I began talking about publishing another book of stories. He suggested that I consider collecting stories about stories. On my search for such stories over the next few years, I began to realize how fascinated I was with stories-within-stories. I also realized that I had already included a number of such stories in my four other Jason Aronson books. Since childhood I had loved the parabolic and recursive structures of stories: my parents, Cantor Samuel and Dora Manchester, had often used them for teaching me values, tradition, and behavior lessons with the "Let me give you an example" or "Let me tell you a story" frame drawing me in to listen to a story inside a story. These stories stayed with me.

So I began to research this genre of tales, which has been especially popular in the Middle Eastern and hasidic oral traditions, the former being influenced by the structure and contents of the Arabic literature, and the latter by the mystical concepts of the *Zohar* and the stories that were told by and about the Baal Shem Tov, Rabbi Nachman of Bratslav, and other hasidic masters.

I have been blessed to know such talented and extraordinary people whom I respect enormously, people who love and know story. The completion of this book is greatly due to the ideas and support of these people.

My thanks go, first and foremost, to my dear friend and editor/ publisher Arthur Kurzweil for initiating this project and for his continued encouragement and support. In addition, I thank him for his wisdom in publishing so many other splendid books of stories.

It has been an amazing search for stories, especially through the Israel Folktale Archives, to which we all owe a tremendous debt of gratitude for collecting and classifying over 20,000 tales from the various ethnic communities in Israel. Most of the stories in this book come from these archives and I am especially grateful to those people who told the folktales they recalled and to the collectors of these great treasures. I have noted their names at the top of those stories. I very much appreciate the work of the folklorists whose annotations of the various stories contributed so much to my understanding.

My great thanks and admiration go especially to Dov Noy, the founder of the Israel Folktale Archives, and to Edna Cheichel-Hechal, IFA Coordinator, for their valuable and exceptional contributions to the world of Jewish folklore. This book—and so many others—could not have been published without this treasured archive. I thank Dov for sharing so generously his encyclopedic knowledge about folktales. I am also grateful for all the faxes exchanged between Edna and me regarding specific information related to the tales. I appreciate her tremendous thoughtfulness and time, always willing to suggest stories and making the archives available to me. Both Dov and Edna also took the time to do a critical reading of my Introduction and offered valuable insights and expert suggestions that strengthened the essay.

I want to express my heartfelt thanks to my dear friend Howard Schwartz who continually and enthusiastically encourages me in my work. As a folklorist and author of major collections of Jewish folktales and essays, he serves as a catalyst to inspire me to set higher standards and do more. I also appreciate Howard's reading a draft of the Introduction and adding his sage comments. I feel very honored that he agreed to write the Foreword to this book. His *menschlichkeit* shines through.

I am deeply grateful to my amazing storyteller-friend, Cherie Karo Schwartz, for her constant friendship and exhilarating dialogues about life and story. I have great respect for her wisdom, creative midrashic connections, her artistry, and her generosity of time and *neshama* in brainstorming ideas and dilemmas and sources.

The librarians at Stern College of Yeshiva University have always been cooperative in helping me get resources and sources needed for my research, and always with courtesy, warmth, and professionalism. I especially want to take the opportunity to thank Edith Lubetski, Director of the library, and Elinor Grumet, librarian.

I want to express my great appreciation to folklorist and author Jack Zipes for his critical reading of my Introduction. Because of his expertise in fairy tales and folktales, he made some worthwhile contributions to my introductory essay.

Thanks need to be given to two other very good friends who have helped me with their excellent suggestions throughout the years: Folklorist/storyteller/author, Barbara Rush; and the Director of the 92nd Street Y Library, Steven Siegel.

My thanks to Hanoch Teller for allowing me to retell a story from one of his books, *Soul Survivors.*

For taking time to discuss ideas with me and for his always positive encouragement, my gratitude goes to my beloved cousin, Dr. Murray Simon.

I want particularly to thank my dear friend, storyteller Roslyn Bresnick-Perry, who used her creative writing talent to transform the literal Hebrew translations of enigmatic stanzas in five of the stories into poetic English verses.

Many thanks go to all the people at Jason Aronson who worked on this book, especially Hope Breeman, production editor, and Elisabeth A. Bruno, copy editor. I owe them a grateful thanks for their professional skill and conscientious attention in transforming my typed manuscript into a real book. They are my behind-the-scenes heroes.

With all the input and rereadings of the manuscript by others, I am ultimately responsible for its content. If I made any errors, I apologize and take full responsibility.

I am very grateful to my wonderful son Mordecai Schram for his supportive encouragement, keen wit, and pride in my storytelling endeavors.

I have saved a special thanks for the end—to my beautiful daughter Rebecca Schram Zafrany. Rebecca has been my translator, primarily of the stories from the Israel Folktale Archives that had all been originally transcribed in Hebrew. But more than just translating literally, she recorded the stories on cassettes so that I carried her voice along with the words. As a result, hearing her voice added a dimension of such heartfelt joy when I worked on those stories. I thank her for her time, attention, patience, and her *neshamah*—as well as her exquisite, perceptive command of languages. I also thank her wonderful husband, my son-in-law Emile, for his patience, his help in so many ways, and his encouragement throughout the lengthy book-in-progress stage. May their children, my grandchildren Dorielle Netta, Aaron Daniel, and Ilan Moshe, enjoy beautiful stories shared in a world of peace!

Preface

In many of these stories-within-stories, there are intricately or confusingly elaborate labyrinths that lead you, the listener or reader, down paths to a point where you cannot stop listening or reading—until you get to the end of the story. A few of these stories you might read in installments—very much like what happened in "The Arabian Nights" or with "The Perils of Pauline," the movie serial—because these stories are very long and keep you, hopefully, in suspense until the next time you pick up the book to continue the story (as, for example, "Queen Hatam and King Tye"). However, many of the stories have one or two simpler stories encircled within a more realistic narrative frame.

I continue to find amazing the discovery that many similar tale types and motifs exist in different stories from various countries. However, that is the process of the fluid oral tradition, which includes repetition and parallelism. Therefore, I chose not to exclude stories on that basis if I found them to have parallel elements, such as similar riddles, enigmatic sayings, parallel tasks, etc. For example, two of the stories, "The Princess Who Would Not Speak" (Iran) and "The Prince of the East and the Princess of the West" (Egypt), share the contest of making a mute princess speak. However, the frames are quite different. Or in "Caliph Harun Al-Rashid" and "The King, Bahlul, and the Clever Maiden" (both from Iran) there are parallel enigmatic conversations between two people who are on a journey. But everything else in the story is different. In other words, these are not retellings of the same story. So I have included all of these stories in this book. And even though the riddles may be the same, sometimes the answers to the riddles are not.

Sometimes there is the same hero type, but each story is different, as we find in three story examples where the hero is a wise and clever shepherd: "The Indian King and the Jewish Shepherd," "Ashmedai's Magic Flute," and "The Lie That Can Stand on Its Own." To explain why I included these recurrent themes/motifs/characters in this book, I will use a corresponding musical analogy. I offer the example of Rossini, who used the same tune for six of his operas. And why not? Placed in another context, the melody takes on different colorations and meanings—and thus becomes a new and different melody.

For the format of the book, I decided to present the fifty stories to you without clustering themes or plots or characters, but rather to intersperse the types so that a humorous story may then be followed by a romantic tale, which is followed by a religious tale, which is then followed by a tall tale, and so on. I added the notes directly after each story so that you can immediately see the sources, tale types, motifs, and my additional discussion regarding the tale.

I begin and end the collection of stories with short tall tales that involve repetition of one event before the problem is resolved. In a way, these two mini-frame stories act as bookends of this volume.

There are many types of stories in this collection:

Tall Tales

Folktales of Magic

Romantic Tales

Religious Tales (with moralistic overtones), including seven stories of three hasidic masters: Baal Shem Tov, Reb Nachman of Bratslav, Reb Levi Yitzhak of Berditchev

Personal stories (primarily in the frame story)

The main types of stories-within-stories include:

Frame Stories

Chain Stories

Cumulative Stories

These stories have been told from generation to generation. They were told not just for entertainment but also for enlightenment and the transmission of values and traditions. The lasting stories pose wrestling-with-life questions, which are then answered best through story. These stories help us resolve some of the questions that intrigue us or make us grapple with them harder, such as:

Can fate be changed?

How can we get closer to God?

Should we look up or down?

Is it better to throw away a treasured object or keep it?

How should we show gratitude?

Who is truly wise?

How should we handle adversity?

What is a true friend?

How should one choose a life partner?

Often, one story will take a particular side of the question, which resolves the question for you. But then you read another story, which takes the opposing point of view. So we then continue to deal with the question. And, of course, we continue to read more stories.

Reading these stories, asking the questions, and maneuvering through the maze of stories-within-stories is like going on a treasure hunt with clues as markers for the next question or answer. I wish my readers a fascinating journey.

—*PS*

An afterword about the end-of-story notes quoting sources:

" 'Like the coolness of snow at harvest time [like a cool breeze during the scorching heat of summer (Rashi)] is a trusted messenger to those who send him; he lifts his master's spirits' (Proverbs 25:13). The messenger in this passage refers to a faithful student who mentions his rabbi's name when he quotes his Torah insights. When the rabbi is deceased, 'he lifts his master's spirits.' Which is to say that when an author is given credit for his sayings (*Megillah* 15a) and his name is mentioned, God restores his soul, so that his lips move gently in the grave."

This teaching is taken from *Sefer Chasidim: The Book of the Pious* by Rabbi Yehudah HeChasid. (Condensed, translated, and annotated by Avraham Yaakov Finkel and published by Jason Aronson, 1997, pp. 16–17).

In other words, if we will all give our sources for Torah insights, [but, I will add, also for the stories we tell], then surely we will hasten the coming of the Messiah (*Megillah* 15a). (The brackets in this paragraph are my addition.)

Introduction
Apples of Gold in Frames of Silver

by Peninnah Schram

"A word fitly spoken is like apples of gold in frames of silver."
Proverbs 25:11

"The Arabian Nights." This title conjures up those cliff-hanging thousand and one nights of storytelling and is the most familiar and vivid example to describe the format of the stories-within-stories structure that is contained in this anthology. In other words, the common thread woven throughout the book is that each story has its own narrative frame, like an artist's frame, on which are stretched many canvases of various colors and differing designs.

As we look around the world, we can see that the design or structure of this type of a story-inside-a-story is everywhere in nature, in personal relationships, in conversations, in sermons and other speeches, and in many of the fairy/folk tales that are in the Jewish oral tradition, as well as in universal folk tradition. But before discussing the structure and tracing the history of these labyrinthian stories, take a moment to look at the concentric circles and spirals that appear and recur all around us, both natural and artist-created: pearls; the conch shell; the grainy rings within a tree trunk; a hall of endless mirrors; nested Russian *matrushka* dolls; mandalas; meditation labyrinths. These mazelike symbols open up

1

our inquiry about our own lives and our search for the sacred as well as the meaning of life. There is great mystery about this journey that we are on as we travel in spirals and labyrinths, going into different levels and spaces, to try to solve the puzzle of human existence. Many times there is that degree of repetition that gives the journey special intensity.

And speaking of repetition, let us consider the pearl. The miracle of pearls is something that especially fascinates me, no doubt because my name Peninnah means "pearl" in Hebrew. How are pearls formed? When a grain of sand or a microscopic sea creature enters the mollusk, it responds by covering the intruder with successive layers of carbonate and lime and an iridescent substance called nacre. Pearls are thus slowly built up in domed layers over periods of two to fifty years. Each layer overlaps another so slightly that it is only detectable by a microscope. But the result is that this repetitive overlapping structure causes light to be evenly reflected, diffracted, and refracted thousands of times, giving the pearl its mysterious glow, as if lit from within. Because of their glow, and because the most valued pearls have a round form, they are called the sacred stone of the moon.

In this sense, we can use pearls as a metaphor for these stories-within-stories. Someone (and I don't know the source of this quote) wrote that a parable is an earthly story with an inner heavenly meaning. Perhaps then we can say that all stories have within them a *sod*, a secret; in other words, a meaning that we must ferret out. The secret is the inner glow of the "pearl." These stories-within-stories, by offering us recursive stories, hold up a mirror to us so we can examine their meanings and, by extension, also interpret our lives refracted through that mirror endlessly bouncing off other mirrors.

In this book, I have retold stories that have the actual structure of a story-within-a-story and stories-within-a-story. According to folklorist Dov Noy,[1] the frame genre is called *Eingeschachtelt*, a German word that means a box-within-a-box; thus this type of story is sometimes called "boxing tales." There are several different conventional structures, identified by the arrangement of the actions in the story, which comprise this sophisticated and clever genre of stories:[2]

1. A *frame* story begins with an independent story wrapped around one or several other stories. The frame sets up a problem but the series

of actions to solve that problem is not linear; rather, each event or character creates more problems. This leads to smaller stories being embedded or boxed in the main frame story. "In a sense, embedded problem sequences 'wind up' like a clock spring as characters get into more and more difficulty, then 'unwind' as characters systematically undo their complicated circumstances."[3] The frame often begins like a fairy tale with a formulaic opening, such as "Once there was" or "A long time ago," and often ends with a wedding and a formulaic ending, such as "I was there and I drank wine with them." However, while the greater frame narrative is usually more realistic in nature, the embedded tales tend to be more magical and fantastic. Sometimes the events and characters of the main story reappear at certain intervals between the inner tale(s), as happens in "The Emperor's Daughter and the King's Son." In other words, the telling of the embedded story alternates with that of the frame story.

Katherine S. Gittes uses the guidelines established by W. H. Clawson to define a frame narrative: "A framework or framing story is to be understood as a narrative which, however interesting in itself, was composed for the primary purpose of introducing and connecting a series of tales, which are the *raison d'etre* of the whole work."[4] The embedded, or interpolated, tales within the frame can stand alone as a complete tale, or even appear within a different frame. Thus, we can find some of the same embedded stories in different contexts or rearranged in their order even within different versions of the same frame narrative, since the arrangement of tales is arbitrary. Even the number of embedded stories can vary from one version to another (as is true of the various editions of "The Arabian Nights"). It is accepted that "all frame tales by their very nature contain structural repetitions or reiterations."[5]

Folklorists generally do not consider a story to be of this genre if the frame includes one singular embedded story.[6] However, I use "frame narrative" in a looser sense to include a frame tale with only one embedded story in this collection. Edna Cheichel-Hechal, Director of the Israel Folktale Archives, recently suggested that I might use the term "a story-within-a-frame" for such a tale where only one story is found within a frame. In these cases, you, the reader, will have to supply the additional inner tales.

2. A *chain* story is filled with stories, midrashim, or proverbs told

one after another, like the links of a chain, each one proving an argument or serving as part of a contest or as part of a search tracing what happened to a biblical object or character that "disappears" from text. For example, Howard Schwartz weaves together a "chain midrash" about the jewel known as the *Tzohar* of Noah's ark and the primordial light. He writes, "Once the glowing jewel of the *Tzohar* had entered Jewish legend, it became the basis of what might be called a 'chain midrash.' This is a midrash that uses some kind of sacred object to link together several biblical generations."[7] In a chain story, the ending does not return to the beginning. An example of a chain story is "The Lie That Can Stand on Its Own."

3. A *cumulative* story presents a problem that is solved through a series of events, each one contributing to the solution. This type of story is often a frame story but there are several variations of the frame story that fall under the rubric of cumulative stories, not all of them structured in the same way. "The cumulative story can be described generally as a setting category plus an episode system containing a problem and a series of events leading to problem solution . . . It is perhaps the most conventional, strictly governed, ritualized formula for story structure in the oral literature."[8] For examples of a cumulative tale see "The King's Daughter and the Choice of Her Heart," "The Princess Who Would Not Speak," and "The Prince of the East and the Princess of the West."

Using the superstructure of a frame to embrace other stories within it is "one of the oldest unifying principles for groupings of tales."[9] During the Second Temple period, "four classic genres of folk narrative make their debut in Hebrew literature in this period . . ."[10] Yassif identifies the framework narrative as one of these international genres. Written as a frame narrative in the seventh century B.C.E., *The Book of Ahikar* greatly influenced the folk literature of the Second Temple period.[11] Although non-Hebrew in origin and translated into Greek, Armenian, and Arabic, it was a popular text among the Jews in an Aramaic version from the fifth century B.C.E. on. Within the frame, there are tales, parables, sayings, and riddles "that serve as means to resolve the conflict exposed in the framework tale"[12] and which characterize wisdom literature. The tale centers around a nephew's betrayal of his uncle and adoptive father, Ahikar the Wise, chief administrator to the king of Babylonia. When the king, who has condemned Ahikar to death, needs a wise man to compete in a contest of riddles with the King of Egypt, Ahikar comes to the rescue and wins the contest and regains his office. "The union of didactic-wisdom orientations with the novelistic tale is a dominant trait of the Hebrew tale of the period."[13] In other words, the tale includes wisdom sayings and also events associated with the hero of the tale. This melding of moral teaching with entertaining tales and riddles in a contest or debate proves to be a durable combination that we see in many framework tales.

One of the earliest texts using this story-within-a-story form is Apuleius's *The Golden Ass*, written in the second century A.D., "one of the three great works of imaginative prose narrative that we own from the ancient world."[14] This tale of magical transformation tells about Lucius who rubs himself with a magical ointment, the same ointment that turned his hostess into a bird, but which turns him into a donkey. Thus, he has a series of adventures, some humorous and some treacherous. In the preface, Apuleius wrote: "In this Milesian tale, reader, I shall string together a medley of stories, and titillate your agreeable ears with a merrily whispered narrative, if you will not refuse to scan this Egyptian paper written with a subtle pen of Nilotic reeds. . . . We begin then, reader, a Grecian tale. Attend, and pleasure is yours."[15] Throughout the book, when one story ends with "Just listen to this story and you'll agree with me," then the next story begins. The original language borders on the line between prose and poetry, according to the translator,[16] and its structure most certainly had an influence on later works, such as Boccaccio's *Decameron*.

In the fourteenth century, two great writers used the frame structure for their famous masterpieces, *Decameron* and *The Canterbury Tales*. As with many of the frame tales, these two works focus on the wisdom theme as well as on entertainment. Framing narratives are ideal for teaching morals and ways of behavior through stories because the listeners/readers eagerly anticipate one tale after the next. And while being entertained, they are all the while learning a variety of wisdom. "Addressing the tales to women who have been unhappy in love, Boccaccio declares that the purpose of the tales is to improve as well as to entertain; . . ."[17]

Giovanni Boccaccio (1313–1375), the Italian writer, transformed medieval literary forms. *Decameron*, written between 1348 and 1353, is a collection of 100 prose tales, many humorous, many satiric and bawdy, all vigorous tales. It is an account of a ten-day stay in the countryside near Florence of ten young people (seven ladies and three gentlemen) who are trying to avoid the plague rampant in the city. This frame tale is merely a literary device for bringing together the 100 tales told by the young people.

The other such collection familiar to the Western reader is Chaucer's *The Canterbury Tales*. Geoffrey Chaucer (c. 1340–1400), the greatest English poet of the Middle Ages, wrote and incorporated tales in this work over a period of time, approximately between 1386 and 1398. Framed by the Canterbury Pilgrimage, there is no overall plan of arrangement evident except for a group of tales that discuss aspects of married life and another group of stories that are connected as part of a quarrel between members of the company.

It is important to note that "the frame story became pivotal in the literary tradition of fairy tales and folk tales after Boccaccio. Almost all of the fifteenth-century Italian writers of novellas and folk tales, whether in Latin or in Italian, used frames. The two most important examples are Straparola and Basile."[18]

Giovan Francesco Straparola (c. 1480–1558) is generally considered the "father" of the literary fairy tale in Europe. His major work is *Le piacevoli notti* (1550–1553), translated as *The Facetious Nights* or *The Delectable Nights*. The collection has a framework similar to Boccaccio's *Decameron*. In this case, the tales are told on thirteen consecutive nights by a group of ladies and gentlemen gathered at the Venetian palace of Ottaviano Maria Sforza, former bishop of Lodi, who had fled Milan with his widowed daughter Lucretia to avoid persecution and capture by his political enemies.

Giambattista Basile (1575–1632) is remembered mainly for two main works written in Neapolitan dialect. The one that pertains to our subject is his fairy tale collection, *The Tale of Tales, or Entertainment for Little Ones* (1634–1636), also known as the *Pentamerone*. The tales were probably intended to be read aloud in the "courtly conversations" that were an elite pastime of this period. This collection is made up of forty-nine fairy tales contained within a fiftieth frame story, also a fairy tale, that opens and closes the collection. In the frame tale, a slave girl deceitfully cheats Princess Zoza out of her predestined prince Tadeo and the princess reacts by using a magic doll to instill in the slave the need to hear tales. The prince summons the ten best tale tellers of his kingdom, a motley group of hags, and they each tell one tale apiece for five days, at the end of which Zoza tells her own tale, reveals the slave's deceit, and wins back Tadeo.

Both Straparola and Basile, through their works of frame tales and inner tales, influenced other Italian and European writers, among them Charles Perrault and the Grimm Brothers. Basile's work, the first collection consisting entirely of fairy tales to appear in Europe, marks the passage from the oral tradition of folk tales to the artful and sophisticated "authored" fairy tale.[19]

Of course when one speaks of a story-within-a-story, the main collection that immediately comes to mind is *The Thousand and One Nights*, better known as *The Arabian Nights*. This marvelous series of stories with its framework narrative is well known: The king Shahryar is betrayed by his queen and turns violently against all women. He commands his vizier to bring a new bride to him every night, and every morning the bride is beheaded. Scheherazade, the vizier's wise daughter, is determined to put an end to these killings by captivating the king and beguiling him with stories every night. The king keeps delaying her execution because he is so intrigued to hear the next story, or the ending to the story of the night before, night after night after night, until, finally, the king realizes his evil ways, and so he and Scheherazade marry and "live happily ever after."

Although the book was first introduced to the West in 1704 with the French translation by Antoine Galland, this book of oriental stories became part of the oral and written traditions in the English-speaking world by the end of the nineteenth century. In fact there were ten volumes published from 1704–1717; they were published in chapbook form during the eighteenth century and were translated in full by the middle of the nineteenth century. Indeed, there was never a fixed version of *The Arabian Nights*. Rather, there were several versions depending on the selections made by translators. Within the Jewish tradition we are familiar with having more than one version of a text, also as a result of the varying choices made by the redactors, namely, our Talmud. In truth, there are actually two Talmuds: the Babylonian Talmud and the Jerusalem Talmud, which differ in style, in content, and even in decisions taken by rabbis. While the Babylonian Talmud is considered the far more important of these two sacred compilations, they are both extraordinary storehouses of history, laws, and lore of the Jewish people.

But let us return to the "Arabian Nights." "These tales in the collection [*The Arabian Nights*] can be traced to three ancient oral cultures, Indian, Persian, and Arab, and they probably circulated in the vernacular hundreds of years before they were written down some time between the ninth and fourteenth centuries. The apparent model for the literary versions of the tales was a Persian book entitled *Hazar Afsanah* ("A Thousand Tales"), translated into Arabic in the ninth century. . . ."[20]

In addition to Egyptian stories added on between the twelfth and fifteenth centuries, the ancient cultures already mentioned furnished many of the stories found in *The Arabian Nights*. However, there was another source for the thousand and one tales, namely, Jewish sources. According to Morris Epstein, "Many Jewish stories have entered Arabic literature. Of the four hundred-odd stories in *The Thousand and One Nights*, some forty-five are Jewish."[21] Epstein continues, "It has even been suggested that the framework story of the whole collection, in which Queen Shahrazad averts execution by telling tales for one thousand and one nights, is the same story as that of the biblical *Book of Esther* (dated certainly not later than the third century B.C.E.)."[22] Shahrazad, in the Persian tradition, is the mother-in-law of Ahasuerus, who in the Biblical story also beguiles his nights by having tales read to him; his wives also hold office only for one night, until Esther obtains a more secure tenure. M. de Goeje thinks that the 'Arabian Nights' preserves a more original form of the story, as the writer of the Bible narrative has modified the fate of Esther's co-wives.[23]

In addition to the Jewish–Persian connection, many Jewish stories with Jewish themes, or derived from Jewish sources, were added to *The Arabian Nights*, along with the Egyptian additions. As already noted, about forty-five, or nearly one-ninth of the whole, can be traced to the Jewish editor of the Cairene edition—and perhaps more. In the "Arabian Nights" entry in *The Jewish Encyclopedia*, twenty-five story titles are identified as tales from Jewish sources.[24] Because of Jews traveling from place to place, Jews played an important role in the transmission of stories from East to West and, along the way, adapted and transformed many of the Oriental and Indian tales into Jewish variants. However, in the fluid folklore process, many Jewish tales were also reshaped as non-Jewish versions.

Before we discuss frame stories found within the Jewish oral tradition, we need to review the background of this type of imaginative and complex narrative structure of the Middle Ages in Spain, a time and place where this form was extremely popular.

These configurations of event sequences that create the story-within-story genre stem generally more from the Middle Eastern countries, clearly due to the influence of the Arabic poetic structure of *makamat*. *Makama* is a rhymed narrative interspersed with short metrical poems. It originated about the tenth century C.E. with the Arab poet Ibn al-Fatih Ahmad ibn Husayni. The word *makam* means "place" in Arabic, similar to the word *makom* in Hebrew. In other words, wherever two Arabic poet-storytellers would appear in a "place," as if by accident, they would engage in amusing conversations and an exchange of improvisational witty remarks and stories. People gathered around to listen, to be entertained and informed of current events in that place. Eventually, these *makamat* were written down.

During this time period of the Middle Ages, Jews lived peacefully in Moslem Spain with the Arab people. The Jews even began to speak Arabic instead of Hebrew and Aramaic. Scholars during the tenth to twelfth centuries, such as Maimonides, wrote halakhic responsa in Arabic as well as Hebrew. Jews and Arabs lived with mutual respect and admiration, influencing each other in the sciences and arts with great mutual benefits. It was indeed a golden age for both peoples. In fact, the rich Arabic civilization and language served as a stimulus to Jews "to create not only religious but secular poetry in Hebrew, employing Arabic forms and principles of meter."[25] Thus, there are a number of works produced by Sephardic authors that utilized the *makama* literary form interweaving rhymed prose with verse, a mix of questions and answers, moral tales, and proverbs.

"The tenth- and eleventh-century Arabic picaresque, or *maqamat* (assemblies), bears an even stronger resemblance than the histories, biographies, and geographies to the frame narrative."[26] And, indeed, we might wonder why the Arabic culture favored the enclosed tale format. Examining the literature, science, mathematics, architecture, and art of the Arabic world, there is a flexible and open pattern that reveals the same outlook, namely that "the suggestion of limitlessness and the stress on the separate unit are prominent traits of literature written in Arabic and help explain why the Arabs framed the *Panchatantra* and much of their literature."[27]

One of the greatest writers of Hebrew *makamat* is Judah al-Harizi. His twelfth-century collection of fifty *makamat* is called *Tahkemoni*, which was written primarily to entertain, but also to give ethical instruction, preach about morality, and praise God. He introduced humor into his work, such as the poem about the flea and the ant. In traditional *makama* style, there is the dialogue form in which a chief narrator tells about curious events and another one asks questions and encourages the first narrator to tell more stories. Through his writings of *makamat*, al-Harizi influenced later Hebrew poets.

This complex Oriental form was utilized by another Jewish writer, Joseph Ibn Zabara. His composition of fifteen *makamat* comprises the satirical-didactic romance called *Sefer Sha'ashuim* or *The Book of Delight*, written in the latter part of the twelfth century. Zabara's book was then published in 1577 in Constantinople. Zabara weaves various disparate stories together, which are encircled by a frame story. This book was written expressly to impart moral and spiritual lessons, and not for amusement. The narrative frame begins when the author himself meets a man, a disguised demon, who persuades the author to go on a journey. The demon's method of persuasion involves telling stories, parables, proverbs, and talmudic sayings, each segment linked together like the links in a chain. Zabara used folklore materials from Jewish, Arabic, Greek, and Indian sources, many known only in the Orient until this work introduced them into Western European literature, such as in *Gesta Romanorum*. The opening story in *The Book of Delight* is itself a frame story, in which are embedded five more stories. I have retold this self-contained opening story that frames other stories, "The Leopard and the Fox" in this book. (This tale can be found also in my *Jewish Stories One Generation Tells Another.*)

The *Book of Delight* also uses another favorite literary device, namely that of riddles. Riddles can actually be considered as tiny stories-within-stories. Some of the same riddles found in these stories can be found in other folktales. This is seen in the story "The Dream Interpreter" in

Jewish Stories One Generation Tells Another and "The King, Bahlul, and the Clever Maiden" in this collection.

In the early thirteenth century, the Indian romance, *Barlaam and Josaphat* (Greek title), was translated into Hebrew by Abraham ben Samuel Ibn Hasdai of Barcelona who called it *Ben Ha-Melech Ve-ha-Nazir* (Son of the King and the Dervish). "This fascinating work, which made itself at home in all medieval European literatures and became one of the most popular books of ethical instruction, sustained many transformations in the course of its wanderings, often changing its form according to the era or the condition of the prevalent culture and religious conceptions."[28] It was written mostly in *makama* style. However, Ibn Hasdai introduced in the Hebrew version various talmudic and midrashic parables, stories, and legends together with homilies.

In addition to all the *makamat* texts, two other important collections using the frame narrative structure of stories-within-stories were popular in thirteenth-century Spain, namely *Kalilah Ve-Dimnah* and *Mishlei Sendebar*. Both texts originally came from India but were translated through the years into various languages, including the Pahlavi dialect (a Persian language), Arabic, and Hebrew.

The first text is *Kalilah Ve-Dimnah*, Bidhapati's original Sanskrit third-century C.E. collection of parables and fables, also known as *Fables of Bidpai*. Originally known as *Panchatantra*, an eighth-century work, it is "the earliest frame narrative of significance."[29] While the boxed tales originated in India, many going back to the second century B.C.E., the frame is most certainly a later addition by the Arabs or Near Easterners who enclosed this collection of tales within a frame.[30] Indeed, each book of the *Panchatantra* has a "boxing" tale of its own. Stressing the wisdom theme of teaching, this frame narrative served as a treatise on human nature for the princes of India, a handbook for rulers. The tales are presented in a frame story by two jackals named Kalilah and Dimnah. Interwoven with ethical sayings and proverbs, the fables and parables explore universal questions of truth and deceit, ambition and loyalty, fear and power. The Hebrew translator, Jacob Ben Eleazar, included many maxims from the Talmud, stressing Jewish values. However, it was Rabbi Joel's Hebrew version of this book that served as the text for John of Capua's Latin translation in the thirteenth century. This Latin version, called *Directorium Vitae Humanae*, became known throughout the continent and was soon transformed into popular European folktales. Some similar stories can be found in *Gesta Romanorum* and Boccaccio's *Decameron*. "Many features of the *Panchatantra* appear, sometimes in altered form, many years later in *The Canterbury Tales.*[31] In India, the story is still popular as the *Panchatantra*. "The Leopard and the Fox" is written in the pattern of *Kalilah Ve-Dimnah*.

The frame structure of *Kalilah Ve-Dimnah* had a direct influence on a twelfth-century frame narrative, *Disciplina Clericalis*. It was written in Arabic and then translated into Latin by Petrus Alfonsi, who "played a central role in transmitting Islamic cultural ideas to Christian Spain and to Europe."[32] Alfonsi was born an Aragonese Jew and became a rabbi, an Islamic scholar, and a physician. He converted to Catholicism in 1106 and, soon after, moved to England. This frame narrative revolves around the theme of friendship with the didactic aim of teaching moral lessons and, above all, wisdom. (See endnote to the story in this collection, "Friends in Deed.") Like other Arabic literary models, "*Disciplina Clericalis* focuses on the concrete, the episodic, and the single unit, while deemphasizing the abstract and the whole."[33] Thus, this work served as a bridge between Eastern and Western narrative traditions and to Boccaccio's *The Canterbury Tales.*[34]

The second text is *Mishlei Sendebar*, which was published in Constantinople in 1516 but was known much earlier in Arabic Spain. Morris Epstein, whose English translation was published in 1967, states, "The oldest of the eight surviving Eastern versions has been assumed to be the Syriac *Sindban*, which has been placed in the tenth century."[35] Other Eastern versions include Syriac, Greek, Old Spanish, Arabic, and three in Persian (which includes Pahlavi, a Middle Iranian literary language of the Indo-Iranian subfamily of Indo-European languages, which flourished from approximately the third to the tenth centuries). The anonymously translated Hebrew version shows the influence of Jewish sources, such as biblical story.

Mishlei Sendebar is the story of a son born to a childless king. The king asks the wisest of his seven sages, Sendebar, to teach the prince wisdom. But when one of the king's young wives makes a false accusation against the prince, the prince is sentenced to die in seven days. To save the prince, each of the seven sages steps forward and tells various tales each day to persuade the king to change the decree. But, after the sage leaves, the king's young wife tries to persuade him, also with stories, to punish the prince. Finally, after this chain of stories, the sages expose the wife's treachery and the prince's life is saved. What is most interesting is the ending in the Hebrew version. "In all the European versions of *Mishlei Sendebar*, the young wife who made the false accusation against the innocent prince is condemned to strict punishment. In the Hebrew text, however, the prince begs his father to forgive her, and when the king reminds the sage Sendebar that, according to their agreement, he has the right to demand a reward consisting of anything he wishes, the sage answers: 'My request is that what you yourself do not like, you do not to another, and that you love your people as yourself.' With this the book ends."[36] (This echoes Hillel's Golden Rule found in Talmud *Shabbat* 31a.) Some of these tales found in *The Seven Sages of Rome*, as the book is known in the West, are similar to Boccaccio's *Decameron*, another frame narrative. Folklorist Jack Zipes has pointed out that there is also a fascinating version of *Mishlei Sendebar* in Richard Burton's translation of *Thousand and One Nights* as "The Ten Viziers or the Story of King Azabakht and his Son." Zipes feels certain that "the *Nights'* version must have preceded and influenced *Mishlei Sendebar*. The ending in which the lost prince forgives the courtesan is similar to the ending of *Mishlei Sendebar*.[37]

As we can see, then, framework story groupings, such as "*Kalilah Ve-Dimnah, The Tales of Sendebar*, and early versions of *The Arabian Nights*, were widespread in Babylonia and Persia at the time; Jews were also familiar with them."[38] This type of frame tale, adopted from the literary models found in Arab culture, influenced other Jewish story groupings (but that are not identified as framework tales) written in the Middle Ages, such as *Midrash of the Ten Commandments* and *The Alphabet of Ben Sira*.

In 1281, Isaac ben Solomon Ibn Sahulah took Arabic and Greek fables and stories and transformed them into more Jewish versions, interweaving the tales with words of Torah, riddles, and talmudic sayings. His collection, *Meshal Ha-Kadmoni*, was also written in the Arabic *makama* style. In each of the five chapters, or "gates," there is a dialogue between the author and a certain *makshan*, one who raises difficult questions. The answers are in the form of stories with animals where the animals quote Talmud and are very learned. These chain stories end with Jewish morals.

Also in the thirteenth century, there lived Berechiah ben Natronai Hanakdan who was born in France. While living in Oxford, he wrote 107 "fox fables," which he collected in his book *Mishlei Shualim*. Written in rhymed prose, many of his fables can be traced to Aesop, and some to *Romulus* collections, while others are similar to the work of Marie de France, but still others seem to be original. Fables are an ancient form of story. "Fables were derived from beast tales in Mesopotamia more than 4000 years ago and spread throughout the Orient and the Mediterranean."[39] Aesop, who lived about 620–560 B.C.E., told his fables in the oral tradition without writing them down.[40] Aesop used the fable so as to couch certain truths about freedom and oppression in a non-threatening form during the time of tyrants and slavery. "And when free speech was established in the Greek city-states after his [Aesop's] death, rhetoricians began using the fable to teach scholars style and rules of grammar and to discuss morals and ethics in debates."[41] Later, during the Middle Ages, the fable was incorporated into lessons and sermons. They are ideal teaching tools with which to impart wisdom and morality because of their brevity, directness, and clarity.

Berechiah Hanakdan's foxes, though, echo talmudic discussion and quote biblical sources. Though his fables include a great deal of quoted Scripture in the *nimshal* (the commentary that supplies the moral of the fable), his goal was not to teach religion. Fables are generally secular in nature. Rather, like Aesop through his fables, Hanakdan, "the Jewish Aesop," sought to give lessons in social behavior. He opens each fable with an aphorism or *pitgam* and closes it with a mini-sermon. Unlike Aesop, this fabulist made sure to write his tales, rather than entrusting them to the oral tradition. Thus, each fable takes on the shape of a story-within-a-story. (See "The Leopard and the Fox.")

The greatest Jewish collector and teller of fables was, without doubt, Rabbi Meir, the student of Rabbi Akiva, who lived during the second century C.E. According to the Talmud, Rabbi Meir collected 300 fables, some of which are found in the Talmud and in midrashim. During the Middle Ages, Jewish scholars, namely Berechiah Hanakdan and Joseph Ibn Zabara, contributed to the rapidly growing number of Jewish fables.

One of the most popular types of stories in Jewish oral literature is a form similar to the fable, and belonging to the same genre, namely a parable. A parable is a teaching tale, usually short and to the point, often using animals as the main characters. However, the main difference between the fable and parable is that fables are absolutely fiction, whereas parables may be fiction but could also be historical examples. A Jewish parable differs from the general parable in that it is composed of two parts: a *nimshal* and a *mashal*. The *nimshal* is really a frame question; in other words, a question that is set up at the beginning followed by a connection at the end that serves as a direct response to the question first posed. It teaches us what we can learn from the embedded story and how to apply that lesson. The *mashal* is the story-example in the middle like a jewel in a ring. Its purpose is to illuminate a verse or passage of Torah or to clarify a Jewish custom or tradition. Sermons delivered by the *darshanim*, the teachers of Torah from the fifth century B.C.E., as well as the *hasidim*, enclosed parables and other aggadic stories within their sermons. In the Middle Ages, the function of the *darshan* was to expound the *aggadah*, with the prime purpose of stressing morality and the observance of religious obligations. While folklorists do not consider a parable to be a story-within-a-story per se, these rabbi-storytellers understood the power and beauty of stories and incorporated parables as examples into their frame teachings.

Parables were supposedly invented by King Solomon, but it was Rabbi Jacob Kranz, the Dubner Maggid (1741–1804), who developed the parable as a primary teaching tool. He imitated the *aggadah* and Midrash by combining lessons from the Bible and its commentaries with the folktales of the people he met on his travels. He adapted these folktales with creativity and imagination in order to teach. An aggadic statement states: "With a penny candle one may often find a lost gold coin or a precious pearl. By means of a simple parable, one may sometimes penetrate the most profound ideas." In "The Maggid of Dubno," I have strung together Dubner Maggid parables to create a linked series of stories-within-stories that enlighten in a beautiful way.

Returning to an earlier century, a mystical movement was developing that would have a profound and rippling effect on interpretations of Torah as well as on stories. In thirteenth-century Spain, the *Zohar* (*The Book of Splendor*) was "written" by kabbalist Moses de Leon, although authorship has been attributed to the second-century *tannah* Rabbi

Simeon bar Yohai.[42] This book, the major work of Jewish mysticism, came to be regarded as the most important Jewish religious text after the Torah and Talmud. It is primarily a mystical commentary on the Torah and contains symbolic descriptions, parables, homilies, and dramatic stories of mystic revelations. It is not within the purview of this introductory essay to delve too deeply into this mystical work and the kabbalistic movement, but a glimpse of them would help understand about the Jewish love of multilayered connections. So first I turn to a "concise" but filled-with-hidden-meaning definition of what the *Zohar* teaches. ". . . [The] *Zohar* teaches that God's nature is ultimately paradoxical: unitary yet multidimensional; transcendent, in its aspect as '*Ein Sof*' ('the Infinite'), concealed from human view, yet also immanent, in the form of the seven lower *Sefirot*, which interact with our own world. The *Zohar* also teaches that the lower world of matter corresponds to the upper world of the *Sefirot*. These two worlds enjoy a dynamic relationship: the lower world receives divine light and blessing from above; the upper world, its primal unity shattered at the beginning of creation, achieves reintegration—*tikkun*, literally 'repair'—as a result of human actions. Both worlds are linked in a chain of energy to the *Ein Sof*."[43]

The *Zohar* made its impact on the mystics of the sixteenth-century Safed who had been forced to leave Spain in 1492. This esoteric movement became known as Lurianic Kabbalah after its leader, Rabbi Isaac Luria, known as the Ari. (It is the book of his stories, *Shivhei ha-Ari*, published in Constantinople in 1766, which would later serve as the model for *Shivhei he-Besht*, the book of Baal Shem Tov stories.) This mystical movement had a great influence on the development of Hasidism in the eighteenth century, although there are differences in their approach of, for example, the kabbalistic concept of *zimzum*.[44] *Zimzum* is, in essence, God's withdrawing in order to make room for creating our world and yet remain *Ein Sof*, the hidden aspect of God who is infinite, endless, and without end.

Kabbalah refers to an intricate esoteric system of symbolism within Judaism that has as its focus the principles of *Sefirot*, emanations of God, and the secret names of God. Each one of the ten *sefirot* represents ten aspects of the unified Divine personality; in other words, they constitute the mystical archetypes for the existence of the world, such as *Hokhmah*

(Wisdom), *Binah* (Understanding), *Din* (Judgment), and *Hesed* (Mercy), etc. The pictorial structure of the *sefirot* is similar to a geometric mandala or an iconographic tree "balanced in dynamic relation to each other, representing the life and actions of God."[45] In other words, eight of the various labeled aspects form a "frame," while two are located in the inner space of the mandala, but all are intricately interconnected, weblike, with at least two or more of the other aspects.

There are many complex interpretations of the *sefirot* as emanations of the divine spirit. One of these deals with the vessels that were filled with Divine light at the beginning of creation (which was alluded to in the above definition of the *Zohar*). The light had emerged from the emanations of the *Ein Sof*. Somehow these fragile vessels shattered and the sparks scattered throughout the world. As a result, everything and everyone contain these divine sparks. It has become the goal of kabbalists, *hasidim*, and indeed all Jews, to gather these sparks in order to bring about *tikkun olam*, the repair of the world, as well as to effect a unity between our world and the upper world of the *Sefirot*. "The essential idea [in Hasidism] is the ongoing battle to redeem and uplift the trapped sparks—to transform evil into good and to help the Tzaddik in his struggle against the satanic forces. Joy and dancing are simple expressions . . . of this basic struggle."[46]

In the eighteenth century these mystical ideas emphasized by the kabbalists and the concepts found in the *Zohar* caught fire with a new religious and social movement, Hasidism. Hasidism was founded in the mid-1730s in Volhynia and Podolia by Rabbi Israel (c. 1700–1760), who was fondly known as the Baal Shem Tov ("The Master of the Good Name" or "The Good Master of the Name") or by the acronym the Besht. The hasidic movement restored the art of storytelling to the peak of creativity. The Baal Shem Tov, a healer and teacher, stressed the joyousness of Judaism through song, dance, and stories. In Hasidism, the human voice, a treasured means for singing wordless tunes (*niggunim*) and telling stories, along with dancing, are the hasid's tools of religious expression, in addition to or even as forms of prayer. In Judaism, words are synonymous with action and Jerome Mintz reaffirms this when he lists one of the functions of stories in hasidic culture: ". . . the *hasidim* believe that tales, like prayers, contain the potential to be active agents . . . Storytelling has been used to shape desired ends, and therefore can be conceived of as the powerful, even magical, equivalent of action."[47] The Baal Shem Tov made story, as well as purity of heart or *kavanah*, more important to the Jewish common folk than great scholarly achievement in Torah study, which was until then the highest ideal of every Jew.

Therefore, the main purpose of stories, in the spiritual hasidic tradition, is to bring the followers back to God, to awaken them through story, to create *tikkun* and reunite the two spheres. Thus, the rabbis used story in a symbolic way to accomplish these goals and reach the hearts of the listeners. There are hidden meanings in the hasidic stories for us to ferret out. For example, in "A Remembered Story" this becomes even clearer when, at the end of the story, the storyteller completes the rich man's story for him and brings him back to his true self, to effect the restoration of the Divine sparks.

All of the great hasidic rabbis who followed the Baal Shem Tov contributed to this body of stories in the oral tradition. A great cycle of stories was formed around each of these leaders, who was called the Tzaddik ("righteous"). Following a specific Tzaddik, who had reached a spiritually superior level, as the intermediary between his *hasidim* and God, is "the most important feature of authentic hasidic religious life."[48]

The tales of the Tzaddik were often transcribed by the rebbe's scribe but published only years later. *Shivhei he-Besht* (*In Praise of the Baal Shem Tov*), published in 1815 (fifty-five years after the Besht's death), are stories told about the Besht and his miracle-making powers. The Baal Shem Tov stories were gathered and retold by many of his followers as they heard them or remembered them, and then they retold them with changes and variations, as happens with all stories told in the oral tradition. Although there was a continuous tradition of stories from the Bible, the rabbinic-talmudic models, the *Zohar*, and the kabbalistic tales, there was now an amazing infusion of wonder and miracle stories, numbskull and humorous tales, and parables and allegories filled with symbolic references. Some of these stories are based on Torah and Talmud, but many of them are about the events of the hasidic rabbis, as well as adaptations from folktales that circulated in that area. While not all hasidic stories are frame tales, a number of them are. In this book, I have included several of the Baal Shem Tov miracle stories. (See "The Wedding Gifts," "The Golden Buttons," and "A Remembered Story.")

Considered the greatest of the hasidic storytellers, the Besht's great-grandson, Reb Nachman of Bratzlav (1770–1810), composed his stories as a single author and told them orally. However, his scribe Nathan wrote them down in a collection, *Sippure Maasiyot* (*Rabbi Nachman's Stories*), which was also published in 1815. Many are in the guise of a fairy tale in the story-within-story format too, but through these simple tales, Nachman could convey mystical Jewish concepts. His long allegory, "The Seven Beggars," is a masterpiece written on many levels with a number of stories embedded within the frame story. To just give you a hint of one of the many allegorical secrets hidden in his story, to show how this story serves as a commentary on *Maaseh Bereshith*, the Work of Creation, Howard Schwartz draws out a connection: "First, the overall structure of the story, with the tale of the seven beggars serving as a frame for other tales within tales, implies the seven days of creation. As in the biblical myth of creation, the seventh day and the seventh beggar are singled out for particular emphasis. The seventh day, of course, represents the Sabbath, while the seventh beggar may be seen as the representative of the messianic era, if not of the Messiah himself."[49] Although the stories can be read/heard and enjoyed as marvelous tales, an annotated volume of Nachman's stories, such as *Rabbi Nachman's Stories*, translated and annotated by Rabbi Aryeh Kaplan, becomes very illuminating as to the secret meanings hidden within the text, which combine both the sacred and the secular. Reb Nachman believed that the only way to wake people up "is through stories."[50] However, the mystery of these tales remains locked within them until we read/hear them so as to open the gates of our hearts. (See "The Emperor's Daughter and the King's Son.")

There are often formulaic openings to a hasidic story. According to Dov Noy, these stories open with praising the Besht as a hasidic introduction to one of his stories. One example is, "I shall tell you a story of the Baal Shem Tov and let his grace rest up unto us."[51] Thus the introduction is connected to the storyteller and not with the story itself. However, this introductory praise serves also to prepare the listener to receive the story. Rabbi Nachman also opened his story with a formulaic beginning: "When the Rebbe (of blessed memory) began telling stories, he said, 'I am now beginning to tell stories' (*ich vell shoin an-heiben maasios der-tzeilen*). His intent was as if to say, '[I must tell stories] because my lessons and conversations are not having any effect in bringing you back to God.' "[52] Then when Rabbi Nachman began telling his "The Lost Princess," he would say: "While on my journey I told a story. Whoever heard it had a thought of repentance."[53] And then Rabbi Nachman told the story.

As there are formula openings of a tale, so too there are formulaic endings. "The end formulas . . . show more variety than the beginning. These go all the way from the simple 'Now it is finished' to the more unusual conclusions with . . . a final rhyme, good wishes (with or without a request for pay), the request to another to tell a tale, or a remark about where the tale was learned, so as to give it proper authority. Especially well-liked are formulistic descriptions of the happy marriage at the end."[54] As you can see from "The Emperor's Daughter and the King's Son," there is an ending paragraph that is found at the ends of folktales in Yemen and Morocco and especially Arabic cultures. The endings lead the listeners out of the story and back to where they are. But it is also a form of a blessing. In the hasidic tradition, giving the source of the tale, the rebbe who heard it from that rebbe, etc., is a way to give it proper authority. "As marks of authenticity, the name of the Rebbe concerned is almost always cited in the legend, and, almost as often, the name of the hasid who was involved or who passed along the tale. In concluding his tale a hasid notes: 'The only way to know if a story is true is if it has testimony from witnesses—that is, true witnesses. This story has been passed by hundreds of people. I heard this story from Rabbi Bernstein from Montreal and from other people also.' "[55]

In some way, any good story always has a "frame" since storytellers find a way to introduce their story by telling about the way they found the story, or say something like, "That reminds me of a story about . . ." or "Have you ever heard about . . . ? Let me tell you a story." It helps to prepare the audience so they can all enter through the gate of story together. And so, too, with the ending, which helps the listeners return from the story mode with a formulaic ending. This approach has helped me to define storytelling as a dialogue between the storyteller and the listeners. Perhaps all stories can be considered as taking place within some framework as stories-within-stories. In this collection, I have taken the liberty to expand the strictly "box-within-a-box" or *eingeschachtelt* genre beyond its stricter folkloristic definition by enclosing a biblical story within a personal story ("A Story of Consolation"); a folktale within another event that happened to me ("We Never Lose Old Treasures"); two folktales about friendship within a created frame situation ("Friends in Deed").

This structure of a center with a frame surrounded by other paths or a structure-inside-a-structure is integral to Judaism if we consider a sacred place and a sacred page. The first is the portable Sanctuary (*Mishkan*) that Israel is bidden to build with its wooden framework, with the inner space divided into the outer Court and its inner Court, which contained the Tabernacle separated into two chambers, the Holy Place and the Holy of Holies, with its ark that will contain the tablets of stone. The detailed description for its construction takes up most of the last part of Exodus beginning with Chapter 25. It is also similar in structure to the First and Second Temples built in Jerusalem in later years. The descriptions for the First Temple are found in I Kings 5:26–6:13.

The second item is the mosaic design of a page of Talmud. Just looking at a page of Talmud, one can understand that it is not a simple matter of reading a linear text, but rather it requires an engagement of all the faculties. The page has an aesthetic mazelike design, and each column of commentaries surrounding the centrally placed Talmud text interprets, enhances, challenges, and deepens the understanding of the central text. Even the typeface of the central text differs from that of the commentaries. It is a "story-within-a-story" structure.

In addition to a physical pictorial page of Talmud, which explores multiple interpretations and dialogue between scholars, we can extend the physical frame designs to the metaphysical Jewish concept of *shivim panim la-Torah*, the seventy faces of Torah, which appears in the *Zohar*. In other words, there are many many ways to read the Torah for if you "turn it, and turn it," you will always discover new ways of understanding. This concept of "the seventy faces of Torah" comes from the eighth–ninth century text that is attributed to Akiva, *Otiyyot de-Rabbi Akiva*.

Furthermore, we see that the idea of multiplicity of explanation can be found in still another Jewish method. In order to get to those deeper and multiple meanings of text, a system called *Pardes* was created or codified by Moshe de Leon, the presumed author of the *Zohar*.[56] *Pardes*, which was originally a Persian word meaning an enclosed area, means "orchard" or "garden" in Hebrew. The word also refers to the Garden of Eden. The metaphor of an enclosed space or garden with its meandering paths has served as an exegetical method of scriptural interpretation to delve further and deeper into four levels of meanings and ultimately connect those meanings with our lives, to find the way to our true identity; in other words, for us to discover who we are and what we are about and how we want to live. PaRDeS is an acronym of four words: *pshat*, the literal level; *remez*, the allegorical level; *drash*, the aggadic level; and *sod*, the mystical level. With these four levels, the journey, which is non-linear and much more complex entering deeper into the center of the garden, can be taken with any text. "This sense that the text (or any life situation!) simultaneously bears several layers of meaning is characteristic of Jewish thinking."[57] Applying these four levels of interpretation, then, can bring us into a forest without an easy exit and without an accessible path to the center. We understand that there is a multiplicity of connections between the text and our lives. But even with the multiplicity of connections, the adventure is always worth it.

When we read the story, the *pshat* is the "simple" or literal meaning, the plot, the sequence of events that we can outline. The story begins with a frame story and breaks into a substructure of smaller stories or events that hinge on a problem that must be solved before the main problem in the frame narrative can be resolved. Sometimes in these more magical convoluted stories, the *pshat* can have some hurdles and prove puzzling.

The second level, *remez*, which literally means "hint," is the lesson or moral, the overall meaning of the story beyond the literal. Here is where you need to apply more questions about the characters in the story and their motives and intentions. The task is to find out what is the moral or message in the story. While many of the stories in the book seem not to be "Jewish," meaning that there may not be identifiable Jewish characters, a Jewish time, or a Jewish place; however, the message must be Jewish in order to be considered a Jewish story. See the discussion below on what makes a story Jewish.

The third higher and yet deeper level is *drash*, the aggadic level. *Drash* literally means "interpretation." This can mean seeing how the story connects to your life. It is more concerned with the specific aspects of the story than with the general message. First there is a subtext to be uncovered, a layer of meaning that will be conveyed because the teller or writer chooses to use certain words and images. The telling of these stories comes from my inner voice and it needs to reach your inner voice. We need to take what is in the story and make it our own. We need to fill in the spaces with questions, such as "What if . . . ?" and "How does this theme/message connect to me?" and "Of what does this remind me?" and "What would I do in this situation?"

The fourth and highest, yet deepest, level is *sod*, secret, the mystical level, and the most difficult to define. It is the unspoken understanding that forces you to take the story into your heart and make it part of you. Do not search for *sod*. *Sod* will find you when it is ready. Sometimes a story will click. Sometimes the meaning, both literal and symbolic, will enter you; the wisdom of the story will fuse with you. It will become your story, this right of ownership passed along because you understand the story to its roots. *Sod* is the inner heavenly glow of the pearl.

A number of the stories in this collection do not "seem" to be Jewish stories because they involve Arabic kings and queens, secular events, tall-tale lying contests, and so on, with no specific Jewish references. You may indeed wonder how do they come to be included in a book of Jewish tales. So perhaps we need to ask what then makes a story a Jewish story? There are two diametrically opposed schools of thought: On one hand there are some who believe that only stories from Jewish sources are truly Jewish stories. However, we know that stories that do not come from Jewish sources have entered into the Jewish body of stories. On the other hand, some believe that any story told by a Jew becomes a Jewish story. In this case, this is automatically true of all of these tales since they were collected either from Jews or retold by a Jew.

However, we need to examine the four components that folklorist Dov Noy has enumerated that characterize a Jewish story: Jewish time, Jewish space, Jewish character, and Jewish message.[58] Jewish time refers to the Jewish calendar, such as the yearly cycle of holidays, the monthly cycle, the weekly cycle of Shabbat, and the daily cycle of prayer; and also refers to the life cycle, such as the *brit*, bar mitzvah, and marriage.

Jewish space deals with the locale of the storytelling event as well as the setting of the story, such as the synagogue or sukkah, etc. Jewish character refers to the acting characters. Certain characters, such as a rabbi, a Chelmite, Miriam, and Elijah the Prophet, would be identifiable Jewish characters in a story. However, in Rabbi Nachman's stories, the characters are symbols, as for example, the king represents God, and the princess, the *Shekhinah*; thus they are very Jewish characters.[59]

However, these three elements are merely markers to indicate the possibility of the story being Jewish. The most important of these elements and the one that is essential for a story to be considered a Jewish story is its message, its lesson that teaches about life and about our duty to God, to another person, and to our people. You will discover as you read these fifty stories—and more if you count all the stories inside the stories—that they teach, inspire, and awaken sleeping hearts.

In modern times, this format of story-within-story has been used by many authors, including Salman Rushdie's *Haroun and the Sea of Stories*. Rushdie based this 1990 novella to a certain extent on Somadeva's enormous Sanskrit story cycle, *Kathasaritsagara* (The Ocean of the Sea of Story, c. 1070). In film, two examples come to mind: the 1951 film *Rashomon*, based on the Japanese folktale of three versions of the same murder; and the 1987 film *The Princess Bride*, based on William Goldman's 1973 novel. The swashbuckling fairytale is embedded in a modern setting opening and closing with the father telling his son a bedtime story.

However, the early writers, much more than most contemporary writers, were very conscious of the oral tradition. This was also the case, and it still remains to some extent, with the hasidic movement. By setting the frame, they acknowledged different kinds of oral telling in lower- and upper-class circles, and they suggest a notion of community that is crucial for the oral tradition. It is through the exchange of tales in the communal setting that people come to understand each other. Since the Sephardim had maintained the oral tradition of storytelling in their communities for centuries, it is then not surprising to find that the richest examples of these stories-within-stories are found among the stories coming from the Middle Eastern ethnic communities, which were collected in the Israel Folktale Archives.[60]

The folk power of invention and fantasy seems inexhaustible. The story-within-a-story is a quest story with *quest*ions asked, *quest*ions answered after a journey or after the fulfillment of a re*quest*. Sometimes we don't "get it" right away because of things that don't seem to make sense in the story. But these stories always fascinate and have deeper meanings that we need to think about. Someday, the meanings may be revealed when we read the story again, or some other story, or have an epiphany, or apply the four levels of interpretation called *pardes*. The fantastic is often tied to the symbolic and stirs our curiosity. These stories bring us into an intriguing maze of images and non-linear plots. We wander through forests, we get lost, we loop back or find a different path, we discover new sides of ourselves before we re-emerge from the woods. All of these stories-within-stories are "like apples of gold in frames of silver" (Proverbs 25:11).

Notes for Introduction

1. Interview with folklorist Dov Noy on March 29, 1995, in Jerusalem.

2. For a more detailed discussion of story structure, see Livo, Norma J., and Sandra A. Rietz. (1986). *Storytelling: Process & Practice.* Littleton, CO: Libraries Unlimited, pp. 27–89.

Also for an in-depth discussion of the folktale as an important art and as an introduction to the great folktales of the world, see: Thompson, Stith. (1977). *The Folktale.* Berkeley, CA: University of California Press. For a comprehensive exploration of the Hebrew folktale, including the frame narrative, see: Yassif, Eli. (1999). *The Hebrew Folktale: History, Genre, Meaning.* Translated from Hebrew by Jacqueline S. Teitelbaum. Bloomington, IN: Indiana University Press.

3. Ibid., p. 34.

4. Gittes, Katharine S. (1991). *Framing the Canterbury Tales: Chaucer and the Medieval Frame Narrative Tradition.* New York: Greenwood Press, p. 3.

5. Irwin, Bonnie D. "What's in a Frame? The Medieval Textualization of Traditional Storytelling" in *Oral Tradition*, Vol. 10/1 (1995), p. 42.

6. Ibid., p. 28. In footnote 2 on the same page, Irwin writes: "I would not, however, consider in this definition a framing story that enclosed only one tale."

7. Schwartz, Howard. (1998). *Reimagining the Bible: The Storytelling of the Rabbis.* New York: Oxford University Press, p. 18.

8. Livo & Rietz, op. cit., p. 41.

9. Yassif, Eli. (1999). *The Hebrew Folktale: History, Genre, Meaning.* Translated from Hebrew by Jacqueline S. Teitelbaum. Bloomington, IN: Indiana University Press, p. 214.

10. Ibid., p. 67.

11. Ibid., p. 39.

12. Ibid., p. 63.

13. Ibid., p. 64.

14. Apuleius. (1960). *The Golden Ass.* Translated by Jack Lindsay. Bloomington, IN: Indiana University Press, p. 13.

15. Ibid., p. 31.

16. Ibid., p. 19.

17. Gittes, op. cit., p. 77.

18. Letter from folklorist Jack Zipes, August 27, 1999.

19. Zipes, Jack, ed. (2000). *Oxford Companion to Fairy Tales*. New York: Oxford University Press. The information on Straparola and Basile was culled from the entries written by Jack Zipes and Nancy Canepa, respectively.

20. Zipes, Jack. (1991). *Arabian Nights: The Marvels and Wonders of the Thousand and One Nights*. Adapted from Richard F. Burton's unexpurgated translation. New York: Signet Classic, p. 585 (Afterword by Jack Zipes).

21. Epstein, Morris. (1967). *Tales of Sendebar*. Philadelphia, PA: The Jewish Publication Society of America, p. 15.

22. Ibid., p. 15.

23. *The Jewish Encyclopedia*. (1902, 1909, 1912). New York: Funk and Wagnalls Company, "Arabian Nights," p. 45.

24. Ibid., p. 45.

25. Zinberg, Israel. (1972–1978). *A History of Jewish Literature*. 12 volumes. Trans. and ed. by B. Martin. Cleveland and London: The Press of Case Western University, Vol. I, pp. 14–15.

26. Gittes, op. cit., p. 44.

27. Ibid., p. 34. See pp. 47–48 for a discussion of the mosque architectural structure resembling those of Arabic literature.

28. Zinberg, op. cit., p. 189.

29. Gittes, op. cit., p. 9.

30. Ibid., p. 9.

31. Ibid., p. 19.

32. Ibid., p. 57.

33. Ibid., p. 65.

34. Ibid., p. 58. For more discussion about *Disciplina Clericalis*, see Gittes, pp. 57–69.

35. Epstein, op. cit., p. 3.

36. Zinberg, op. cit., p. 199.

37. Letter from Jack Zipes, August 27, 1999.

38. Yassif, op. cit., p. 246. Also see footnote 2 on pp. 508–509 for many further sources about Arabic and Jewish frame narratives.

39. Zipes, Jack, Selected and Adapted. (1992). *Aesop's Fables.* New York: Signet Classic, Afterword by Jack Zipes, p. 276.

40. Townsend, George Fyler, translator. (1968). *Aesop's Fables.* New York: Doubleday & Company, p. 28.

41. Zipes, *Aesop's Fables,* op. cit., p. 278.

42. For more about kabbalah, the *Zohar,* and *sefirot,* see books by Gershom Scholem:

(1995). *Major Trends in Jewish Mysticism.* New York: Schocken Books.

(1965). *On the Kabbalah and its Symbolism.* New York: Schocken Books.

(1977). *Zohar: Book of Splendor.* Edited by Gershom Scholem. New York: Schocken Books.

43. Frankel, Ellen, and Betsy Platkin Teutsch. (1992). *The Encyclopedia of Jewish Symbols.* Northvale, NJ: Jason Aronson, p. 86.

44. For a discussion of these differences regarding *zimzum,* see: Dan, Joseph. (1983). *The Teachings of Hasidism.* New York: Behrman House, pp. 18–19.

45. Frankel and Teutsch, op. cit., p. 87.

46. Dan, op. cit., pp. 31–32.

47. Mintz, Jerome R. (1968). *Legends of the Hasidim: An Introduction to Hasidic Culture and Oral Tradition in the New World.* Chicago, IL: The University of Chicago Press, p. 8.

Four valuable resources on hasidic story are:

Dan, Joseph. (1975). *The Hasidic Story—Its History and Development.* (Hebrew). Jerusalem.

Ben-Amos, Dan, and Jerome R. Mintz, Translators and Editors. (1993). *In Praise of the Baal Shem Tov.* Northvale, NJ: Jason Aronson.

Newman, Louis I. (1987). *The Hasidic Anthology.* Northvale, NJ: Jason Aronson.

Citron, Sterna. (1994). *Why the Baal Shem Tov Laughed: Fifty-two Stories about Our Great Chasidic Rabbis.* Northvale, NJ: Jason Aronson.

48. Dan, op. cit., p. 30.

49. Schwartz, Howard, ed. (1991). *Gates to the New City: A Treasury of Modern Jewish Tales.* Northvale, NJ: Jason Aronson.

50. Kaplan, Aryeh. (1983). *Rabbi Nachman's Stories: The Stories of Rabbi Nachman of Breslov. (Sippure Maasiyot).* Brooklyn, NY: Breslov

Research Institute. Aryeh Kaplan has translated twenty-nine of Nachman's stories and parables, supplying extensive annotations for the stories.

51. Interview with folklorist Dov Noy on March 29, 1995, in Jerusalem.

52. Kaplan, op. cit., pp. 8–9.

53. Ibid., p. 31.

54. Thompson, Stith. (1977). *The Folktale*. Berkeley, CA: University of California Press, p. 458.

55. Mintz, op. cit., p. 6.

56. Scholem, Gershom. (1995). *Major Trends in Jewish Mysticism*. New York: Schocken Books, p. 400, note 15.

57. Green, Arthur. (1999). *These Are the Words: A Vocabulary of Jewish Spiritual Life*. Woodstock, VT: Jewish Lights Publishing, p. 25.

58. For more about this model of Jewish folktale, see Dov Noy's Introduction in:

Schwartz, Howard. (1988). *Miriam's Tambourine: Jewish Folktales from Around the World*. New York: Oxford University Press, pp. xi–xix.

59. See Aryeh Kaplan's annotations in *Rabbi Nachman's Stories*.

60. The Israel Folktale Archives was founded by Dov Noy in 1956 and the archives are at the Haifa University. The IFA Coordinator is Edna Cheichel-Hechal. Through the work of volunteers, they have gathered over 20,000 folktales from the various ethnic communities that live in Israel and classified them according to folk motifs and tale types. The IFA is the source of thirty-nine of the fifty stories in this anthology.

1

The King Who Loved Stories

There once was a king who loved stories. He could never get his fill of stories. One day the king announced, "Whoever can tell me a story that will make me say 'Enough!' will receive a great prize." Of course the king thought that could never happen. And, in this way, the king was certain he would hear many many stories. And so he did.

One person after another came to the king and told him stories, stories, and more stories. Each one wanted only to win the generous prize from the king. Meanwhile the king heard many many stories. He listened to all the stories, each of which gave him great delight, so he never said "Enough!"

One day a man came to the palace and told the King this story:

> Next to the king's palace there was a gigantic hut. Inside the hut there was wheat. One day a mouse came, a tiny tiny mouse, and he made a small small hole in the wall of the hut until he could get into the wheat. He crawled into the hole, ate the wheat, became full, and went out. Then the next day, another mouse came, a small small mouse who then made a small small hole in the wall of the hut until he could get into the wheat. He crawled into the hole, ate the wheat, became full, and went out.
>
> The next day, a tiny tiny mouse came and made a small small hole in the wall of the hut until he could get into the wheat. He went in, ate the wheat, became full, and then went out.
>
> The next day, . . .

At first the king listened with interest. But then when the king had heard this same story for the seventieth time, the king became more and more impatient. Finally, he got so angry that he shouted, "Enough!"

"Aha," said the man, "I have won the prize." And so he had!

End of Story Note

IFA 18.146 Told by Hinda Scheinfarber from Poland and recorded by Hadara Sela. This story was never published.
Tale Type: AT 2300 (Corn Carried Away Grain at a Time).
Motif: Z11.1 (Endless tale).

There are many universal as well as Jewish folktales concerning contests where a king offers a reward if someone can make him respond a certain way:

1. by making the king say, "That's a lie!" (see "A Tall Tale" in my *Jewish Stories One Generation Tells Another*);

2. by making the king laugh and cry at the same time (see "Laughter and Tears" in my *Tales of Elijah the Prophet*);

3. by telling the king a story that does not have an ending (see "The Horse That Got Stuck in the Mud" in this collection.)

In this tale, the king who loves stories offers a prize to anyone who can make him say "Enough!" to a story. This is a Formula Tale, tale type AT 2300 with motif Z11.1 (Endless Tale). It is similar to tale type AT 2301A (Making the King Lose Patience). This is also accomplished by telling how an ant came to a huge heap of grain and took a grain home with him; the next day the same thing happens; and so on. Hearing this repeated over and over, the king loses patience and rewards the storyteller.

For a variant of this story, see "The Storyteller" in *The Fire on the Mountain and Other Ethiopian Stories* (Courlander and Leslan).

As you begin reading this collection of involving stories, may you have patience to follow the maze and enjoy the stories "grain by grain."

—PS

2

We Never Lose Old Treasures

Several years ago I was in the Albuquerque airport waiting to board the plane for my return to New York. I had been in New Mexico for a storytelling booking combined with a vacation. Since I still had some time before boarding, I decided to go to the gift shop to look at picture postcards of the views that I had seen or had missed seeing. As I was standing there at the carousel of postcards, a man stepped up to the counter and asked the young saleswoman, "Do you have any string?"

"String?" She repeated the request in a puzzled tone as though she had never heard of string in this package-taped world. "No, we don't," she answered, ready to turn to the next customer. However, the man kept asking that she look in the storeroom and she kept insisting that they had no string. Meanwhile, I said to myself, "Peninnah, stay out of this!" At that moment, I suddenly turned to the man and asked, "How much string do you need?" He held out his arms about three feet apart and said, "About three times this length."

Without a word, I reached into my canvas carry-on bag and, after a few seconds of rummaging around, found the packet of used string wound around with a rubber band and handed it to the man. It was not new string, but old string with knots, many knots tying together different lengths of used string. "I always carry old string with me . . . in case . . ." After exchanging our names, smiles, and a thank-you, the man left.

As I boarded the plane, I looked around and saw the man standing against a wall reading his newspaper. Next to him was a box wrapped around with my string.

Suddenly I realized what my mother had often told me all through my childhood was really true. "Don't throw anything out. It may come in handy." She used to use the Yiddish expression: *Dos vet kumn tzu nitst.* My mother never threw anything out, and even when she tried, it somehow always turned up again and again—and it always came in handy. And that reminds me of a story that perfectly illustrates my point.

Many years ago, in the town of Baghdad, there lived a man and his name was Abu Kasem. One day Abu Kasem received a great inheritance and he became very rich. So what did he do? He bought a house with a garden and new clothes. Only he did not want to part with his old sandals. After all, they were very comfortable.

But his neighbors said to him, "Abu Kasem, here you have become so rich. It is not nice that a rich man, like you, with such nice new clothes, should walk in the streets with such old sandals."

So what did Abu Kasem do? The next day he went and bought new shoes and wore them even though they pinched his feet. And the sandals, well, he took them and threw them into the river.

The next day, two fishermen came to him and said, "Abu Kasem, Abu Kasem, look what we caught in our net." And they threw his old sandals on the floor of the house and left.

What did Abu Kasem do? He went to the bath house and left them there, thinking to himself, "Surely someone who needs them will take them."

The next day, a young boy came to him and said, "Abu Kasem, Abu Kasem, you forgot your sandals at the bath house." The young boy threw the sandals on the floor and left.

What did Abu Kasem do? He decided to bury the sandals in the ground. So he waited until night and he dug a hole and buried the sandals.

The next day, the police came to him and said, "Abu Kasem, Abu Kasem, we heard that last night you found a treasure in the ground. You have been seen digging in the earth. This treasure belongs to the country and you must give it to us."

Abu Kasem told them the whole truth about the sandals. The police left him alone and went away. And ever since then, Abu Kasem has worn only his old sandals.

And so, my mother's advice keeps turning up—over and over again, like those old sandals, and her wisdom "comes in handy." How did my mother, Dora Markman Manchester, become so wise to understand that that would happen? Maybe it's because she knew so many stories.

That's how Jews have kept our stories in the oral tradition for all of these centuries. We, too, need to continue to tell our "old" stories and circulate them, like gifts of string, until they feel like comfortable old sandals. And we must never discard these old stories. These stories connect people, heart to heart, and bind us with strong knots as friends wherever we journey in life. Stories are our treasures.

End of Story Note

IFA 8898—titled "The Old Sandals," in *A Tale for Each Month 1970*, Story #5, collected by David Gid'on from his mother Sarah, from Turkey (Noy).
Tale Type: AT 745 (Hatch-penny or The Reproducing Coin).
Motifs: N211.2 (Unsuccessful try to be freed of a pair of slippers); H602.3 (Symbolic interpretation of names).

I begin with a personal story as the narrative frame of an episode that actually happened to me. In retelling this incident, I realized that it is connected to my philosophy of life and to the ways of oral tradition. I then embedded a popular folk tale of the old sandals within the personal story frame.

According to the folkloristic annotations, the international tale type (AT 745) is also connected to AT 736A (The Ring of Polycrates) where a king throws a ring into the sea and it is found the next day in a fish brought to him. However, the motives for each of the characters is different: throwing the precious ring away is to avoid the jealousy of the gods, a religious motive; while throwing away the sandals now that the man has become rich, and, therefore, it is no longer seemly to wear old tattered sandals, is social.

There are variants from Libya (IFA 9326) where a man loses all the money he inherited but for one coin, which keeps returning to him. The coin helps him prosper once again. IFA 9400 from Iraq is similar except that, instead of a penny, it is sandals that keep turning up. This tale also belongs to *The Arabian Nights* and medieval European tradition.

Common to almost all the variants is the name of the main character, Abu Kasem, which means "father of fate" from the Turkish and Arabic. This story has the quality of a joke or a humoristic story. It touches us in a delightful way to see how Abu Kasem cannot get rid of the sandals, no matter what he does, and then gives up trying. Sometimes we have to know that there are some things we cannot control—or should not throw away.

This is a story for all time.

For other stories dealing with the question of "fate" in this collection, see "Can Fate Be Changed?" and "The Luck of Faradj, the Rope Maker."

—PS

3

The Emperor's Daughter
and the King's Son

Once there was a merchant whose wife had no equal in her beauty and grace. One day, the merchant told his wife, "I must go on a journey to a distant country. As soon as I buy the merchandise I need, I will return to you."

But his wife began to weep. "Dear husband, when you leave, I will be alone. How shall I spend my time?"

The husband replied, "I will go to the marketplace today and buy you something that will amuse you during the time I am gone." As soon as the husband entered the marketplace, he heard someone call out, "Buy this wonderful bird. Whoever buys this bird will bless this day; but whoever buys this bird will forever pay."

Puzzled by these words, the merchant approached the seller and asked, "What do your words mean?"

"Only the buyer can know and understand. I'll sell you the bird for one thousand dinars."

The merchant hesitated. After all, it was a great deal of money. But, he also realized that the little bird, with all the colors of the rainbow in its feathers, would be a good companion for his wife during his journey. As he paid the money, the seller added, "Remember, this bird eats only almonds and raisins and drinks only milk and honey."

The merchant returned home with the rainbow bird and gave it lovingly to his wife, adding all the instructions the seller had given him. Then the merchant prepared for his journey.

Waving to her husband from the balcony, the wife lingered a while longer to enjoy the gentle breeze stirring the trees and watch the drifting clouds.

At that moment, another carriage was riding by with the son of the Sultan. Looking up, he saw the merchant's wife. Smitten by her beauty and grace, the Sultan's son returned to the palace and fell into bed with a raging fever. The Sultan's physicians were called but no one could cure the prince because they did not know the cause of his sudden illness.

The Sultan finally called in a wise old woman and said to her, "Stay with my son to try to find out what is wrong." The old woman sat near the prince's bed all throughout the night. In his sleep he cried aloud, "My love, where are you? Come to me and delight my heart, my love."

In the morning, the wise old woman went to the Sultan and said, "I know what is the matter with the prince. I will bring the cure for him." And she went directly to the merchant's house.

She knocked on the door and said to the merchant's wife, "There is a wonderful celebration which you must attend. I have come to escort your personally."

But the merchant's wife replied, "I cannot go with you as I wait for my husband to return."

However, the old woman kept insisting that she come with her, until finally the merchant's wife agreed. However, first she went inside to change her clothes and put on her perfumes and powders. As the merchant's wife was about to leave the house, she turned to the rainbow bird and said, "Goodbye, my little bird."

"Oh, dear, dear lady, you have already forgotten me," answered the bird.

"Is there something you would like?" asked the wife.

"Well, I want to tell you a story, if you will listen," said the bird.

"Of course I will listen. Tell it to me at once," answered the merchant's wife.

Once there was a great emperor who had no children. There was also a king who had no children. Each ruler traveled to many countries to try and find a remedy in order to have an heir. Once it happened that both the emperor and the king arrived at the same town and met while staying at the same inn. Since they became friends very quickly, each revealed to the other the reason for the journey. The emperor said to the king, "If it should happen that one of us has a son and the other a daughter, let us take a vow that our children will marry each other." The king agreed and they gave each other their word. Then the emperor and the king returned to their homes.

Within the year, the emperor's wife gave birth to a daughter. At that same time, the king's wife gave birth to a son. However, their vows were forgotten.

As the children grew, the two rulers each sent his child away to study in a certain land. The two children happened to meet since they studied with the same teacher and they came to love each other very much. The king's son gave a gold ring to the young woman as a token of his love.

One day, when their fathers had heard about the vows of love their children had given to each other, they commanded their children to return home. The emperor wrote that he would not approve of this marriage. The king wrote the same thing.

The two young people did not know what to do. They could not leave each other, perhaps never to see each other again. They talked about what they could do. "We love each other more than anything else in the world. We must remain together and marry." So they decided to hire a ship and set sail.

One day they reached a coast and went ashore to walk and rest. As they lay down to sleep, under the trees in the forest, the emperor's daughter handed the gold ring to the prince and he placed the ring next to her. When she woke, they returned to the ship. Just then he remembered that he had left the ring on the ground under the tree. He ran back to the woods to look for it, but he could not find the place where they had been. He searched deeper and deeper in the forest and soon he was lost in the maze of paths and bushes, and far from the shore. Finally, he saw a clearing and a city in the distance. He went to an inn and got work as a servant.

After waiting for the prince for a long time, the emperor's daughter decided to go searching for him. But soon she, too, was lost in the labyrinth of the forest. She finally found a path that led to the shore—but it was a different shore, because their ship was nowhere in sight. She decided to wait there, sleeping in a tree at night so that animals would not harm her. During the day, she ate the fruit of the trees nearby and she walked along the shore waiting and hoping that the king's son would return to her.

In a foreign country, there was a great merchant who had traded everywhere and who was very old. He had one son who was the apple of his eye. One day the son said to him, "My dear father, I need to gain some experience in the ways of the world and I need to learn about business. In that way, I will be able to take responsibility for the business one day. Give me a ship and goods and let me sail the seas."

And the merchant gave his son what he had asked for and the son set sail. He traded the merchandise and did well. One day his ship sailed near the shore where the emperor's daughter was waiting for the prince. He did not see her, at first. But as he was looking in the water, he saw the reflection of a top of a tree and what looked like a woman sitting in the branches. He got into a small boat and went ashore. He called up to the young woman to climb down.

She replied, "I will come down on one condition, that you do not touch me until we return to your home and are married according to the law. However, you must promise not to ask who I am until then."

The young merchant's son promised to do as she asked.

When the emperor's daughter went aboard his ship, the merchant's son found out that she could sing and speak in several languages and could play musical instruments. He was enchanted with her and very happy that he had met her.

As they were getting closer to his home, the emperor's daughter said to the young man, "You must go to your parents and family by yourself first and tell them that you are bringing a very important woman home. In that way, they will all come to the dock to welcome me. And it is also proper that you should give the special wine you have on the ship to all the sailors on board so they should also know that you are marrying an important woman."

The merchant's son agreed. He brought out barrels of the special wine and gave it to the sailors to drink and celebrate while he returned to his home to tell the news to his family.

Meanwhile, the sailors went ashore and fell down all over the place in a drunken sleep. Then while the merchant's family were preparing to greet the mysterious young woman, the emperor's daughter untied the ship and spread the sails and set out to sea in the ship.

When the merchant's family arrived at the dock, they did not find a ship. "Believe me, father, I brought the ship filled with excellent merchandise— and a bride, too. Ask the sailors and they will tell you that what I speak is the truth." But when they looked around, they saw only the drunken sleeping sailors. Finally, a few of them awakened but they did not have any idea what had happened to them. However, they did remember that there had been a ship there.

The old merchant was so angry with his son that he said, "Leave my house. I never want to see you again." And his son became a wanderer.

"And so you see, dear lady," the rainbow bird said to the merchant's wife, "that if you go with this old woman to the celebration, you will regret it, just as the young man did."

Then the young wife turned to the old woman and said, "I will not go with you after all. Perhaps another day. But today I must wait for my husband."

The old woman returned to the palace. The prince still remained with a fever, calling out for his love.

On the next day, the old woman returned to the merchant's house and knocked on the door. "Dear lady, come with me today for there will be an even greater celebration at the palace."

"I will gladly go with you today. Let me put on some proper clothes and perfumes."

Just as she was about to leave the house, she again turned to her rainbow bird and said, "Goodbye, my little bird."

The bird said, "Dear lady, have you forgotten about me already?"

"Is there something you would like, little bird?"

"Not really, except that I would like you to listen to a story. Do you not want to know what happened to the emperor's daughter?"

"Yes, I do," answered the merchant's wife.

"Then listen," replied the little bird.

The emperor's daughter continued sailing the ship until she came to a land where the king of that place had built his palace near the sea. When the king looked out at sea and saw the ship, he was puzzled because he did not see any sailors or other people on the ship. The king sent his sailors out to bring the ship to the shore. When they did, the king saw the emperor's daughter and he wanted her very much. He had never married since no one had ever pleased him.

The young woman said to the king, "You must promise not to touch me until we are wedded according to the law." And the king gave his oath. Then she added, "And you must not board the ship nor touch any of the goods on board. The ship must remain anchored out at sea until our wedding. Then, at that time, everybody will see the vast and goodly things I have brought with me. In that way, people will see that I am an important woman, and not just someone that you had taken from the marketplace. Only at our wedding will I also reveal who I am." The king promised to do as she wished.

The king built a special palace for his bride, the emperor's daughter. She also demanded that eleven noble maidens be brought to her to keep her company. The king immediately ordered that princes and ministers send their daughters and he built eleven palaces for these young women. These young women kept the emperor's daughter company as they played musical instruments and sang and also played games.

One day, she said to them, "Come, let us board my ship and spend some time on the water." And so they all went on board. While they were singing and playing games, the emperor's daughter said, "Let us all drink some of my special wine. It will make us feel good." And she gave them the wine to drink. As soon as they became drunk and fell asleep, the emperor's daughter pulled up the anchor, spread the sails, and set sail out to sea.

Meanwhile, one of the king's men was looking toward the water and saw that the ship was no longer in sight. He ran to tell the king, but the king said, "My bride will be very upset by this news that her ship is gone. Let us send one of her noble maidens to tell her the news in a gentle manner."

But when they went to find one of the eleven maidens, they could not find any of them. Then they went to the chamber of the bride, but she too was missing.

Meanwhile, the fathers of those eleven maidens were alarmed that they had not heard from their daughters. When they found their daughters missing, they became furious with the king and decided to banish him from the kingdom. The king had to leave his land and become a wanderer.

"And so, dear lady," said the rainbow bird, "if you go with this woman to the celebration, you too will regret it as the king was filled with regret."

The merchant's wife turned to the old woman and said, "I cannot go with you today after all. I will most certainly go tomorrow."

The old woman became angry but she quickly left the house.

On the next day, the old woman returned to the merchant's wife earlier than usual. After a long time, the young woman once again agreed to go with her and ran upstairs to change her clothes and put on her oils and powders and perfumes. As she was on her way out of the door, she turned to bid farewell to the bird.

The bird said, "Oh you have really forgotten me."

The merchant's wife became angry, "Why are you always stopping me and why don't you let me go to the celebration so I can dance?"

"But aren't you curious to know what happened to the emperor's daughter on the ship with the eleven maidens?" asked the bird.

The merchant's wife wanted to shout "No" since she had no more patience. But she was intrigued to know what had happened to the women in the story.

"Listen a while longer, dear lady, and you will know all," answered the bird.

The emperor's daughter was sailing on the ship when, after a time, the eleven companions woke up from the wine-induced sleep. "Let us return to shore. All I see is water in every direction," they said. Then a storm came and they again pleaded, "Let us go back home." But finally the emperor's daughter told them they were already far from home and she planned to continue sailing.

"But why did you do this?" they asked her.

"Because of the storm. I was afraid that the ship would split apart and be wrecked. I had to release it and spread the sails."

They began to sail the seas and sing and play their instruments day after day.

Finally they saw an island in the sea and approached it and landed on it. There they found twelve pirates facing them.

"Which one is your leader?" asked the emperor's daughter. And the leader stepped forward.

"And who are you?" he asked her.

"We are also pirates, but while you rob with bravery and strength, we rob with our wisdom and cleverness. We know many languages and music, so what would you gain by killing us? You would have everything to gain rather by marrying us. Each one of you would gain a wife—as well as the great riches we carry on the ship," and the emperor's daughter.

The pirates were persuaded by her words and, after seeing the treasures on the ship, the pirates showed the young women their great wealth. Then they also agreed that each man should be matched with a woman that suited him best. The leader who was drawn to the beauty of the women's leader, chose her. After all of that was settled, the emperor's daughter offered them the special wine that she had on board ship.

"Let us drink to our good matches since this is a special occasion," she said. And she gave each pirate a goblet filled with wine. They all drank and fell into a drunken stupor.

The emperor's daughter turned to her companions and said, "Take knives and each one slaughter your pirate-partner." And they did as she instructed. Then they went to the pirate's treasuries where they found greater wealth than any king possessed. They threw overboard some of the merchandise already on the ship and loaded the ship instead with the pirate's gold and jewels, leaving behind copper and silver.

As they were about to leave, they also decided that they would dress as men. They quickly sewed men's clothing, put it on, and sailed away from this place.

After a time, the ship arrived at a port and the twelve of them went ashore. As they were walking in the town, they heard the sounds of wailing and cries of mourning as they saw crowds of people walking toward the palace. When they asked the people what had happened, they answered, "The king has died and there are no children to sit on the throne. When that is the case, there is a custom in our land for the queen to climb to the roof of the palace and throw the crown down upon the crowd of single men who gather below. On whose ever head the crown falls, that man must marry the queen and become our new king."

Just as she heard the word "king," the emperor's daughter, in the disguise of a man, felt something land on her head. It was the royal crown. A great shout went up, "God bless our king!" She was lifted onto the shoulders of soldiers and carried to the palace. Of course, no one knew that the person chosen to be king was not really a man, but the emperor's daughter.

While plans were being made for the royal wedding, the disguised king ordered that fountains be set up around the city for all travelers to refresh themselves and that "her" portrait was to be placed at every fountain. Then the announcement was made in every country that all strangers, wanderers, and vagabonds should all come to the royal wedding. Meanwhile, the disguised king ordered that guards should stand next to the portraits to observe those who approach and, if someone stared for a long time at the portrait or expressed astonishment or grief, then that person was to be brought immediately to the "king."

The guards brought three people. The first one was the young prince who was the real bridegroom of this emperor's daughter. The second one was the son of the merchant whose father had thrown him out of his home on account that she had fled with his ship. The third person was the king who had been thrown out of his country because she had fled with the eleven noble maidens. Each of them recognized a resemblance to her in the portrait, so they stared and grieved and were arrested.

Just before the wedding was to take place, the disguised king—the emperor's daughter really—ordered that the three prisoners be brought in. She recognized them, of course, but they did not even imagine that this king could be the young woman they had wanted to marry.

The emperor's daughter said to the third man, "You who were a king thrown out because of the eleven lost maidens, here they are alive and well. Return with them to your kingdom with my gratitude."

To the second young man, she said, "You whose merchant father drove you away from home because of the lost ship, there is your ship with greater wealth than what you had brought and now return home with my appreciation."

Then she stood up from the throne and left the room. She took off her king's robes and dressed in a golden gown. When she entered the throne room again, she walked up to the first young man, and said, "And you, my prince, let us return home together."

When the merchant's wife heard the end of the story of the emperor's daughter and the king's son, she turned to the old woman, now ready to leave for the celebration. At that moment, a carriage appeared and the merchant himself arrived from his journey. When he noticed her clothes and perfumes, he asked her where she was going. Then he saw the old woman and demanded to know what was happening. Out of fear, the old woman told him the truth about the Sultan's son's love for his wife, but that it was the rainbow bird that had detained her with stories.

The merchant gently took the rainbow bird in his hand and asked, "Now I know why the seller said 'Whoever buys this bird will bless the day.' But what did he mean by 'Whoever buys this bird will forever pay'?"

"I will gladly explain it to you, but first open your hand and you will see," said the bird.

The merchant opened his hand and the little bird flew away, disappearing into the sky.

As for the Sultan's son, we are told that he died of love and the Sultan ordered that the old woman, who had delayed bringing the son's love, to be drowned.

That happened to them, but this happened to us. On their roof is sheep dung; on ours, almonds and raisins. If we have spoken the truth, it is God's truth; if we have lied, God forgive us. Go home quickly, or the dog will eat up your supper, and forgive us for wearying you. We, in turn, forgive you for being such a nuisance to us.

End of Story Note

Based on Reb Nachman's story "The King and the Emperor" in Rabbi Nachman of Bratslav's *Sippure Maasiyot* (Warsaw, 1881) combined with a Yemenite variant.

Tale Type: AT 1352A (Seventy Tales of a Parrot Prevents a Wife's Adultery). This tale type is well-known as a frame tale.

Motifs: K1837 (Disguise of woman in man's clothes); H1385.4 (Quest of vanished husband).

Rabbi Nachman of Bratslav (1770–1810), the great-grandson of the Baal Shem Tov, was the greatest hasidic storyteller. He was so revered by his *hasidim*, that, after his death, they have kept him as their "rebbe."

This well-known hasidic story (sometimes titled "The Broken Betrothal") was told by Reb Nachman probably during the winter of 1806–1807. All of Reb Nachman's classic stories (there are thirteen primary tales) are among the most imaginative folktales, yet filled with spiritual and mystical allusions and insights revealed to those who study and delve into those "secular," apparently simple tales. If one reads Rabbi Nathan's Introductions (Reb Nachman's scribe) and Aryeh Kaplan's translations of the stories along with the commentaries by Reb Nachman's students and followers, one sees the complexity and mysteries embedded in these stories. However, these stories can also be read on a literal (*pshat*) level with great enjoyment.

But where did Reb Nachman get these wondrous stories? "[The Rebbe] would sometimes relate ordinary folk tales, but he would embellish them. He would change the order of the story, so that it was very different than the original folk tale" (*Rabbi Nachman's Stories*, Kaplan, 8). Incorporating folklore motifs in a literary creation, Reb Nachman would create an allegory and infuse his tellings with a higher holy purpose—to teach Torah and moral lessons and ultimately to bring people back to God. "When Rabbi Nachman first started telling his stories, he declared: 'Now I am going to tell you stories.' The reason he did so was because in generations so far from God the only remedy was to present the secrets of the Torah . . . in the form of stories. There was no other way to achieve the necessary impact in order to heal us" (Introduction by Chaim Kramer, *Rabbi Nachman's Stories*, viii). It was

Reb Nachman who said (and I paraphrase), "Stories bypass the intellect and enter directly into the heart." And so it continues.

The inner story begins with a vow taken by the Emperor and the King to marry their future children to each other. A vow is sacred and, thus, cannot be broken easily in Judaism, at least not without some consequence. (See the stories "A Promised Betrothal" and "A Bride's Wisdom" in my *Jewish Stories One Generation Tells Another.*)

The enigmatic Hebrew rhyme by the parrot vender was rendered into rhyming English by Roslyn Bresnick-Perry.

Versions of this story can be found in *Mimekor Yisrael* (Bin Gorion), *Rabbi Nachman's Stories, Classic Hasidic Tales* (Levin), *Elijah's Violin* (Schwartz), and *From the Land of Sheba: Tales of the Jews of Yemen* (Goiten). The basic elements of the story can also be found in *The Arabian Nights.*

The motif of the parrot who keeps a certain young woman intrigued with stories is also found in another Jewish text, namely *Mishlei Sendebar*, as well as in international folktales. In *Mishlei Sendebar* (see my discussion of this text in the Introductory Essay) the King, in the frame story, hears a cautionary story told about a rich man who had an unfaithful wife. The rich man buys a parrot in the marketplace, and asks the parrot to spy on his wife and report all that he witnesses. Then the husband gives the parrot to his wife ordering her to care for the parrot. But how the story continues does not concern us here. However, the inclusion of a parrot as a spy telling "tales" or as a teller of tales to deter the wife from leaving is a known motif.

We find the storytelling parrot also in a Sicilian folktale (from Giuseppe Pitrè's *Fiabe, Novelle, e Racconti—Folktales, Fictions, and Stories*) that forms the core of Gioia Timpanelli's lyrical novella, "A Knot of Tears" in *Sometimes the Soul.* In a conversation with Gioia, she told me that she remembered hearing this folktale as a child. Being the respected poet/storyteller/teacher that she is, she incorporates the source of the folktale in her novella as part of a letter that the main character Constanza writes to her friend. "Please remember to write me about the Pitrè. '*Lu Pappagaddu Chi Cunta Tri Cunti?*' I can't quite remember the frame story of that one. Is it about a husband and wife? I know the motif of a parrot storyteller exists in Arabian, Spanish, even Asian versions. But I think the Sicilian one is not about marriage but about stories themselves" (p. 72).

Integrating folklore material into contemporary literary works continues—a form of recycling that revitalizes the culture and nourishes the soul. This is the process of oral tradition, even one step beyond, that reassures us that the oral tradition remains vital and vigorous.

For more in-depth discussion of Reb Nachman, see *Reimagining the Bible* (Schwartz, pp. 163–175), *Tormented Master: A Life of Rabbi Nachman of Bratslav* (Green), and *Rabbi Nachman's Stories* (Kaplan).

The ending paragraph of this story is a formulaic ending found in Yemen and Morocco, and especially Arabic cultures, as a way to lead the listeners out of the story mode and back to where they are. It is also a form of a blessing.

—PS

4

The Gates of Tears

It was a year of drought. No rain had fallen for many months. Holidays had come and still the prayers for rain had not been answered. The earth was parched and hardened. The people had little food to eat and water to drink. The rabbis prayed and fasted. The people prayed and fasted. Still no rains came.

One night the rabbi had a dream and in the dream he heard a voice that said, "Call Rachamim to the bimah to pray before the congregation. Only if he prays, then will God hear his prayers and the rains will descend from Heaven."

In the morning, the rabbi remembered the dream and what the voice had told him to do. He was astonished because Rachamim was an ignorant man who didn't know how to read. However, the rabbi ran to the synagogue and told the shammas, "Go to Rachamim's house and bring him here—and go quickly."

Soon Rachamim arrived at the synagogue and the rabbi told him, "Rachamim, it is you who must go in front of the congregation to pray for rain. You have been chosen by God to plead before Him. Only then will God send rain to us."

"But rabbi," stammered Rachamim, "you know that I do not know the prayers. I do not know how to read the prayers. Please choose a more learned man. I cannot stand in front of everyone."

"No, Rachamim, you must be the one to pray on our behalf. Shammas, summon the people to come to the synagogue so we can begin the prayers for rain."

Immediately the shammas left the synagogue to gather the congregation. And Rachamim also left the synagogue—to return home.

In the meantime, everyone in the community had gathered in the synagogue. They waited for the rabbi to begin the prayers. But instead, the rabbi called out, "Rachamim, come to the bimah." Everyone looked around. Where was Rachamim? And why was the rabbi inviting him to begin the service when everyone knew that Rachamim was a simple man who did not know how to study Torah or even how to read.

A few moments later, Rachamim came back into the synagogue and he went up to the bimah. He was holding a small clay pitcher with two spouts. He turned to the congregation and asked everyone to begin the prayers. As the Holy Ark was opened and everyone stood and began to recite Psalms, Rachamim stood on the bimah and brought one of the spouts up to his mouth and whispered some words into the spout. Then he turned the pitcher and held the second spout up to his ear.

A short time passed. Then from a distance, a small dark cloud began to appear at the horizon and spread quickly. Soon the rain cloud covered the entire sky and a torrential rain began to fall.

The rabbi went over to Rachamim and asked, "Rachamim, your prayers brought the rain. But why did you bring this clay pitcher? What did you do? What did you say?"

This is the story that Rachamim told. "Rabbi, I am a poor man with a wife and many children. I am a cobbler and, no matter how hard I work, I cannot earn enough for my family. How many nights have I seen my children go to sleep hungry crying for bread and there is no bread. My heart breaks to hear their cries. So what could I do? I would go to the corner of the room and I would weep bitterly. I began to collect my tears in this clay pitcher. I asked my wife to bury this pitcher with me when I die. So when you asked me to pray for rain, I brought this pitcher from my home and spoke into one of the spouts and said, 'Rebono Shel Olam, You know what each tear means to me. You understand how much each tear contains the outpouring of my soul. So, Rebono Shel Olam, if you do not bring rain, I will break this clay pitcher in the presence of the entire congregation.' Then I put the second spout up to my ear to hear the response and a voice said, 'Do not shatter the pitcher!' Then it began to rain."

The rabbi began to weep and said, "It is because of your tears that the rains came. How true are the words of our sages: 'The Gates of Tears are never locked.'"

End of Story Note

IFA 9229 From *A Tale for Each Month 1971*, Story #10, collected by Moshe Rabi from Josef Statya, from Syria (Noy).
Tale Types: AT 752*D (IFA) (Simpleton's prayer brings down rain); **AT 827*A** (IFA) (Simpleton's successful prayer).
Motifs: V 51.1 (God wishes the heart); D2143.1.3 (Rain produced by prayer).

This theme of an innocent and unlearned man asked to pray for rain is very popular in both oral and written Jewish literature. A special kind of Jewish tale that appears in no other culture, it is a Jewish oikotype of AT 827 (A Shepherd Knows Nothing of God). This comes from the saying, "Rakhmana lieba ba'ee" (God Wants the Heart), which, according to Dov Noy, is based upon the talmudic maxim in *Sanhedrin* 106b, which stems from I Samuel 17:7. In Psalms 116:6 there is also a reference to the simple man: "God guards the simple." See "A Hero of the Spirit and a Hero of the Flesh" in *Moroccan Jewish Folktales*, story #28 (Noy).

The tale type "God Wants the Heart" is clear in another parallel tale from Syria (IFA 7728) in *A Tale for Each Month 1967* (Cheichel-Hechal): I. A rabbi preaches about the impossibility to offer at present the showbread in the Temple in Jerusalem. The simple man thinks that his synagogue is meant and offers bread in the ark, which is taken away by the shammas. The simple man thinks that God has accepted his offering and is delighted. A version of this tale, titled "Challahs in the Ark" by Rabbi Zalman Schacter, can be found in *Gates to the New City* (Schwartz).

There are many other variants, but the four essential elements in the tale type AT 752*D (IFA) are always the same: There is a drought; the community's fasts and special prayers do not bring rain; someone in the community who is often illiterate must pray for rain; God answers his prayers alone, and sends rain. In other words, it is not the formal representative of the normative religion whose prayers are heard, but rather the illiterate simpleton, because of his simple faith or simple deeds.

Throughout the Torah God promises to bring the rain according to its season as a blessing as long as we, the Jewish people, hold to our partnership of the Covenant. (Leviticus 26:3–4 and Deuteronomy 11:13–14) There are many prayers for rain at various times of the year: for *geshem* (rain) on Sh'mini Atzeret, for *tal* (dew) on the first day of Passover when we add in, "You cause the wind to blow and the rain to fall."

According to folklorist Dov Noy, "In many Oriental countries Arabs regard Jews as rain makers and hence think of drought as caused by unwillingness of the Jews to pray for rain" (*Folktales of Israel*, p. 14). (See IFA 719, "The Drought in Mosul," in *Folktales of Israel*.)

In all of these stories, the simple man asked to pray for rain is an honest and earnest person. In one parallel, the man is an honest grocer who speaks directly to God in front of the congregation by demonstrating his honest balance scales; another is a potmender who has kept Shabbat and demands that God bring rain according to the partnership agreement between Jews to keep Shabbat and God to bring rain. However, in this story, the man who is asked to pray for rain is someone who has collected his tears in a clay pitcher. His weeping was caused by seeing his children frequently without food. How similar this is to Jacob's dilemma (Genesis 42:1) when he, too, regards his sons and sees that there is no more food because of the famine. As it notes in Midrash ha-Gadol (compiled by Rabbi Dovid al-Aldeni in the thirteenth century), what we can learn from Jacob's story is that it is a parent's worst trial to have his children ask for food when there is nothing to give. No doubt Jacob shed tears at those moments too.

In the Talmud, as in the folklore of many cultures, there is a mythical connection between tears and rain. Ginzberg draws from the Aggadot various comparisons between man and the world: "The body of man is a microcosm, the whole world in miniature, and the world in turn is a reflex of man . . . his tears [correspond] to a river . . ." Therefore, tears can become a symbolic action that can bring rain, as is illustrated in a story from the Babylonian *Taanit* 25b: "Our masters taught: Once it happened that R. Eliezer decreed thirteen fasts for a community, and no rain came. Finally, when people began to leave [the synagogue], he said, 'Have you got graves ready for yourselves?' At this, the people broke into sobbing, and rain began to fall" (Bialik and Ravnitzky, *The Book of Legends*, 753:278).

The idea of collecting tears in a clay jar can be found in Psalm 56:9,

"Put Thou my tears in Thy bottle." According to folklorist Theodor H. Gaster, "This curious image may well have been suggested by the widespread practice of conserving tears in a bottle at funerals and other occasions of lamentation." This kind of tear-pitcher is used by the hero in this story to collect his own tears of sorrow and to have it buried with him when he died. Being buried with such a tear-collector was actually carried out in some ancient societies.

There are many versions of this tale type in the Jewish oral tradition, with over twenty versions in the IFA, as well as variants in *The Exempla of the Rabbis* (Gaster), *The Ma'aseh Book* (Gaster), *Mimekor Yisrael* (Bin Gorion), *Seventy and One Tales for the Jewish Year* (Rush and Marcus), and *The Classic Tales* (Frankel). For a creative adaptation of this story, see Cherie Karo Schwartz's "Midrash of Mayim: A Water Story" in her "Three Stories from the Heavens" trilogy in my *Chosen Tales*.

See also "A Question of Balance" in my *Jewish Stories One Generation Tells Another*.

—PS

5

Which Way Should One Look—
Up or Down?

Two friends had just finished lunch. One of them was very impatiently rushing to his next appointment. "Slow down," said the first friend. "The day is beautiful. The flowers are in bloom. And besides, you still have time left before your work starts again. Life is so short. So slow down, my friend, and look up at the sky!"

"That's fine for you to say, friend, but I have to get to my next appointment. I have so much to do that I rarely take even this much time for lunch with a friend."

"Wait one more moment, and let me tell you a story," answered his friend.

One day Rabbi Nachman of Bratzlav was looking out of the window of his study. From there, he could see the people in the marketplace hurrying from place to place. Suddenly the rabbi saw a familiar face.

"Yaakov! Come in and talk a while, dear friend," said the rabbi.

"Shalom, rabbi, how are you?" asked Yaakov.

"Fine, Yaakov. Come in and have a glass of tea." And he opened the door. "Tell me, what are you doing here in the marketplace?"

"Oh, today I'm very busy. I have a lot of business to take care of and very little time. I have no time for tea."

"Yaakov, have you looked up at the sky today?" asked the rabbi.

"At the sky, rabbi? No, of course not. I'm too busy to look at the sky!"

"Yaakov, look out the window and tell me what you see."

Yaakov looked puzzled but replied, "I see men and women, horses and carriages, all rushing around doing business and shopping."

"Yaakov," the rabbi said, "in fifty years there will be other men and women in other carriages, drawn by other horses, but we will not be here. And in a hundred years who knows if either the marketplace or this town will even exist. Look at the sky, Yaakov, look at the sky!"

Hearing this story, the friend smiled thoughtfully and then said, "But looking up is not always the answer. Listen to this story."

One dark night, two friends, one wise and one foolish, were walking through the forest. They had been walking and tripping their way through the thick underbrush since they could not see the path. There were no stars in the sky. Suddenly the wind began to blow and there was a great bolt of lightning. The sky lit up like it was the middle of the day and the foolish man looked up at the sky in wonder. But what did the wise man do? He quickly looked *down* so that he could see where he was. Close by he saw a tree that had been struck by the lightning and he ran over to the tree and blew on a branch that was still a glowing ember. Soon he had a fire, which warmed them both through the night. And all night long the wise man told his friend stories so that by morning, the foolish man was no longer so foolish.

The two friends had exchanged these stories as they walked into the park and sat down on a bench. "And so, which is better, to look up at the sky or down at the ground?" they asked each other.

The last time I saw them, they were still sitting in the park and debating that question by telling each other more stories.

As for the answer, I will leave it to you to decide.

End of Story Note

In this story, there are actually two stories encircled by a frame, which sets up the title question.

The first story of "The Mirror and the Window" from *Gemeinde der Chassidim* by Chaim Bloch, Vienna, 1920 (German) can be found in *The Hasidic Anthology* (Newman), *The Classic Tales* (Frankel), and *Lessons from Our Living Past* (Harlow). I've also heard this story throughout the years. I always recall the story when I read in Genesis 13:14, "And the Lord said unto Abram, 'Lift up now thine eyes, and look from the place where thou art, northward and southward and eastward and westward'"; and when I read in Genesis 15:5, "Look now toward heaven . . ." and again in Genesis 22:4, "On the third day Abraham lifted up his eyes . . ." To look up—to reach for the sky and to see beyond ourselves—these are our Jewish goals, a spiritual elevation.

The second story comes from Hanoch Teller's book, *Soul Survivors.* I retell this story with his permission. When I asked him for his source, he could only say that he heard the story from a hasid who heard it from a hasid. And that's the way of the hasidic oral tradition, and the oral tradition generally.

It struck me that looking, like listening, is such an amazing gift. We need to learn how to use it wisely and with good judgment. And so we must continue to ask which way we should look—up or down? Or does it depend on the context?

—PS

6

The Most Peculiar Thing in Life

One day King Solomon decided to hold a banquet for all the animals—from the biggest animals that were in the forest to all the smaller animals that crawled on the ground. Everyone was told the exact date and the exact time. The day came and every animal went to be received by the king. However, when they saw that the eagles were missing, they postponed the beginning of the party. After about a half hour of waiting, the beating of wings in the distance was heard. In a few moments, seven young eagles arrived. The king asked them, "Why were you late?" And the eagles replied, "We have a very old father. He is crippled and not able to fly. And therefore we were taking care of him and feeding him. This evening, only after we put him to bed, were we free to come to the party."

Then the king asked, "But why didn't you bring your old father to this important party?" And he immediately ordered them to bring him and added, "We will delay the start of the party until the old eagle arrives." The eagles returned to their nest, which was on a high cliff, and they put their father into a big basket and brought him to the party. The old eagle was almost without feathers and he wasn't able even to stand up on his legs.

King Solomon got up and welcomed him and blessed him. Then the king asked him, "How old are you?"

"I am three hundred years old," answered the eagle.

Then the king continued, "Please, tell us at this party what is the most peculiar thing you have seen in your long life?"

The eagle answered, "I don't remember anything special because my years were not very many but I heard about a woman who is four hundred years old and that she is from a very large family. The bracelet that is around her foot is as big and as wide as a barrel. I'm sure that she has seen something important in her life. But she has died a long time ago."

"Do you know where she is buried?" asked King Solomon.

"I know where the place is. But it is very far from here and I cannot fly there," answered the old eagle.

And the king prayed over the eagle and his strength returned to him. Then King Solomon got on the back of the eagle and they flew together as with the speed of an arrow shot from a bow—that fast—until they arrived at that certain place in the forest. When they landed, the eagle looked around to find the exact place of the grave. But there was no grave. Then he saw a place on a small hill. "There, I think that is the place," the eagle called out.

But now there was another problem. How is it possible to dig in a place in order to find who is buried there? So King Solomon prayed until the earth opened up and the body of the great woman was there. And again King Solomon prayed that her soul would return to her. And that's what happened. And the king asked her, "What is the most special thing that you have ever seen in your long life?"

And the woman answered, "What is the length of my life when you compare it with the length of the lives of my other family members. My life was not long at all. And during my life I have not seen anything peculiar. Oh yes, I saw a gigantic skull. It was so big that a whole army could fit in it."

"And where is it?" asked the king.

And the woman described the place where the skull was. At the end of her story, she returned her soul to King Solomon. Then the king returned her body to her place. Immediately he got on the eagle's back again and went to the place of the skull.

Solomon and the eagle indeed found this gigantic skull in that certain place and King Solomon prayed and the breath of life went into the skull. The king asked the skull, "What is the most peculiar thing that the man who belongs to the skull had seen?"

The skull answered, "Even if I were a thousand years old I have not seen anything peculiar. But I could send you to a frog that has been alive since the beginning of the world. He lives in one of the wells and it is possible that that frog has seen something."

King Solomon thanked the skull and got on the eagle's back and they flew to where the well was.

When they arrived at the well of the frog, King Solomon asked it, "What is the most peculiar thing you have seen in your life? Something that deserves special attention?"

The frog answered, "In ancient days, there was a pulley with a bucket and a rope hanging in this well. Both the bucket and the rope were made of pure gold. People would come and draw up water from the well and they would leave the bucket and the rope for other people who would come to drink. You see, there was absolute belief and faithfulness in the world. But years passed and generations passed. And then we realized that the bucket and rope of gold had disappeared. In their place there was a bucket and rope of silver. And again years passed and generations passed. Also this bucket and rope of silver disappeared. In their place was a bucket and rope of brass. And years passed and generations passed and instead of the bucket and rope of brass, there was only those of leather. And these are the only things I can remember that were special and peculiar that deserved any kind of attention paid to it."

Then the frog leaped back into the well and King Solomon and the eagle flew back to the gathering.

End of Story Note

IFA 5088 from *A Tale for Each Month 1963*, Story #11, collected by Miriam Sheli from Shelomo Uzzan, from Tunisia (Kagan).
Tale Types: Elements of AT 726 (The Oldest on the Farm); AT 920A* (The Inquisitive King).
Motifs: F571.2 (Sending to the older: Old person refers to his father, who refers to *his* father, and so on for several generations); B841 (Long-lived animals); H1235 (Succession of helpers on quest).

Solomon succeeded his father, David, as king when he was eighteen and ruled for forty years (961–920 B.C.E.). Solomon, or Shlomo, which means "peace," since peace and prosperity reigned in his kingdom during his rule, was given the honor of building the Temple in Jerusalem. His achievements were many, but perhaps the most widely known were those stemming from his gift for poetry. He wrote Song of Songs and probably the book of Ecclesiastes. He was also known as the inventor of the parable. Parables are like riddles and, since Solomon was also famous for posing and answering riddles, perhaps we can rightly conclude that he did shape the first parable.

When a biblical hero becomes a folklore hero, he is transformed into a character who specializes in a particular domain. In this case King Solomon, who is the second most popular acting hero, becomes especially known for his great wisdom. (Elijah the Prophet, the Master of Miracles, is the most popular character in folktales.) There are many legends of Solomon as wise judge. In fact, when a difficult decision must be made, the phrases "Solomonic wisdom" or "We need the wisdom of Solomon" are often heard. There is a tale type classified as AT 926C ("Cases solved in a manner worthy of King Solomon"). (See the story "100 Grams More or Less" in this collection.)

Solomon is also known for his ability to communicate with animals and birds. The famous story of "King Solomon and the Bee" is one example. Another one is the story of Solomon and the Hoopoe bird. The Hoopoe birds save Solomon's life and Solomon wants to repay them by granting whatever they would wish for unanimously. The birds all agree to ask for a golden crown of gold. As promised, although warning them that this wish might cause them danger, Solomon grants their request.

However, when the birds see that hunters desire those crowns of gold so they are about to become extinct, they plead with Solomon to help them. Solomon turns their gold crowns into crests of feathers. And to this day, the Hoopoe live in the land of Israel. (See "Solomon's Gift" in my *Jewish Stories One Generation Tells Another*.)

In this story, the question "What is the most peculiar thing you have seen in your long life?" posed to the old eagle prompts the rest of the story. It is indeed a puzzling riddle question worthy of King Solomon.

—PS

7

Friends in Deed

Several friends sat in the coffee house drinking and talking about life and friendship. Suddenly one of the friends asked, "What is true friendship, after all?" The oldest of the friends answered, "True friendship is as it is written in Shabbat (32a) 'Numerous are the friends at the gate of the palace, meaning when you are rich, but few at the gate of the prison, meaning when you are poor.'"

"How is that? What do you mean?" asked the youngest of the friends.

"I will explain my meaning by telling you this story." So the old man began:

Once there were two merchants who had conducted business with each other for years. However, they had never met since they lived in different countries, one in Egypt and the other in Babylon. One day, the Babylonian merchant decided to travel to Egypt to deliver some goods himself to the Egyptian merchant. When the Egyptian merchant heard about the arrival of his friend, he went out to greet him and welcomed him royally into his home. Singers and musicians entertained at an eight-day feast arranged in his honor.

On the eighth day, the Babylonian merchant became ill. His host was very concerned and hastened to bring the wisest sages and the finest physicians of Egypt to cure his faithful friend. One sage finally said, "This man does not have any physical illness, but rather he has become ill with lovesickness."

The host asked his friend, "Is it true? Who do you love so deeply? Is it anyone in my household?"

The guest answered, "Show me all the women of your household and I will tell you the one whom my heart desires."

The merchant then called for all the maidens in his house, but none did his guest choose. Then the merchant called for his daughters to appear, but still the guest did not choose any of the man's daughters. Finally, the host invited a young maiden who was exceedingly beautiful to appear before the guest. This young woman had been brought up in his household from a very young age and she had been carefully guarded so that when she would become a certain age, then she would marry the Egyptian merchant.

When the sick merchant saw this young maiden, he called out, "This is the woman whom my heart desires. She is my life or death."

When the Egyptian merchant heard these words, he turned to his friend and said, "If the young maiden gives her consent, then you will marry her." The merchant gave them gifts and so arranged for their wedding. After that, the Babylonian merchant returned in peace to his land with his wife.

It came to pass that the Egyptian merchant's wheel of fortune turned and he lost all his money and his business. "I shall go to my faithful friend and ask him to take pity on me and help me out of these dire troubles." He set out and traveled to Babylon and finally arrived one night. But since he was barefoot, wearing rags and dirty, he hesitated to go directly to his friend's home. "Surely he will not recognize me and think me only a beggar, perhaps even turning me away. I will wait until morning." And he found an empty building where he lay down, shivering in the cool night air.

Meanwhile, in the city two men had quarreled. This fight became more and more violent until one of the men killed the other and fled the city. Many began to run after the murderer and some of them came to the building where the merchant was lying miserably alone. Assuming he was the murderer, they asked him, "Who killed the man?" And thinking that he preferred to die than to live in poverty and shame, he answered simply, "I did."

The impoverished merchant was immediately arrested and thrown into prison. In the morning, when the judges sentenced him to die by hanging, he was led to the gallows tree. Many people came from the city to see that justice was carried out. Among the crowd was the Babylonian merchant. The merchant recognized his friend and remembered, too, all the favors and kindnesses he had done for him on his visit to Egypt. And he thought to himself, "Now I can repay him for all that he had done for me."

Without hesitation, the merchant ran over to the judges and pleaded, "Do not kill this man. He did not commit this crime, but rather it was I who did the killing."

When the judges heard this, they ordered for this man to be arrested and brought him over to the gallows tree for hanging.

Now the actual murderer was in that same crowd and watched what was going on and said to himself, "I was the one who killed the man, but soon an innocent man will be punished by hanging for my deed, while I will remain alive. Perhaps there is a plan that I do not understand. After all, the Blessed God on High is just. I cannot allow another to be hanged for my misdeed."

The murderer pushed his way through the crowd, shouting, "Judges, do not let an innocent man be punished. Indeed, neither of these two men are the killers. I confess to this brutal murder. I killed the man and ran away. It is better for me to perish in this world and not in the next."

The judges turned to the two merchants and asked for an explanation. The Egyptian merchant replied, "When I lost my entire fortune, I decided to come to this city to ask my friend for help. But I could not appear at my friend's home at night in such a disgraceful condition because I feared that he would send me away. When the men found me in the building and accused me of the murder, I thought to myself, why should I continue to live in such shame and dire poverty. I had lost all hope so I preferred death over life. That is why I confessed to the murder."

At this point, the Babylonian merchant spoke up: "Honored judges, I was in the crowd to see the hanging. When I recognized my friend and realized how much he had done for me, even offering his chosen one to become my beloved wife, then I felt I loved him more than a brother, that our very souls are entwined together. I knew that I could even give up my life for his."

When the judges heard these words of the three men, they freed the two merchants and arrested the true murderer and hanged him on the tree.

The Babylonian merchant welcomed his merchant friend to his home, gave him proper clothing, and honored him with an eight-day feast. After that, the wealthy merchant gave his friend many gifts and gold so that he could pay his debts. In that way, he returned home with honor and once again became a successful merchant. The two merchants remained faithful friends for the rest of their lives.

Then the old man turned to his young friend and said, "The best advice I can give you is as it says in *Avot* (1:6), 'Acquire yourself a companion.'"

The young man asked, "What do you mean?"

The old man said, "Let me explain my meaning through a story." So the old man began:

There were once two friends who loved each other very much and were inseparable companions. However, because of circumstances, they had to settle in different kingdoms, far from each other. One day, one of the friends decided to pay a visit to his long-time friend in this other country. Just at that time, a war broke out between the two countries and the visiting friend was unable to return home. In fact, because he was a citizen of this other enemy country, he was accused of being a spy and brought before the king. He was sentenced to death. He immediately fell to the ground imploring him to grant him one last request before he died.

"What is this request?" asked the king.

"Your Majesty," the man said, "I am a respected merchant in my city and frequently conducted my business on trust and a handshake. I never wrote any contracts or letters of agreement. So now when I will die, my wife and children will become paupers since they will not even know who owes them money from my business transactions. I therefore beg Your Majesty to allow me to return to my country for a short time to settle my affairs and put my house in order. I solemnly promise to return here and suffer the penalty you have imposed on me."

The king was surprised at this request. "How will I know if you will return? What guarantee do you offer that you will keep your word?"

"Your Majesty, I have a trusted friend and companion who lives in this city who will be my security. He will not refuse to stand bail for me."

The friend was immediately summoned to the palace. "Will you serve as security for this friend of yours? If he should fail to return when promised, are you prepared to suffer the penalty of death in his place?" asked the king.

Without hesitation, the friend answered, "Yes, Your Majesty, I will willingly substitute myself for my friend, for I have complete faith in him."

The king was surprised at this response. "Is it possible to have such a devoted friend? I must see whether such a thing can really happen." Then the king gave the merchant a month's time to return home while his friend was taken into custody.

On the last day of the month the king waited until sunset to see if the merchant would really return to be executed. Just as the sun was about to set, the man had not yet returned, so the king gave the executioner the order to begin. The prisoner was brought from the prison and led to the place of execution. Just as his head was placed on the block, there was a commotion in the crowd. "Wait, the prisoner has returned!" they were shouting.

And indeed, the merchant was hurrying to the place of execution and pushed his friend out of the way and took his place, saying, "I am the one who must die."

The friend pushed his way closer to the block, insisting, "No, my friend, I am the one who will die in your place."

Meanwhile, the astonished king, who never believed that such friendship was possible, was greatly moved. He immediately pardoned both friends and set them free, giving them both great riches. Then he spoke to both of them, "I see that there exists such a strong friendship and love between you. I would be honored if I could be your companion too!"

From that day on, the two friends became close companions of the king.

At this point, the young man turned to the old man, and in tears said, "I now understand what true friendship means. How wise the sages were when they said, 'Acquire yourself a companion.' How fortunate is the man who has such a companion."

End of Story Note

Motifs: H1558 (Tests of friendship); H1556 (Tests of fidelity); H1558.1 (Test of worthiness for friendship).

There is a popular saying, "Friends in need are friends in deed." And, indeed, there are many stories, biblical and folk, that explore the meaning of true friendship.

For this story, I have created a frame story and embedded two tales with the same theme of deep friendship that is truly devotion unto death. In other words, I have taken two folktales and used them as illustrative tales to explain two talmudic sayings, one in *Shabbat* 32a ("Numerous are the friends at the gate of the palace") and the other in *Avot* 1:6 ("Acquire yourself a companion"). This idea is already found in folklore but with different questions prompting the telling of similar stories of friendship. The thirty-four stories in *Disciplina Clericalis*, an important frame narrative that bridges Eastern and Western narrative traditions, revolve around friendship. This manuscript was written in the twelfth century by an Argonese Jew, Petrus Alfonsi, who converted to Catholicism and then moved to England. He wrote the manuscript originally in Arabic and then translated it into Latin. The main framing story of the *Disciplina Clericalis* is about a dying Arab who imparts wisdom to his son by asking, "How many friends have you gained during my life?" The son responds, "A hundred friends, I think, I have gained." The father then tells him what to do to prove whether his "friends" are truly friends who will help him in a time of trouble. The son discovers that only his father's "half friend" will help him. Then the son asks his wise father, "Have you ever met a man who was a perfect friend?" The father answers, "I myself have never met such a man, but I have heard of one" and relates a version of the first of these inner stories (in my story) to his son. This creates a dialogue in which the father teaches the son wisdom through a series of stories and proverbs.

The theme of willingness to give one's life for a friend is a recurrent theme in Jewish folklore, a form of *Messirat Nefesh*, devotion unto death. The Hebrew phrase means, literally, "the handing over of the soul," to a cause, a person, or God. This theme is inextricably interwoven in both of these stories-within-stories. (For a beautiful love story with this theme, see "Messiras Nefesh" by I. L. Peretz.)

The first story of friendship can be found in several sources: *Beit Ha-Midrash* (Jellinek), *Otzar Midrashim* (Eisenstein), *Sefer Hanokh*, *Melanges de litterature Orientale* (Cardonne), and *Fabliaux* (d'Aussy). In English it is found in *The Folklore of the Jews, Mimekor Yisrael* (Bin Gorion), *The Exempla of the Rabbis* (Gaster), and *The Classic Tales* (Frankel). The theme of literal "lovesickness," which, when diagnosed, creates the search for and affirmation of love from the woman whom the man desires so intensely, is found in a number of folktales such as "The Emperor's Daughter and the King's Son" (in this collection) and "The Life-Giving Flower" in my *Tales of Elijah the Prophet*.

The second of the inner stories, a well-known tale, can be found in a number of sources: *Ma'arikh* (di Lonzano), *Beit Ha-Midrash*, *Otzar Midrashim*, and *Oseh Pele* (Farhi); and in English sources, *Mimekor Yisrael, Gates to the Old City* (Patai), *Jewish Folktales* (Sadeh), and *The Classic Tales*. There are parallels to this folktale found all over the world, including a version in *The Arabian Nights*.

—PS

8

The Leopard and the Fox

A t one time, many wild animals lived together comfortably in a land of plenty. In this place was a leopard with his mate and cubs. For a time all continued well with them, according to the patterns of nature.

Nearby lived a fox. And though the leopard and the fox were neighbors, and even friends, the fox kept thinking, "I am safe so long as the leopard feeds on other animals. But why should I always live in fear and uncertainty? Who knows when he will become hungry and angry and pounce on *me*?" So the fox talked around and around, acting according to the sage advice of the rabbis, "Before evil comes, seek a good solution and act upon it."

Finally, the fox hit upon a plan to get the leopard and his family to leave their home for a place where they would not survive. Thus the fox would be rid of the leopards without fighting or bloodshed, because actually, in any battle with the leopard, the only blood that would be shed would be the blood of the fox. And the fox was too shrewd to let that happen. And again he drew his advice from the rabbis, who said: "If someone comes to kill you, kill him first."

The next day, the fox visited the leopard. They greeted each other warmly.

"*Sholom aleikhem*," said the fox.

"*Aleikhem sholom*," replied the leopard.

And as they were talking, the fox said, "There is a beautiful countryside I found not far from here—a land of flowers and food—which would delight you. It is a paradise to behold."

The fox painted such a glowing picture of this paradise that the leopard was indeed eager to see it. And yes, the leopard found it to be as the fox had described it and began to consider the move, but. . . .

"Well," said the fox, "what's the matter? If you like the place, bring your family there *today*. Why do you hesitate? Remember what the sages say, 'He who hesitates is lost.'"

"True, true," replied the leopard. "But such a decision must not be made alone. I always consult my wife first. She is my wise partner in life. And her wisdom is beyond the price of rubies."

The fox's spirit fell, for he knew how wise the leopard's wife was.

"You ask your *wife* before you make a decision?" cried the fox suddenly in outrage. He was not about to let *her* foil *his* plan. Then he changed his tone and spoke softly to the leopard, as if they were conspirators. "A woman's advice is *foolish*," he said, "and sometimes even evil. Ask her advice, by all means, but then do the *opposite* and *that* will show you what to do." And the fox worked very hard to convince the leopard not to trust his wife's counsel.

Fired up by the fox's words, the leopard returned home and said to his wife, "*Wife*, we are leaving this place to go to a paradise. I have seen it and it is so."

"Who brought you to that place? What made you decide on this sudden change of residence when we have been happy and content right here?" asked the leopardess.

When the leopard explained that it was the fox's idea, his wife simply said, "Beware of the fox!"

And then she continued, "The two craftiest creatures in God's creation are the snake and the fox. So, before you follow the fox's advice, you should know how the fox defeated the lion."

"How did he do that?" the leopard asked.

This is the story the leopardess told her husband:

> There once was a lion who was a friend to the fox. But the fox kept thinking of ways to cause the lion's death. He knew he could not fight the lion and win. So the crafty fox thought of a plan. He came to the lion, pretending to have a pain in his head. Oh, he could go on the stage, he was such a good actor.
>
> "What can I do to help you feel better?" asked the lion, his friend.
>
> And the fox cried out, "OOooooh, my head hurts so. OH, I remember

an old remedy that my grandmother always used for such a pain. But I will need your help to bind up my feet and hands—for that is the remedy."

The lion agreed and tied up the fox according to his directions.

A moment later, the fox began to smile, and he shouted "Yes! Yes! YES! It is indeed a remedy for pain—my head hurts no longer. It's a miracle remedy."

So then the lion untied the fox. But one day the lion's head began to ache. He ran to the fox's den and cried, "Brother fox, tie me up, for my head hurts me terribly."

And, of course, the fox tied the lion with long flexible twigs. Then taking some heavy stones, he crushed the lion's head.

"So much for the fox's friendship, my husband," concluded the leopardess. "It is false and evil. Tell him to go to this paradise himself. *We* will stay *here*."

"O wife," replied the leopard impatiently. "They are right when they say women are foolish and have no head for decisions. The fox is my *friend*. I have confidence in him." And the leopard went to find the fox.

By the time the leopard located the fox, he had calmed down and realized that the story his wife had told him had disturbed him, after all. So he told the fox about his doubts.

The fox replied, without taking a breath, "Well then, if you follow your wife's warning, you might end up like the goldsmith."

"What do you mean?" asked the leopard.

And the fox replied with the following tale:

Once a goldsmith was working when his wife came into his shop and said, "Listen, husband, we can be rich if you follow my advice. The King has one daughter whom he loves more than anything else, even more than his life. Make a gold statue of the princess as a gift. It will please him beyond measure, and surely he will reward you greatly and we will be rich."

The goldsmith took the suggestion, and his wife brought the statue to the King. When the monarch saw it, he became enraged. "It is written," he declared, "that no idols should be created. Whoever made this statue, let his right hand be cut off."

And so it was done. The poor goldsmith never again fashioned anything out of gold. Instead, he cried out, "O husbands, look at me and learn a lesson! Never heed your wife's advice, for it will cause you suffering in the end."

The fox watched the leopard's reaction, and he continued, "If this hasn't convinced you, then remember what King Solomon often said, 'One good man among a thousand I have found; but a virtuous woman among all those have I not found.'

"Listen, and I will tell you how the great King proved the truth of what he said."

Everyone knows about King Solomon's great wisdom and understanding of people. One day, he proclaimed that women are selfish and love not their husbands more than themselves. His advisors disagreed. So he decided to test his statement and prove he was right. He sent his attendants to find a married couple who were known for their virtue and deep love for each other.

When such a couple was found, the husband was brought to the King, who said to him: "We have searched the entire city for a man worthy to marry my beautiful daughter and love her as befits a person of high rank. You have been chosen as that man. After your marriage, I will appoint you my chief advisor. But since you are now a married man, go home and slay your wife so that you will be free to marry my daughter and enjoy the new position I offer you."

At first the man protested, but the King insisted.

"How shall I do this deed?" asked the man finally. And the King gave him a sword, but it was made of lead and in fact would not hurt or kill anything. *Remember*, the king was only testing the man's love for his wife, and did not mean to do her bodily harm.

The man returned home, his heart heavy with the thought of what he now had to do. When he saw his wife, he was overcome with love and emotion. "No, I cannot do this terrible deed when she is awake," he thought. "I will wait until she is asleep."

But when she was asleep, he leaned over her—and then sprang back. "No," he cried, "not even for the entire Kingdom will I kill my wife, the woman who has brought such joy to my life. What joy would I have from marriage to the King's daughter but a bitter joy?" And he went to Solomon and told him he could not accept his offer.

A while later, the handsome Solomon sent for this man's wife in secret, declaring his passion and love for her. "Since I cannot marry you while your husband lives," he declared, "you must slay your husband tonight, and tomorrow you will be my queen." And as he said these words, he handed her the sword, which looked like steel but was made of lead.

The woman returned home with the sword. That night she fed her husband well and gave him plenty of wine to drink. And in the middle of the night she took the sword and struck him while he slept. Of course, the sword did not hurt him, but it did wake him up. And she had to confess what she had planned to do.

They went together to King Solomon, and Solomon turned to his scoffers and said, "Now no one can ever tell me that a woman is to be trusted."

Then the fox again waited a moment before he added, "More than that. Not only can a woman not be depended on to advise you while you live. She will betray you even in death."

"How is that?" asked the leopard.

"Listen and I'll tell you," replied the fox.

There was a custom in ancient Rome that whenever a criminal was hanged, the body remained on the gallows for ten days as a warning to everyone. To make sure that no relatives came to cut down the body and bury it before the tenth day, an officer of the King stood on guard at the gallows. If the body of the condemned man was stolen, the officer on guard was hanged in its place.

One night, as an officer was guarding the body of an executed criminal, he heard shrieks that pierced his soul, and cries that went directly to his heart. He ran toward the cries and found himself in a nearby cemetery. There on the ground, lying across a fresh grave, was a young woman, weeping, lamenting the death of her beloved husband.

"My good woman," said the officer, "what terrible thing has happened to make you weep with such pain?"

"My lord," answered the woman, between sobs, "my husband, whom I loved more than life itself, has died and my grief is too great for me to bear. So I weep and pray for my death to come quickly now." The officer calmed her, persuaded her to return home, and accompanied her to the city gates. Then he went back to his post at the gallows.

But the next night, and the next, the grieving widow returned to her husband's grave and would not be consoled. The officer meanwhile had begun to embrace and kiss the woman, and before long their love was kindled and they lay together.

Returning to the gallows together with the woman, the officer discovered that the body he had been guarding was gone. He was suddenly terrified and whispered to the widow standing next to him, "Go home quickly. I must run away or I will be hanged for neglecting my duty."

But the widow replied, "Do not run, my love. We can dig up the body of my husband and hang him in place of the stolen body. Your life will be saved."

"I cannot dig up a body from its grave," protested the officer.

"Then I will do it for you," said the widow, who only hours before had wept over her husband's grave. "Helping a live person is more important than worrying over a dead one."

When the body of the woman's husband was dug up, the officer took one look and cried, "Alas! All your efforts are useless. They will know this is a different man, because the criminal they hanged was bald and your husband was not."

"Oh, that should not cause you any concern," said the woman. "I will make him bald, too." And saying that, the widow plucked out all her husband's hair and hung him on the gallows. As for the officer and the widow, they got married.

That's the end of the tale.

The fox did not have to say anything more. With fire in his eyes, the leopard ran to his wife and commanded, "Woman! Take our children and *follow me* to our *new home*." And so the leopard family arrived at their new home with the happy fox accompanying them most of the way. Then they waved farewell to each other, and the fox skipped joyfully to the leopard's abandoned home.

"Good," chortled the fox. "Now I can take over their spacious, comfortable home. They will certainly not return and threaten my freedom ever again." And he stretched out and went to sleep.

Just as the leopards settled into their new home, in paradise, the season of rains and floods began.

In the middle of the night, the rains poured down, the river rose over its banks, and the leopards were carried out of their home over the raging waters.

And the leopard cried out, "Woe to me, and woe to the man who does not listen to his wife's good counsel."

And a cold angry wave swept over the leopard.

End of Story Note

From Ibn Zabara's *The Book of Delight* plus four didactic stories found within the frame of the leopard and fox tales, in the pattern of *Kalilah Ve-Dimnah*.

The first of these, the miracle remedy, and the second, the cutting off of the goldsmith's hand, are found in similar stories throughout the Near East and have close affinities to materials from India. The King Solomon tale comes from the *Legends of Solomon*. The last of the stories is one of the most famous of all fables: the "Widow of Ephesus," and Perry, *Aesopica*, number 543. It is found as an independent story in *Tosafot* (*Kiddushin* 80b). The fable is also very much a part of Jewish traditional story telling and is found in numerous fable collections, such as *Mishlei Shualim* (Hanakdan). It is called "The False Widow" in *Mimekor Yisrael* (Bin Gorion).

Tale Types: AT 1510 (The Matron of Ephesus); AT 4 (Carrying the Sham-Sick Trickster).

Motifs: Elements include: K2213.1 (Substitutes husband's corpse on gallows so the knight can escape); T231 (The faithless widow).

Fables are short, didactic, and simple. As a relatively modern development, fables have a clearly stated moral (although they also contain multilayered values) and use animals and plants, men and gods as characters. In earlier Jewish fables, many of them probably translated and adapted from Indian, Roman, and Greek sources, the animals were not only endowed with human personalities, but also spoke wisely about Torah. The greatest collector and teller of Jewish fables was without doubt Rabbi Meir, a student of Akiva, who lived in Hellenic Asia Minor during the second century C.E. According to the Talmud, he collected 300 fables, some of which are found in the Talmud and Midrash.

During the Middle Ages, three other Jewish scholars contributed to the body of Jewish fables:

1. Berechiah Hanakdan (about 1190 C.E.) was born in France but, while living in Oxford, he wrote 107 "fox fables" (*Mishlei Shualim*). While many of his fables can be traced to Aesop, and some to *Romulus* collections, others are similar to the work of Marie de France. Confusion over their respective birth dates makes it unclear who influenced whom. Berechiah Hanakdan's

foxes, though, echo talmudic discussion and quote biblical sources. Though his fables include a great deal of quoted Scripture in the *nimshal*, his goal was not to teach religion. Rather, he sought to give lessons in social behavior. He opens each fable with an aphorism or *pitgam* and closes it with a mini-sermon. He made sure to write his tales, rather than entrusting them to the oral tradition.

2. Jacob ben Eleazar (1195–1250) and later Rabbi Joel in 1250 C.E. translated *Kalilah Ve-Dimnah*, a well-known collection of fables, from Arabic into Hebrew. Originally written in Sanskrit, *Kalilah Ve-Dimnah* was first translated into Persian, and then, in 750 C.E., into Arabic. These wondrous tales, presented in a frame-story by two jackals named Kalilah and Dimnah, served as a treatise on human nature for the princes of India, a sort of handbook for rulers. Interwoven with ethical sayings and proverbs, the fables and parables explore universal questions of truth and deceit, ambition and loyalty, fear and power.

Containing many maxims from the Talmud and stressing Jewish values, the book was popular among the Jews of that time.

It was, however, Rabbi Joel's Hebrew version of *Kalilah Ve-Dimnah* that served as the text for John of Capua's Latin translation in the thirteenth century. This Latin version, called *Directorium Vitae Humanae*, became the source of the European versions, which became known throughout the continent and were soon transformed into popular European folktales.

3. In the thirteenth century, the Hebrew poet Joseph ibn Zabara, collected fables from ancient Hebrew, Greek, Arabic, and Indian sources for his *Sefer Sha'ashuim* (Book of Delight). Influenced by the Arabic pattern of such books as *Kalilah Ve-Dimnah* and by the Indian Bidpai fables, the author weaves several shorter tales into one major frame-story. The book has a "chain" structure with various tales serving as links.

This story is also in my *Jewish Stories One Generation Tells Another*.

—PS

9

A Match Made in Heaven

The philosopher Moses Mendelssohn, who lived in the eighteenth century, had such deformities that it was difficult for people to look at him, and, when people did not know who he was, they often turned away when they saw him approach. Children made fun of his hunchback. But as ugly as Mendelssohn was, so was his wife beautiful.

How could a man so ugly in physical appearance have such a beautiful wife? True, it was a time of arranged marriages, but did not the young woman, so desirable in every way, not have a great choice of mates? And did she not have to give her consent to the marriage? How did this strange pair meet and become acquainted?

The wealthy family Guggenheim, who lived in Berlin, had a beautiful daughter who was the apple of their eye. One day, the father decided to hire a tutor for his daughter. He chose the young Mendelssohn. And why? Besides his excellent qualifications as a teacher, the father reasoned that, because of such an uncomely appearance, there would be no risk of distractions, or better yet no attraction to each other. In this way, his daughter would be safe from any unwanted attentions.

And so Mendelssohn, as the tutor, began to come to the Guggenheim house. Soon the tutor and the student became good friends. They sat around a large table studying and reading for many hours. Sometimes they walked in the gardens talking of their love of books or discussing a rabbinical debate. After a time, the young tutor realized that he loved this beautiful student of his, but he said nothing to her about his deep feelings for her. How could he ever hope to win her heart? How could he even speak of his love for her? Would she not laugh and look at him with disdain and derision? And so he remained silent for many months. As for the young woman, while she enjoyed the lessons and his great wisdom, she was not at all attracted to her tutor because of his ugliness.

One day, while they were studying a particular passage about Leah and Rachel and Jacob, Mendelssohn began to ask her questions, as was his way of teaching. Suddenly Mendelssohn asked:

"My dear student, do you believe that a match is made in heaven?"

"Yes," she answered. "I do believe that a match is made in heaven as we can see from this example . . ."

"Then listen," Mendelssohn continued, "I want to tell you a story."

It is written that forty years before the birth of a baby, an angel sings out an announcement in heaven: "The daughter of this certain man will be married to the son of this other man." Before my birth, I heard the angel announce: "The daughter of Guggenheim will be the betrothed of Moses Mendelssohn." When I heard my name, and the news that I would be the one to be married, I became very happy, but also very curious. I wanted to know what my future bride was like, and so I asked the angel: "What does my match look like? Is she beautiful?"

The angel hesitated and said, "You cannot know this in advance. You can only know this when you meet her in person. It will come as a surprise."

But I was always a curious person, and also stubborn, and so I asked the angel every day about my bride-to-be. I hounded this poor angel with so many questions, that finally the angel answered me, but in a soft pitying tone:

"No, your future match is not beautiful. She is very ugly, deformed— and hunchbacked."

"Hunchbacked?" I whispered. When I heard this, I became filled with sorrow and, yes, even anger, and I called to the angel: "Go and tell the Creator that I am willing to take her ugliness on me. And I am willing to give her whatever I have that is pleasing and beautiful. A deformity in a woman is a terrible thing for the eye to see. I will take upon me this deformity only on condition that she should stay the most honest and the best of all the young women."

Mendelssohn ended his story and then sat quietly looking down at the floor and waited.

The young woman listened to this story, and the story touched her heart so that tears began to flow down her cheeks. Slowly she looked at the young tutor, touched his hand gently, and said, "This is truly a match made in heaven. It will be my great honor to become your wife."

End of Story Note

This love story reveals the power of persuasion through story. Even when events actually happen in real life, these occurrences are often interpreted by drawing on the folk tradition. Therefore, similar stories have been told throughout the ages, although sometimes with different main acting characters or protagonists. In this supposedly true historical tale, told here about Moses Mendelssohn (1729–1786), one finds a number of versions elsewhere with other main characters. I first heard Elie Wiesel tell a version of the Moses Mendelssohn story years ago as part of a lecture at the 92nd Street Y—in fact twice, but several years apart. And the second time, I was struck by his evident added sense of humor and delight in the retelling.

The story is also attributed to the Sanzer Rav, in "Look Not Upon the Flask," which originally appeared in *Souled! Stories of Striving and Yearning* (Book 2) and is reprinted in my *Chosen Tales*. In this latter collection, Hanoch Teller writes that his version "is based upon the true story of the match between the famous head of the Sanzer Chasidim, Reb Chaim, and his wife Rachel Faigele." He further writes, "The message of this story has been instrumental in bringing countless couples to the bridal canopy."

However, this story type also appears in *Me'otzranu Hayashan* (Hebrew), edited by B. Yushzon (Sifriyat Maariv, 1976). Recently, a version of the Mendelssohn story was transformed into an illustrated book as a Japanese fairy tale. And so it goes: a good story always triggers another version.

—PS

10

The Wedding Gifts

When the Baal Shem Tov, the Besht, was with his students, they would *daven* together, sing *nigunnim*, and tell wondrous stories. And sometimes in the evenings, the Besht would ask his friend, Alexis, to hitch up his horses to the wagon so that he and his students could go for a ride in the woods—or wherever the horses would take them.

One winter snow-filled evening, the Besht suddenly said, "Let us go on a journey." Alexis took the reins of the horses, all the *hasidim* got into the wagon, and they began to ride in the forest. The students knew that when they traveled with the Baal Shem Tov, they would witness astonishing things.

As they finished reciting their evening prayers, a wagon with one horse came rolling up to them and stopped. At first, they didn't see anyone in the wagon. But when they approached it, they saw a young man and a young woman, almost unconscious, slumped in their seats. The students immediately began to revive the couple by rubbing them with snow and then covered them with their own blankets to keep them warm. Finally, the couple awakened and told the *hasidim* their story.

The young man said, "My name is Isaac and this is Miriam. Both of us are orphans and we worked as servants at an inn. We had decided to get married. But because Miriam could not always please the innkeepers, the innkeeper's wife would beat her unmercifully. One time, I tried to come to her aid. So what did that innkeeper's wife do? She threw us both out of the inn. We had a little money between us so we bought this horse and wagon. For the past few weeks, we have traveled from place to place, trying to find work and a place to live. We have no more money and we have not eaten for several days. Now with the cold, well . . . that's how you found us."

Immediately the *hasidim* brought some food and drink from their own wagon for the couple. When the couple felt stronger, the Baal Shem Tov said, "Come, we will go to an inn and this young couple will be married."

The two wagons rode through the woods until they came to an inn. But when the couple saw the inn, they realized with fright that this was the same inn where they had worked. At that moment, the innkeeper and his wife came out to greet the guests in the wagons. However, when they recognized the young couple, their dismissed servants, they began to rage at the couple, "Get out! You are not welcome to step foot inside here, you ungratefuls. Leave or we will throw you out again."

The Baal Shem Tov stepped forward and declared, "This couple are my special guests who are about to be married. I would like to make the arrangements for their wedding celebration."

The innkeeper and his wife burst out laughing. "This couple are to be married *here*? And who will pay for all the food and drink? Will they pay for it all?"

The Baal Shem Tov showed them some gold coins. Suddenly the innkeeper and his wife stopped laughing and opened the doors wider to welcome everyone. Then, with great haste, the innkeepers went to the kitchen to prepare an elaborate feast for their guests.

After the Baal Shem Tov performed the wedding ceremony, everyone sat down at the wedding banquet. When they had finished eating and drinking a *l'khaim* to the bride and groom, they began to sing in celebration of the *simkha*. Then the Baal Shem Tov got up from his place and said to the couple, "We are obliged to give gifts to you, bride and groom. So I give them this inn and all its furniture, and all the buildings around it, as well as the sheep and cattle."

When the innkeepers heard this, they laughed and ran to tell their neighbors, "Come quickly and hear the outrageous gifts that are being promised at the wedding feast. You will laugh heartily, I promise you that."

Now it was the turn of the *hasidim* to offer their gifts. One after another stood up and said, "I give you a gift of the forest around the inn."

A second one said, "And I give you the water mill."

A third student said, "And I give you one thousand bushels of grain from the granary of the duke."

A fourth student said, "I give you one hundred barrels of wine from the cellar of the duke."

As each of the students made these gift offerings, the innkeepers and the neighbors were howling with laughter. At this point, the innkeeper himself ran over to the head table and, hardly being able to keep from doubling over with laughter, announced, "And I give to this fine couple ten thousand silver pieces, which the duke received today from the innkeepers."

The wife of the innkeeper shouted, also with great laughter, "And I give this lovely bride the gold necklace and earrings which the duchess wears."

The Baal Shem Tov turned to the innkeepers and said, "Innkeepers, perhaps you want to give them something of your own. After all, they once were servants in your house."

Hearing this, the innkeepers, roaring with laughter, said, "We give them the palace that stands at the end of the village."

When the neighbors heard this, they bellowed with even more laughter because what stood at the end of the village was an old broken-down palace, without a roof, without doors and windows.

"And what more will you give them?" asked the Baal Shem Tov.

"Nothing more," the innkeepers answered.

At that moment, the Baal Shem Tov got up, and with a heavy sigh, paid the innkeepers for all the expenses of the wedding feast. He also took the tablecloth and told the bridegroom to gather up the remnants of the banquet in the cloth and take it with them in the wagon.

"But where should we travel? In which direction?" asked the young groom.

"To the right," replied the Baal Shem Tov.

The bride and bridegroom then got back into their wagon, with the tablecloth filled with food and wine, and continued on their way "to the right." In the middle of the forest, their horse stopped suddenly. When the couple looked to see why the horse had halted, they saw an unconscious man lying in the snow. They rubbed him with snow until he began to open his eyes and move. Then they brought the food and wine from their wagon and gave it to the man. When he felt stronger, he told them this story.

"I am the duke's son. I had gone out hunting, perhaps it was yesterday, or before yesterday, I can't seem to recall how long ago it was. But I was thrown from my horse and became lost in the woods. I went to an inn, but because I must have looked bedraggled like a wanderer, the innkeeper drove me away. After wandering a long time, I must have fainted from the cold and the lack of food."

Just as the duke's son was speaking, suddenly there was the sound of trumpets. The duke's soldiers had been searching for the son throughout the wooded area. They spotted the duke's son and immediately returned him to his parents, leaving the young couple behind.

With great happiness the duke and duchess welcomed their son home. The son told them about his experience and about the young couple who had found him and saved him from death.

"Find this couple and bring them here immediately," said the duke. "I want to reward them for their kindness."

When the couple arrived at the duke's home, the duke asked them questions and they spoke about their adventures as well.

The duke listened and then said, "So the same innkeepers drove you and my son away from the inn. In that case, I give you permanent possession of the inn, its furniture, the building around it, and all the sheep and cattle."

And the duchess added, "And I give you the forest that surrounds the inn."

The duke's son offered his gift, saying, "And I give you the water mill, one thousand bushels of wheat from our granary, and one hundred barrels of wine from our cellar."

Then the duke spoke again, "You will need money to run the inn. So I give you the ten thousand pieces of silver that I received from the innkeepers yesterday."

The duchess then said, "Since this young woman was married yesterday, and she has no jewelry for her dowry, I give her the gold necklace and earrings that I am wearing."

The young couple stood silently, astonished at all that had been happening to them. They felt as though they were in a dream. But suddenly they felt a sense of pity for the innkeepers. "What will happen to the innkeeper and his wife, now that they will no longer have their inn? Where will they go?"

And the duke replied, "Very well then, I shall give them the old palace that stands at the end of the village."

And everyone there began to laugh. But the young bride and groom, who had seen all that the Baal Shem Tov had promised fulfilled, wept tears of joy.

End of Story Note

This Baal Shem Tov story has been attributed in several anthologies to the ethnographer/playwright S. Ansky with the title "A Good Laugh." Ansky may have collected it during his ethnographic expeditions to Eastern Europe early in the 1900s. There is even a version of this story by Isaac L. Peretz called "The Wedding Gift" in *The Book of Fire*, translated by Joseph Leftwich. "David's Harp," a similar story of Reb Shmelke of Nikolsburg, is in Martin Buber's *Tales of the Hasidim—Early Masters*. Still another version is in *Great Tales of Jewish Fantasy and the Occult* by Joachim Neugroschel.

There is also an interesting version in Beatrice Weinreich's *Yiddish Folktales* called "The Happy Pair and the Baal Shem Tov." Her source was the Vilna Ethnographic Commission Archive. However, only in this version has the ending been extended. At the end the Besht returns to test the memory of the former greedy innkeepers and to see whether they have learned their lesson. In disguise as a beggar with filthy clothes, he goes to their village. This time, the woman welcomes him in and offers him hospitality. The next morning the Besht reveals who he is and blesses the couple with happiness and abundance. The story ends with "That's the sort of thing the Baal Shem Tov used to do" (281).

For other Baal Shem Tov stories in this collection, see "A Remembered Story" and "The Golden Buttons."

—*PS*

11

The Fire That Didn't Warm

There was once a king and he had a pool of cold water. One day, the king ordered, "Whoever can sleep in this pool all night and come out alive on the next day will receive 100 liras and a new suit." Many people tried to sleep all night in the pool, but the next day they were all found dead. One woman had an only son who didn't have any money. He said to his mother, "I want to try my luck and sleep in the cold pool. I don't have one penny in my pocket and I don't care if I die." The mother begged her son, "My only son, I don't have any other sons or daughters. I have no one else. Please don't go and leave me." But the son had decided to go and that's the way it was.

And the mother stood at a distance of approximately fifty meters from the pool in order to know the fate of her son. And in the meantime, she took some branches and lit them so that she would be warm during the night. The next day, the son came out alive and healthy and went before the king to ask for the prize that the king had promised. But the king claimed, "You don't deserve any prize because your mother lit a fire and you were then warmed by it. That is how you stayed alive."

The son answered, "I did not feel any warmth from the fire." However, his claims did not help him and the king refused to give him the prize. The son returned to his home and his mother cried and said, "I told you not to go. And now it should be enough for you that you went into the pool and came out alive and healthy."

But the son was very angry that the king did not give him his earned prize and he decided to bring him to the court of King David. King David heard about the claims of the two sides and judged. "You do not deserve any prize because your mother lit the fire near the pool." At that time, Solomon, King David's son, was present in the great hall where the king heard these two claims in his court. And in his heart he was very angry about the lack of justice that was done to the young man. So what did he do?

Solomon ordered a meal to be prepared for that evening. He invited his father to eat with him. King David arrived for the meal. He waited for a long hour for the meal to be served, but still the tables remained empty. David asked his son, "Where is the meal?" And Solomon answered, "The food has not been cooked yet." And the king looked and what did he see? He saw that the pot, which contained the meat, was tied close to the ceiling and the fire was below the pot, but on the floor. King David asked his son, "How will the food ever be cooked in this way, with the fire so far away from the pot?" Solomon answered, "You are right, father, the food will not be cooked because the pot is too far from the fire. But if that is the case, why did you judge that the son could be warmed by the fire lit by his mother outside of the pool? And if that is the case, then you did not give a right and true judgment."

And King David answered, "Yes, my wise son, I see now you are right. And we can still correct my wrong judgment." And so what did they do? They called the young man and gave him the prize and asked his forgiveness.

The young man returned to his house and to his mother and his happiness was doubled.

End of Story Note

IFA 6858 from *A Tale for Each Month 1965*, Story #11. Collected by Billy Kimhi from Ester Elizra, from Morocco (Noy).
Tale Types: This story is a combination of two types: AT 1262*A (IFA) (The Distant Fire That Did Not Warm) and AT 920* E (IFA) (The Story of the Child That Taught the King to Judge).
Motif: J123 (The child's wisdom decides the judgment).

There are two parallel versions of AT 1262*A from Israel (Druse and Iraq) and twelve versions of AT 920*E recorded from Tunisia, Israel, Yemen, Iraqi Kurdistan, Persia, and Afghanistan.

These versions can be found in the Israel Folktale Archives. The trickster Nasreddin Hoca appears in a Turkish version titled, "The Hoca and the Candle," which is in Barbara K. Walker's book, *A Treasury of Turkish Folktales for Children* (1988). Hamden, CT: Linnet Books.

There are a number of stories involving children who point out to a king the right way to judge. For example, in stories with King David and his young son Solomon, it is often Solomon who teaches his father to resolve the case in a clever and wise way. In "100 Grams More or Less," in this collection, it is also young people who demonstrate, through their play reenactment of a certain court case, how the king can judge rightly to resolve the conflict he faces. A variant of this tale is "The Lamp on the Mountain" in *A Coat for the Moon* (Schwartz and Rush).

—*PS*

12

The Princess Who Would Not Speak

One king had three sons, King Mahamad, King Gamshid, and King Chourshid. The first two didn't show any wisdom or any understanding of leadership, so the king didn't see them as fit to succeed him on the throne. However, the third son was very clever and also had a keen understanding of things. And the king decided that this third son would be the one to succeed him as the new king. And while the king was still alive, he declared that it would be his youngest son who would succeed him on the throne.

The two older brothers looked at their youngest brother with eyes of great jealousy. And they talked between them how to make him fail and even to get rid of him altogether. And in their hearts the jealousy grew greater and greater, until one day they appeared before the king and said to him: "We have happily accepted your decision to give your throne to our youngest and clever brother, King Chourshid, because, in your opinion, he will be able to hold the king's scepter. However, the king, in our opinion, should be one who knows how to ride a horse and how to shoot arrows straight into the heart of the enemy. Please, dear king, dear father, send him with us to hunt for three days. During these three days, we will teach him everything he needs to know."

The king accepted this proposal and so the two brothers took their youngest brother and went out into the forest, accompanied by a whole unit of the army. There they set up their tents. During this time, a light-footed deer appeared in the distance. The two older brothers ordered their soldiers to surround the deer from all four sides. "Whoever is in the path of the deer as the deer runs to you, must catch the deer and capture it alive." But to themselves they thought, if the deer goes toward

Chourshid, he will then have to go after the deer and try to catch it, and he will surely fall helpless on the way and die. That's how we will get rid of him.

However, the deer turned toward King Mahamad. Mahamad rode on the horse following the deer until the deer disappeared from his eye. And he could not find his way back to the camp they made in the forest. In the distance he saw a city. He got closer, and to his great amazement, he saw many heads stuck on the wall. When he asked the passers-by to explain this, they answered, "Our king has a beautiful daughter. Whoever succeeds in making her speak, will be her husband. But if he doesn't fulfill this goal, his head will be stuck on the walls of the city, next to the other cut off heads of previous suitors."

Mahamad came before the king and asked for his beautiful daughter's hand in marriage. The King responded kindly, "Please do not try, my son, because it will be your fate to be like the others. Because if you don't succeed to make my daughter speak three times, you will be taken out to be killed. It would be a pity for the son of a king who is young and alive, like you, to die before his father."

"If you have to chop my head from me, I am still willing to try my luck to make your beautiful daughter speak." All of a sudden the king's daughter appeared, in all her beauty, and she charmed all those around her. She appeared next to the window. All Mahamad had to do was to see her, and because of all her beauty, he lost his senses and fell down and fainted. And that's the way it happened with Mahamad, three times in a row, he couldn't make her speak because he could hardly stand in front of her. And Mahamad was taken out to be killed and his head was stuck on the wall with all the other heads.

Meanwhile, Gamshid saw that the brother had not returned to the camp and so he followed his tracks and went in search of him. He was riding on the horse of a knight. He also arrived at the same city and he was also surprised to see all the heads on the wall. Among the heads, he saw the head of his brother Mahamad. And when he was told the reason for all the heads, he also presented himself before the king and asked for his beautiful daughter's hand in marriage. But he also did not succeed in making the daughter talk, so he was taken out to be killed and his head was placed next to his brother's on the wall.

Then, when Chourshid saw that his second brother had not returned, he followed his tracks in search of him. He also arrived at that same city and saw, stuck on the wall, the heads of his two brothers. What did he do? He went to find out the meaning of this from a wise old storyteller. He gave the teller a gold coin and asked the storyteller to tell him a story so that he could sleep even beneath his sword. Then the storyteller told him a story and he fell asleep. When he woke up from his short sleep, Chourshid gave the storyteller another gold coin and asked him to tell the secret of all the heads around him. And the old man told him, "It is better for you, my son, that you shouldn't know this because this could mean your soul as well." But Chourshid begged him until finally the storyteller told him about the King's only daughter who was beautiful and clever. That only the person who would make her speak three nights in a row would marry her. And if not, he would die and his head stuck on the wall.

The next day, Chourshid presented himself to the king and asked for his daughter's hand in marriage. And the king said, "You must forsake this idea because it could mean your soul." But Chourshid begged and pleaded until the king agreed to his request. The two of them signed the agreement.

Chourshid was obligated to make the princess speak three times. But first he asked the king to prepare three items in the room where they would sit together. He asked for a pitcher for washing, a candlestick, and a wax candle. That night the king ordered all those things and Chourshid sat together with the king and his advisor in that special room in the palace. The king rang a bell and immediately his daughter appeared before him in royal clothing in all her beauty. Chourshid didn't raise his eyes to see her, but looked at the three items before him, the pitcher, the candlestick and the wax candle, and he spoke to them:

> Wax candle in tall candlestick, and purifying pitcher too,
> Listen, listen to what I say, This story is for you.

> *Pa'amot v'sha'ava shimu et asher essahper*
> *Hazen l'dvarai gam ata hakiyor hamitaher*

There were once three Persian priests traveling together. A man passed by them and asked, "How are you?" The priests spoke among themselves and one said, "When that man asked that question, he meant *me*." And the second one said, "No, he said hello to *me*." And the third argued, "He said hello to *me*."

And the three then decided to ask him directly. They ran after the man and asked him, "Which one of us three did you greet?" And the man answered them, "To the most foolish among you." And then each one of the three told a story about how stupid he was.

The first one said, "I was a new teacher and I used to hit my students often. So the bigger children decided to get revenge on me. So what did they do? One day all of them looked into a pit and started to scream, 'Priest, priest, here is a thief in the pit.' And I asked the students to go into the pit and get the thief out. But they refused. I gave each one a whip and told them 'I will go down myself into the pit. Then I will come out with the thief. When you see him, you must hit him with terrifying blows with your whips.' So I went down into the pit and looked into every corner of it but I didn't find a living soul. I came up out of the pit with empty hands. But when my students saw me, they began to yell and scream, 'Here is the thief! Here is the thief!' and they all began to hit me with intensive blows with the whips that I had given to them myself."

The second priest told this story: "I was also a new teacher and my students hated me because I hit them so much. And everytime I sneezed, everyone called out, 'God bless you.' They also made such noise and a mess in the classroom, that I said to them, 'When I sneeze again, you should all clap.' One day my chicken fell into a pit and I asked my students to go down and get the chicken out of the pit. But they refused. So what did I do? I tied a rope around my hip and asked them to lower me into the pit and afterwards to pull me out. And while they were pulling me out of the pit, I sneezed. Everyone let go of the rope and they all started to clap. I fell back down into the pit and only by the grace of God was I saved from death."

And the third priest told this story: "I was also a new teacher and I hit my students all the time, from the right and from the left. It is no surprise that I was hated by all of them. Once the children wanted to get revenge on me and what did they do? One morning in the classroom each student approached me and asked me, one by one, 'O priest, why are you frowning? Why are you so sad?' And this was very bad for me, so the students took me to a doctor who had received a bribe from them beforehand. And the doctor said to me, 'You must close yourself off in your classroom, for three days without food. If you try to eat, you will surely die.' So my students locked me in the classroom and they all went outside into the courtyard where they started going crazy, going wild, making noise and playing. One of the mothers brought some bread and meat to her son and she heard all the noise. She left quickly, but, because of my hunger, I took the bread and meat and put them in my mouth. Immediately one of my students caught me with the food in my mouth and gave a great cry, 'Our priest is going to die.' They called the doctor and he looked at my swollen cheeks and he had no choice but to operate on my cheek and to take out all the swelling. He took out a sharp knife and opened up the cheek and took out the partly chewed up meat."

And now Chourshid turned to the three items in front of him and asked, "Who is the greatest fool among the three priests?" The king called out, "The first priest." And the advisor cried, "The second priest." And the king's daughter called out in a loud voice, "The third priest because he was the greatest fool among them because he could have swallowed the meatball or thrown it out and he didn't need an operation at all."

And that is how Chourshid got the king's daughter to speak for the first time.

Then on the second night, the king had a great party in the palace ballroom and invited all his advisors. Chourshid sat in his place where he had sat the night before. In front of him was the candlestick, the wax candle, and the pitcher. And the king's daughter appeared in royal clothes and in all her beauty. Again Chourshid did not look at the princess but rather kept his eyes on the three items in front of him. And he said,

> Wax candle in tall candlestick, and purifying pitcher too,
> Listen, listen to what I say, This story is for you.

There was once a carpenter, a tailor, and a priest who were traveling together. One night they had to sleep in the forest and they decided among them that two would sleep while a third would stand guard. And each would take a turn. They drew lots and the first to stand guard was the carpenter. In order not to fall asleep, the carpenter took a piece of wood from a tree and carved a lifelike figure of a man. And then it was the tailor's turn and so he occupied himself by sewing a suit of clothes for this figure. Then the priest guarded his friends and when he saw the figure, he prayed to God to breathe the breath of life into it. This doll figure came to life and began to walk around. And now tell me, all of you, as he turned to the three items in front of him, who is the smartest, the carpenter, the tailor, or the priest?" The king called out immediately, "The carpenter." The advisor said, "The tailor," but the princess yelled out, "The priest who prayed to God for the breath of life into the inanimate object."

And that is the way Chourshid succeeded in making the king's daughter talk a second time.

On the third night, again the four people came together. Chourshid sat in his usual place and again did not look at the king's daughter. But again he called to the three items before him,

> Wax candle in tall candlestick, and purifying pitcher too,
> Listen, listen to what I say, This story is for you.

There once were three women, the wife of the king, the wife of the advisor, and the wife of the kadi. Once the three were walking in the field and, on the ground, they found a ring with an expensive jewel. And the king's wife said, "This ring should be on my finger." And the advisor's wife said, "You have many many beautiful expensive jewelry. This ring should be mine." And the kadi's wife said, "You both have beautiful jewels and rings. This ring should be mine." And so it was decided that whoever can tell the shrewdest or most sly story would win the ring.

And the kadi's wife told this story. "I once had a friend that visited me from time to time whenever my husband was not home. Once I said to my friend, 'I want the kadi to perform a marriage ceremony for us.' And my friend said, 'How is it possible for a kadi to perform such a marriage between his own wife and another man?' 'Oh yes, I will find a very shrewd way so that my husband, the kadi, will perform this marriage ceremony between us.' So what did I do? I ordered that a tunnel be built from my house to my friend's house. And I asked my friend to invite the kadi to his house so he could perform a marriage ceremony between him and his betrothed. My friend did as I advised and he invited the kadi to his house for the ceremony. By the time that the kadi walked very slowly to the house of my friend, I went very quickly to the tunnel and, in no time at all, I was sitting in my most festive clothes at my friend's house waiting for the kadi to arrive.

When the kadi arrived, he was shocked to find me there. So he made an excuse that he had forgotten his prayer book and left to go back home to bring it. I quickly ran home through the tunnel and quickly changed my clothes and I started doing some housework. When the kadi came in, I asked him, 'Did you perform the wedding ceremony so fast?' And my husband said, 'I forgot my prayer book and so I must return to the wedding now.' When he left with his book, I quickly changed back into my bridal clothes and ran through the tunnel and I was sitting at my friend's house. When the kadi entered the house for the second time, again he was surprised to find me there and said, 'I forgot my official seal. I will go back and bring it.' Again I quickly ran home through the tunnel, again changed my clothes, and started doing housework. When my husband got there, 'You will lose your salary if our neighbor will call a different kadi to perform the wedding ceremony.' My husband took the seal and returned to the wedding house for a third time. Again I got there before him and was waiting for him. My husband didn't dare leave the house again and so he performed the wedding ceremony between me and my friend. When I returned home through the tunnel, I again started doing some household chores when my husband returned. And he never caught on to the underground tunnel connection.'"

Then the advisor's wife told this sly, shrewd story. "I also had a friend who would visit me from day to day, especially when the advisor would go out on business. Then once, before he had to appear before the king, I bet him who could make up the greatest lie. That same day my friend came to visit me. And I set a beautiful table with delicious food and good wine. All of a sudden, my husband knocked on the door. Quickly I put my lover in a big box and closed it at the top. My husband entered the room and was shocked to see the mess and yelled in a booming voice, 'What is this great meal I see here? Who was here and what did he do with you?' I gave to my husband the key that I used to lock the box and said, 'Here. My friend was here and I locked him up in this box. Here is the key and you can open up the box and see for yourself.' And my husband turned to me and said, 'I know your meaning here. I understand what you are doing. You are trying to win the bet about who can make up the greatest lie. That is why you set all of this up.' He laughed and returned the key to me and left."

And the king's wife also told a very sly story. "I also had a lover friend and once I said to him, 'I feel like making love with you, in front of my husband, the king.' And her friend asked, 'How can you do something like this without incurring the wrath of the king?' But I promised him that I would do what I wanted to do and what my heart desires. So what did I do? I invited a carpenter and ordered him to dig a hole inside a tree, the size of a man, and to put a door there that could not be seen by the eye. I put my friend into the heart of the tree. And I said to the king, 'You have great strength in riding a horse and shooting arrows. You could also show me your strength in climbing this tree?' The king climbed the tree until he was at the very top branch. In the meantime, I signaled to my friend to come out and we made love to each other. And the king cried out from the top, 'Who is there next to you?' And I answered quite happily, 'You are mistaken, there is no one here next to me.' And when the king climbed down from the tree, I put my friend back into the heart of the tree, closed the door carefully. Then I said to the king, 'Your eyes are mistaken to see another man with me. I will climb to the top of the tree and I will look down into the nature around me.' And when I reached the top of the tree, I called down, 'Who is that with you, lying next to you?' And the king thought that from the top of the tree it appeared that there was another person with him. He yelled back to his wife, 'There is no one here with me.' And then I climbed down and we went on our way."

When Chourshid finished his story, he said, "Now tell me all of you who is the smartest of the three women?" And the king said, "The kadi's wife." And the advisor said, "The advisor's wife." But the king's daughter all of a sudden exclaimed, "The king's wife. She is the smartest." And that is the way Chourshid made the princess speak for a third time.

As promised, the king gave his daughter in marriage to Chourshid because he succeeded in making her speak three times. And after the marriage ceremony and the seven days of the wedding celebration, Chourshid went back to his town and told his father all that he had done and about the fate of his two older brothers.

In time, Chourshid became a very wise king.

End of Story Note

IFA 7156 from *With Elders Is Wisdom*, Story #16, recorded by Hanina Mizrahi from memory, from Iran.

Tale Types: AT 1332 (Which Is the Greatest Fool); AT 945 Part II (The Wooden Doll: a. A mute princess is offered to the man who can make her speak; b. The gardener tells his dog (a picture) in her presence of a woodcarver who made a wooden doll, a tailor who clothed her, and himself who gave her the power of speech: to whom shall she belong?; c. The princess breaks silence.) AT 1406 (The Merry Wives Wager); AT 1419 (The Returning Husband Hoodwinked); AT 1419E (Underground Passage to Paramour's House); AT 1423 (The Enchanted Pear Tree); AT 1419K* (Lover Hidden in Chest).

Motifs: J1712 (Which is the greatest fool); H343 (Suitor test: bringing mute princess to speak); F1023 (Creation of person by cooperation of skillful men; D435.1.1 (Transformation: statue comes to life); H621 (Skillful companions create woman: to whom does she belong?; F954.2.1 (Mute princess is brought to speech by tale ending with a question to be solved); Z16.1 (Tales ending with a question); J2301 (Gullible husbands); K1545 (Wives wager as to who can best fool her husband); K1510 (Returning husband hoodwinked); K1518 (Husband believes that he has seen double from tree).

The first inner story, as to who is the greatest fool, is also a variant of a Nasruddin Hodja trickster tale. The second inner story deals with a carpenter, tailor, and priest. (See also "The Prince of the East and the Princess of the West" in this collection as well as "The Mute Princess" in Howard Schwartz's *Elijah's Violin*.) The third inner story deals with infidelity stories of three wives as to which one can tell the shrewdest story. In some international variants one wife will make her husband believe that he is dead; in another she spins, weaves, and sews clothes so fine that they cannot be seen; a third makes her husband believe that he is a dog and so he barks at people who pass.

There are many variants of this story from Morocco, Tunisia, Iraqi Kurdistan, East Europe, Afghanistan, Persian Kurdistan, and Iraq. In all of these stories, a man has the challenge to make a princess, who refuses to speak, willing to speak. He does this by telling stories that have a dilemma question at the end as to who is the wisest, or the greatest fool, etc. Through talking to three objects, the vase, candlestick, and candle, and receiving their responses, the princess listens but rejects those responses and speaks, setting forth her judgment. These three objects/symbols, which are replaced by witnesses in some versions, have sexual connotations, which makes this clearly a story always told by a man to a woman.

The repeated couplet that the young king speaks to the various objects before telling "them" his dilemma stories was recast in English by Roslyn Bresnick-Perry.

—*PS*

13

The Luck of Faradj, the Rope Maker

Faradj was a rope maker. A simple Jew and very naive, his earnings were just enough to live hand to mouth and not more. One day, two strangers came to Faradj. And what did they see? A Jew who had many blisters on his hands and he could hardly support himself. They asked him, "What are your earnings every day?" And he answered, "Eight rupees. But I have been blessed with seven children and I don't make enough to support them."

They asked him, "Why don't you buy some machines in order to increase what you produce and increase your earnings?" And the rope maker answered, "Everything depends on money. Where would I find this money?"

One of the strangers, who was a very wealthy man, took pity on Faradj and lent him 200 rupees so that he could improve his business. "If you make a profit, then, one day, you will repay this debt," the stranger told the rope maker.

The rope maker took this loan and put the money under his hat for safekeeping. On his way home, he bought some meat for his children with some money he had. An eagle flying high overhead smelled the meat, swooped down, and tried to take the meat from its owner. In the struggle, the eagle became very angry and snatched the hat of the rope maker, with the money inside, and flew away.

The rope maker put the meat on the side of the road and ran after the eagle. But the eagle flew away and disappeared from his view. When the man returned to take his meat package, he saw that dogs had eaten it. Faradj was very tired and very angry. Embarrassed, he returned to his home and told his wife all that had happened to him.

Some time later, the two strangers returned to Faradj's shop and there they saw that he was just as poor as before. The rope maker told them all that had happened to him on that day. Again they had pity on Faradj and again the wealthy man gave him another 200 rupees.

This time Faradj decided to put the money in a grain jug that was at the entrance to the house. This is where the money would stay until he would be able to buy the right machinery. Faradj returned home and was filled with great happiness. But then, one day, he discovered that the grain jug that had stood at the entrance to his house for many years had disappeared. When he asked his wife about the jug, his wife told him, "I didn't have any bread for the children so I sold the jug for ten rupees." Only one sentence came out of Faradj's mouth, "God should have pity on me."

Many months passed. And Faradj's old friends returned again. They were even more surprised to see his poverty had not changed since they had been there. Again Faradj told them all that had happened. And again the two strangers comforted him and one of them said, "In our first two meetings, we gave our friend 200 rupees each time. This time I will give him a piece of coal and, with the help of God, this will bring him blessings because everything depends on luck."

That night, at midnight, there was a knocking on the door. Faradj's wife went to the door and saw her neighbor. "Please have pity on me and help me. My husband, the fisherman, lost a piece of coal that he uses to fish. And if he doesn't go out to fish tonight, we will have nothing to live on."

And the wife was surprised at this request. Where would she get any coal? Faradj overheard the women talking, so he got up and gave the neighbor the piece of coal. After all, what use did he have for this piece of coal? And the fisherman's wife was very grateful and said, "You are a very generous neighbor. And for all your generosity, whatever my husband will catch in the first net that he puts down will be yours."

The fisherman left to do his work. And indeed, after a short time, he brought up a very big fat fish. He brought the fish home and gave it to his good neighbor, Faradj. Faradj cut open the fish and he was very surprised for inside the fish he found a very great brilliant stone. Faradj didn't know what this stone was, so he gave it to his children so they could play a game with it. During the evening, one of the neighbors was curious and asked, "What is different tonight that is different from all other nights? What is the cause for such a great light in your house?"

Faradj's wife told him about the strange stone. The neighbor replied, "My husband is a diamond merchant and he will pay you a great amount of money for this wonderful miraculous stone."

The next day, the diamond merchant appeared at Faradj's house to check the stone. He examined it from all different angles. He immediately offered them fifty rupees. Now, as naive as he was, Faradj was certain that this merchant was trying to trick him. So he said, "Of course not." According to this answer, the diamond merchant, mistakenly of course, thought that the amount was too little for Faradj. He kept multiplying the amount and Faradj kept repeating, "Of course not." In this way, the negotiations continued until the merchant offered the great amount of 100,000 rupees. The diamond merchant took out of his pocket an advance of 10,000 rupees and he promised to bring the remaining amount in one hour's time. Faradj finally believed that this man was not trying to trick him, after all.

One day the diamond merchant heard that the king was searching to replace a diamond that had fallen from his crown into the water while he was sailing in his boat. When the merchant arrived at the palace, the king was surprised and overjoyed to discover that this diamond merchant had found the original stone.

As a commission, the king gave this diamond merchant 20,000 rupees as a reward, in addition to the price of the stone. Then the king asked the diamond merchant, "How did this diamond come into your possession?"

"I purchased it from my neighbor Faradj, the rope maker," replied the merchant.

Then the king invited the rope maker to his palace. He embraced Faradj and asked him to tell him his life's story.

Faradj told the king about his poverty in the past and about the two strangers who had tried to help and save him from his troubles. "It was only because of the piece of coal that I attained this great wealth," added Faradj.

And the king said, "Until now you have been a poor man. And now I will give you a place to live, servants, two bodyguards, and many horses. And you will also receive my royal permission to be the only rope maker in my kingdom. Nobody but you will be allowed to do this work here. From now on you will be the king of the ropes. And every day, in the middle of the day, you will eat at my table."

Many days passed, and the two strangers returned to Faradj's house. Now they were very surprised to see, instead of the small rundown cottage, a great house with many servants and workers and many machines. When the visitors asked for Faradj, the workers told them, "Faradj is the owner and the manager of this factory." The visitors went from room to room—and each room was more beautiful in this factory—until they found Faradj.

Faradj received them very happily. He showed them his beautiful house and groves. Then he wanted to bring them to his friend the king. As they were riding noble horses to meet the king, suddenly, Faradj called out, "Look over there, on the tree. My old hat is caught on one of the branches." They brought down the hat that the eagle had taken and they found in it the 200 rupees.

Then when they passed through the center of the town, they saw the old grain jug that was being sold in a market. Faradj bought it for a small amount and inside they found the other 200 rupees.

"We always believed in you and in your honesty, even if you had not found the lost money," said the visitors who were very excited. Faradj returned their money in addition to many valuable gifts.

At the palace, the king of the ropes presented his loyal friends to the king and told him everything that had happened to him, again from the beginning, and about his friends' generosity.

Then the king, who was impressed by their honesty and faith, gave them the right to be exempt from taxes all the days of their lives. Whenever they would visit the city, the two friends, along with the rope maker, were always invited to eat at the king's table.

End of Story Note

IFA 8620 from *A Tale for Each Month 1968–69*, Story #15, collected by Ben-Zion Yehoshua from his father, Refael Yehoshua-Raz from Afghanistan (Cheichel-Hechal).
Tale Types: AT 935** (The Poor Rope Maker); AT 946D* (Fortune and Coincidence); AT 736 (Luck and Wealth).
Motifs: N183 (The third time he recovers all his money); N421 (In the net is a fish with a precious stone in his body); N529.2 (Pearl found in fish).

There are many variants in universal folklore and versions of this story type come from *Stories of 1001 Nights*. In addition, there are also many parallels in the Israel Folktale Archives from Morocco, Iraq, Afghanistan, Tunisia, and Poland. The theme of retrieving a diamond in a fish recalls the story of Joseph the Sabbath Lover who buys a beautiful fish to honor the Sabbath and finds a diamond, his reward for his love of Shabbat. However, in this story, the diamond is given to the rope maker as a result of a deal between the poor rope maker and the fisherman. It is the reward for Faradj loaning the fisherman the piece of coal for bait. The wife promises to give Faradj whatever her fisherman husband will land in his first catch. Perhaps we should retitle the story "Faradj's Fate."

In the story "We Never Lose Old Treasures" (in this collection), the old man wants to get rid of his sandals but can't. Obversely, in this story, the old man can't seem to hold onto his valuable gifts. However, in both stories, the objects are all recovered, with happy results and with a sense of not being able to escape one's fate.

See also "Can Fate Be Changed?" in this collection.

—*PS*

14

The Broken Betrothal

Once there was a leather merchant. While he did not follow any hasidic rabbi, and was in fact an opponent of Hasidism, his wife was a follower of the Belzer rabbi. This couple had been married for over ten years but remained childless. Twice a year the wife would go to Rabbi Joshua ben Shalom Rokeah of Belz and plead with him to pray for her.

"What is my life without a child," the wife cried. "I will do whatever you tell me that I have to do in order for my husband and me to have a child."

But as time went on, the husband scoffed at her visits to the Belzer rebbe and her prayers, saying to her, "You see how much your rebbe and your prayers are helping. Do you really think he has divine power? I will not stay with you any longer. According to talmudic law, a man must divorce his wife of ten years if there are no children. And so I will see the rabbi, too, but for another reason."

At once the woman went to her rabbi and began to weep, "Holy rabbi, help me. I do not want that we should be divorced, but tell me what can I do. My soul cries out for a child, but I remain barren."

The rabbi looked at the woman and was deeply moved by her tears. "My dear woman, go to a certain city to buy leather. You will find your answer there."

"But, rabbi, how is that possible? Who should I meet there?"

"Ask no questions. Just do what I told you to do. It will become clear in the right time," replied the rabbi calmly.

The woman made arrangements to go to that certain city and to the tanning factory where she would purchase the leather, as the rabbi had instructed her to do.

As she was choosing the leather, a man, wearing a vest and silver buttons, entered the shop and spoke to her, "What are you doing here? Do you live near here?"

The woman looked up at the man, but did not recognize him. "Why do you ask me these questions? Do you know me?"

"Yes, of course I know you. Is it possible that you do not recognize your own betrothed? We were going to be married, but then you left me without explanation and moved away. I was left a bitter and shamed man. No one would marry me because of that—and I did not want to marry anyone either because I no longer felt worthy. At the time, I cursed you that you should not have any children. All these years I have remained alone."

When the woman heard this, she was shocked and amazed at what she was hearing. She had not thought of him for so long, and had forgotten about him. Then, with a sudden burst of tears, she said, "Forgive me, please, for the injustice I have done to you. It is because of this broken betrothal that I have not had any children and I want a child more than anything in the world. It is the Rabbi of Belz who sent me here for he knew that we would meet. I will do whatever you ask of me in order to receive your forgiveness and lift your curse. Do not add any more sorrow to my soul."

Seeing how much she truly felt repentant, the man replied, "Yes, I will forgive you because the rabbi has sent you here. But first you must do something to help me. In a certain village, a distance from here, lives my widowed sister. She has two sons of marriageable age, but she has no money to find good brides for them. If you will agree to marry them off, I shall completely forgive you and you will have a child who will be a light to the world with Torah learning."

As soon as the woman heard this, she immediately agreed to this condition and began asking the sister's name. Suddenly, the oil lamp fell, causing the flame to flare up. The woman looked away for that moment—and when she looked again—the man had vanished.

The woman began to search for the man in all the streets but she could find no trace of him. When she asked people about him, no one even knew who he was and, in fact, assured her that they had never seen such a man in that town. So she decided to spend the night at an inn there, thinking she would find him again the next day.

That night she had a dream. In the dream, the same man appeared, still wearing the same vest, and said, "My sister's name is Sarah and lives with her sons Jacob and Isaac in this certain village. Go there and visit her, as you have promised." When she woke up, she hired a wagon and driver and set out for that village. While driving in the woods, they became lost and soon the sun set and it was night. Since the wagon driver could no longer see the path, he stopped his horses but did not know what to do. The woman began to weep, but after a long while fell into a deep sleep. Suddenly the driver saw a man coming toward him. The man got up on the seat next to him, took the reins, and drove the horses to the path. By the time they reached the edge of the forest, it had begun to rain lightly. Just at dawn, the man disappeared. The wagon driver woke the woman and told her what had happened.

"Describe this man," she asked.

From his description, she knew that it was the same man she had met in the leather shop and in her dream. She began to shiver with wonder.

They continued to ride in the village until they came to a house and stopped when they saw a woman in front. "I am looking for Sarah and her two sons, Jacob and Isaac."

The village woman answered, "Yes, I am that Sarah."

"Your brother has asked me to come to your home and to marry off your sons. I am here to fulfill my promise to him."

"Why do you tell me this? Have you lost your senses? For, if you have, then you surely belong in the madhouse. When did you see my brother?"

"I assure you that I am not a madwoman. It was just a few days ago that I met your brother in the leather shop. My driver saw him in the woods last night when he helped us find our way out of the forest," answered the woman, sensing that something was out of the ordinary. "What is wrong?"

Sarah was silent for a long while. Tears filled her eyes and she said, "Please come with me."

The two of them walked until they reached the edge of the village and entered the cemetery. "Here is my brother," Sarah spoke softly, pointing to a gravestone bearing her brother's name. "He died ten years ago. How could you have seen him a few days ago?"

Sarah and the woman walked back to the house, in silence. At the house, Sarah asked, "Describe the man you met."

The woman described the man and his clothing. "And he wore a vest with unusual silver buttons."

Sarah said, "Wait a moment." And she went into the house but returned a few moments later holding in her hands the exact vest that the man had been wearing. "This was my brother's vest, which I kept as a remembrance of my brother. No one has worn it for ten years." But as the woman touched the vest, she saw that it was damp with beads of water as though it had been in the rain. And the two women looked at each other, realizing that the brother had returned from the other world.

The woman kept her promise and gave Sarah a thousand gold coins to arrange good matches for her two sons, and to buy the wedding clothes and the food for the wedding feasts. She then stayed for the Sabbath. After the Sabbath she took part in the celebration of the marriages.

When she returned home, she told her husband everything that had happened to her. The husband listened with wonder and finally said, "I see now that your rabbi is really a great man after all." And he too became a hasid of the Belzer rabbi.

A short time after this, the woman conceived and nine months later the couple knew great joy when a child was born to them. They celebrated the birth with a joyous feast.

End of Story Note

Sources: From *Kehal Hasidim* (Hebrew), compiled by Aharon Valden (Warsaw: no date) and *'Adat Tzaddikim* (Hebrew), compiled by M. L. Rodkinson-Frumkin (Lemberg, 1877). In *Mimekor Yisrael* (Bin Gorion) there are two variants: one from *'Adat Tzaddikim* with the Seer of Lublin; the other from *Petirat Rabbenu ha-Kadosh mi-Belz* (Hebrew) (Lemberg, 1894), with the Belzer rebbe. This story has also been attributed to the Maggid of Kosnitz.

Tale Types: AT 512B* (Ghost Is Avenged).

This is one of the most powerful tales I have encountered. In the telling of Howard Schwartz's version in *Lilith's Cave*, I really felt the ghostly presence of the betrothed woman who was wronged, and, with a shiver, immediately understood the essence of the message. As in "The Emperor's Daughter and the King's Son" (in this collection) and in "The Promised Betrothal" (in my *Jewish Stories One Generation Tells Another*), the story revolves around a vow taken but then broken. In Judaism, a vow is sacred and must be kept. To break it is to incur punishment, often in the form of being barren, as in this story. In Jewish folklore, as in at least four biblical stories, the theme of barrenness is dominant. Often, as the story unravels, we discover that the hero or heroine had broken a vow once taken in the past, a vow that had been forgotten. However, as in this case, the Belzer rabbi brings it to her attention. Only when the hero or heroine is redeemed is the curse lifted.

In *Mimekor Yisrael*, there are two versions of this story, and both make reference to the well-known talmudic and medieval Jewish folktale of "The Story of the Weasel and the Pit" (which is the story of "The Promised Betrothal" mentioned above). In almost all the variants of "The Broken Betrothal" story, it is the Seer of Lublin who can see in the past and future, a wondrous role set by the Baal Shem Tov in his many roles as a master of miracles, wonder-worker, and prophet.

For other versions of this story, see "The Dead Fiancée" in *Lilith's Cave* and "The Broken Betrothal" in *The Classic Tales* (Frankel), as well as the two versions of "The Story of the Weasel and the Pit Repeated" in *Mimekor Yisrael*.

—PS

15

A Story of Consolation

Yitzhak ben David died suddenly late one night. A heart attack, they said. Yitzhak ben David (Irving son of David) had been my husband. We had been at a dinner party when he started feeling seriously ill. And when our host called the emergency ambulance, it seemed to take hours before it arrived. It was already starting to snow lightly as we followed the ambulance to the hospital in that town, one hour's drive from Manhattan and our home. As some friends and I waited impatiently in the hall of the hospital for some news, hopeful news, I looked up and saw the men, perhaps they were orderlies or the emergency ambulance crew, whispering among themselves. I looked up and found myself able to decipher two of their whispered words: "Heart attack." My life changed in that moment. I was no longer a wife, but a *widow*.

That night, after the long drive back to New York City, I kept trying to understand what was happening, trying to decide how I could tell my mother-in-law that her youngest son, Yitzhak ben David, was dead, and his death coming only seven months after her own husband's death, David's death. This was the reversal of nature. A child should bury his parents, and not a parent a child. And how could I tell our two young children that they would never see their father again? This too was not natural. Everything was topsy-turvy with my whole world spinning into chaos.

During the *shiva* period, my father, a cantor, wrote a letter, in Yiddish, of compassion and consolation to my grieving mother-in-law. Following a Jewish tradition to use a story to comfort, my father told the biblical story of another David's son, which is found in the second book

111

of Samuel (Chapter 12, lines 15–23). This story, set in the letter like a jewel in a ring, comforted my mother-in-law.

> David's son became ill. And when King David heard of his illness, he took off his crown and replaced his kingly robes with sackcloth, went to an inner room of the palace, and sat on the ground. He refused to eat any food, but only recited psalms day after day, praying to God to heal his child. The elders of his house approached him and pleaded with him to rise up and eat with them, but David refused to leave his place.
>
> And it came to pass that, on the seventh day, David's son died. But the servants feared to tell David. "How can we approach him with this news when he refused to eat and rest while his son was still alive? How will he be able to bear his son's death? What will he do now?"
>
> And so none of the servants dared to tell David what had happened to his son.
>
> When David looked up, he saw his servants standing at a distance, whispering among themselves. And seeing this, David realized that his son was dead. "Is my son dead?" he asked them. And they answered, "Yes, he is dead."
>
> Then David arose from the earth, and washed. He put on his robes and went to his house to eat and resumed his kingly duties.
>
> His servants were puzzled by the King's actions. They approached him and asked: "We do not understand what you have been doing. While your son was ill, you sat on the ground, refused to eat, and only fasted and wept and prayed for your child. But now that your child has died, you rose from the ground, you ate and you are now sitting again on your throne."
>
> And David answered: "While my child was still alive, there was hope. And so I fasted and wept and prayed that God would be merciful and restore my child to health. What else could I do for him? But now that he is dead, why should I fast? I must now go on with life. Can I bring him back to life? No, I shall go to him in time, but he shall not return to me."

And when my mother-in-law read this story, she too wept and understood what she had to do. She was not alone in her sorrow.

Then she read my father's letter out loud to me. Just as she ended the story, my son began to cry. His diaper was full. I looked at my mother-in-law and she gave me a nod. I knew what I had to do. I picked up my crying child, this grandson of David. Laughter burst out of me as I went to change his diaper. *L'Khaim!* To life!

End of Story Note

This is a personal family story that is based on an actual experience in my life.

However, when I share this story—the frame story along with the biblical episode (found in II Samuel)—I have found that it is a story that has helped many who have gone through a crisis, or are going through a crisis, especially the death of a loved one. There are no explanations to the unexplainable events of life. I know, though, that we can draw strength and direction from our tradition and our stories. Somehow one doesn't feel so alone in the universe after sharing a story with someone. As King Solomon once said, "A man should speak of the anxiety in his heart in order to help lighten it." A story helps to lift the spirit and lighten the heart.

See "Twelve Sons of the Emir" in this collection.

My father, Cantor Samuel E. Manchester, knew biblical text and understood well the power of words. He wrote the letter, which is quoted in the story, at a deeply sad time of loss. The story-within-the-letter helped us all through the grieving time because it helped us gain a perspective and keep our balance.

It is also interesting to note that the same chapter of II Samuel, Chapter 12, opens with a very well-known story-within-a-story. In Chapter 11, David had sent Uriah the Hittite to the front line of battle so that he would be assuredly killed. And why? Because David coveted Uriah's wife, Bathsheba. As soon as Uriah was reported killed, David married the wife and together they had a son. All of this displeased God.

Chapter 12 begins as God sends Nathan the Prophet to rebuke David. And how does he rebuke him? How does he get David to understand his actions, the repercussions of his actions, and to take responsibility for those actions? Trusting the power of story, Nathan rebukes David by telling him a parable.

"There were two men in the same city, one rich and one poor. The rich man had very large flocks and herds, but the poor man had only one little ewe lamb that he had bought. He tended it and it grew up together with him, and his children: it used to share his morsel of bread, drink of his cup, and nestle in his bosom; it was like a daughter to him. One day, a traveler came to the rich man, but he was loath to take anything from his own flocks or herd to prepare a meal for the guest who had come to him; so he took the poor man's lamb, and prepared it for the man who had come to him.

"David flew into a rage against the man, and said to Nathan, 'As the Lord lives, the man who did this deserves to die! He shall pay for the lamb four times over, because he did such a thing and showed no pity.'

"And Nathan said to David: 'That man is you! Thus said the Lord, the God of Israel: It was I who anointed you king over Israel and it was I who rescued you from the hand of Saul; and I gave you . . . and gave you . . . and if that were not enough, I would give you twice as much more . . . Therefore the sword shall never depart from your House—because you spurned Me by taking the wife of Uriah the Hittite and making her your wife.'

"David said to Nathan: 'I stand guilty before the Lord!' "*

As we see, David understood his part in this tragic situation only when he heard a parable paralleling his actions in a non-threatening way. Without realizing it, he took what he needed to learn from the story and transferred it to his own life. Stories illuminate and teach in a beautiful and lasting way, as shown by this biblical example.

The son who is the subject of the biblical story that my father wrote about is the child of the union of David and Bathsheba. The prophet Nathan follows his rebuke to David with: "The Lord has remitted your sin; you shall not die. However, since you have spurned the enemies of the Lord by this deed, the child about to be born to you shall die."

Thus, within one chapter of II Samuel, there are two stories-within-stories, which are continually being interpreted and used as models to help us unravel the mysteries of life.

—*PS*

---

*The translation used is from *The Prophets* (1978). Philadelphia: Jewish Publication Society.

16

The Golden Buttons

It was Friday night and the Baal Shem Tov was sitting with his disciples around the Shabbos table making *kiddush*. Suddenly the Baal Shem Tov burst into laughter.

His disciples looked around, looked at each other, searching for an explanation. They were mystified about this occurrence. Yet they could not ask the Baal Shem Tov.

After they had eaten the soup, the Baal Shem Tov laughed again, a hearty laugh. And then after the dessert, he laughed a third time.

After *Havdalah*, it was the custom for the *hasidim* to ask their master questions on matters that they had been puzzling over during Shabbos. So they finally asked, "Tell us, Holy Master, we want to know why did you laugh three times on erev Shabbos?"

The Baal Shem Tov got up from his chair, called for Alexis to harness his horses to the carriage, and said to his *hasidim*, "With patience the reason for my laughter will become clear. Come, let us go for a ride."

The *hasidim* left Medziboz and rode throughout the night and, by morning, they had reached the town of Kozenitz. Everyone in the town heard that the Baal Shem Tov had arrived in their town and they all came to see him, some even hoped to receive a blessing from him. Everyone wanted to be in the same place with him.

When the Baal Shem Tov had finished his morning prayers, he turned to the head of the community and said, "Send for Reb Shabsi, the bookbinder, and his wife."

Surprised that he had asked for Shabsi, an old man who was a good man, but certainly not a scholar, the head of the community hesitated.

Perhaps he had not heard the name right. But the Baal Shem Tov repeated, "I need to see Shabsi and his wife."

A messenger went immediately to the poor hut where Shabsi and his wife lived and brought them to the center of the town.

The Baal Shem Tov said gently to them, "Shabsi, tell me what you and your wife did on Friday night during the Shabbos meal. Leave nothing out and do not be afraid to tell me the truth."

Shabsi replied,

> Dear rabbi, I will tell you the truth. All my life I have been a bookbinder earning a very good living. Then on Thursdays, I would give my wife money to buy the best food for our Shabbos meals and for *tzedakah*. But now, as you can see, we are old, and I do not have much work anymore. I earn very little. We have no children to help us in our old age.
>
> This past Friday morning I realized I had no money for the shopping in order to prepare properly for Shabbos. I cannot beg and I have never borrowed from anyone. I have always put my trust in God to help us out of difficulties. But since we would not have anything for Shabbos, I was determined that that is what will have to be and we would fast this Shabbos. So I spoke to my wife and pleaded with her not to borrow anything from neighbors, no matter what. I knew it would be especially hard for her to be without candles, wine, and challah. But what could I do?
>
> Then I went to *shul*, telling my wife that I would be later than usual because I would leave after everybody else. I didn't want anyone to ask if we would be their Shabbos guest if they saw our dark house without candles. I would burn with shame. So instead I walked home alone, slowly. But when I approached my house, I saw candles had been lit. I thought to myself, "My poor wife could not withstand this test. She surely borrowed candles from the neighbor." I felt pity for her. Then when I entered the house, I saw the wine and challahs on the table. Still I didn't want to say anything to spoil the sweet silence of Shabbos. I made kiddush.
>
> By then my wife saw my disapproving look, and she said, "Shabsi, today I had no food to cook, so, after I had done all the regular cleaning, I opened the old trunk to rearrange some things. Do you know what I found there? An old jacket with golden buttons. I snipped them and I went and sold the buttons. It is with that money that I bought all the best foods for our Shabbos meals."
>
> Dear rabbi, that's when I started to laugh. There was such joy in my heart. Above all, we could observe Shabbos with the help of God—and all

because of those long lost golden buttons. Suddenly I took my wife's hand and we began to dance.

Then I realized we were perhaps breaking the holiness of Shabbos, so we sat down and continued our meal. But after the soup, I broke into joyful laughter again and we danced some more. And then after the dessert, we danced and laughed once more. We only wanted to express our thankfulness for God's goodness when we laughed and danced. If I have sinned against God in any way, then you will tell me how to atone for the sin. You judge me and I'll do whatever you say.

The Baal Shem Tov and everyone else listened until Shabsi finished his story, and the Besht said to his disciples, "You see, when Reb Shabsi and his wife laughed and danced with joy, all the angels laughed and danced with them. And, if the angels laughed and danced in the heavens, then how could I not join in. So I laughed three times too."

And turning to Shabsi and his wife, the Baal Shem Tov said, "This was no sin, but rather a blessing. And so I will grant whatever your fondest wish is. Do you want to be rich, to have great honor, or perhaps to have a son to be a comfort to you in your old age?"

"Holy rabbi, do not mock us. We are already old and do not have children. But yes, our heart's greatest desire is to have a child."

"God will bless you with a son. I will return for the *bris* and be the *sandak*. Give him a name after me, Israel."

As the Baal Shem Tov said, so it happened. Within the year, the bookbinder and his wife had a son and they named him Israel. Rabbi Israel Baal Shem Tov came, as he had promised, and blessed him. And this child Israel grew up to be the holy Maggid of Kozenitz.

End of Story Note

Source: *Niflaoth ha-Maggid Koznitz*, published by A. J. Kleiman, Piotrkov, 1911 (Yiddish).

This Baal Shem Tov story is one of my favorites that I have told for years. I love the idea of laughter as a joyous response, especially adding to the joy of Shabbat. In one version, in *The Hasidic Anthology* (Newman), instead of a coat with golden buttons, what is recovered is a pair of long-lost gloves with silver buttons.

Baal Shem Tov stories often begin with his *hasidim* sitting around the table. Throughout Shabbos stories are told at such a *farbrengen*, a gathering of the *hasidim*. Then something precipitates an after-Shabbos journey to a distant place to reveal some mysteries.

Versions of this story can be found in *The Hasidic Anthology* and *The Classic Tales* (Frankel).

For other Baal Shem Tov stories in this collection, see "A Remembered Story" and "The Wedding Gifts."

—PS

17

100 Grams More or Less

In a certain town two neighbors lived; one was rich and one was poor. There came a day when the poor man had no money left, not even enough money to buy food for his hungry children. So what did he do? He went to the rich man and asked him for a loan of 1000 lires. The rich man agreed on one condition, saying, "If you return the money at the end of the year, then it will be fine. But if you don't return the money at that time, then I will cut 100 grams from your flesh in exchange for the debt." The poor man hesitated in his heart to take the loan. But then he thought to himself, "Great are the deeds of God and He will help me bring the money back to repay the debt." And the poor man went out of the rich man's house with a lighter heart and 1000 lires in his pocket.

But the year passed and again the poor man didn't have any money in his pocket. And he thought to himself, "Now what will I do? The rich man will cut 100 grams from my flesh."

While he was deep in thought, the door of his house opened and the rich man was standing on his doorstep. "Return now the 1000 lires that I lent you." The poor man had to tell him that he did not have any money after all. But then he suggested, "Don't cut my flesh. Rather let us go to the king. He will judge between us." And the rich man agreed because he knew that the law was on his side.

So they came before the king and they told him the whole story. Surprisingly, the king was embarrassed because he did not know how to give them a judgment. So what did he do? He suspended his decision for thirty days.

The king then called for his advisor, who was a vizier, and told him about the situation and said to him, "You must solve this problem. If you don't find a solution in thirty days, you will die."

And the vizier went out to travel around the country saying to himself, "Maybe I will find a solution among the country people." And in the meantime twenty-nine days had already passed and there was still no solution.

On the thirtieth day the vizier was still roaming around the city and thinking about his impending death. And he was still thinking when he heard a voice calling out, "What is mine is yours, one gram more, one gram less. *Sheli shelkha gram pakhot gram yoter.*" And the vizier thought to himself, "Am I dreaming?" And then he looked and he saw two children playing and he decided to listen. "Perhaps what they say will be of use to me," he thought.

Then he heard one of the children saying, "You be the poor man and I'll be the rich man." And they started to play. The child who was "poor" said, "I agree that you may cut 100 grams from my flesh, but on this condition: if you cut one gram more or one gram less, I will kill you." And the second child resisted this for a moment by saying, "If that is the case, then I don't want your money and I do not want your flesh."

When this play discussion had finished, the vizier ran to the king's palace, burst inside without paying attention to the people around, and yelled out, "I have the solution." And the king was very curious to know what the solution would be. But the vizier would not agree to reveal this solution until the day of the trial.

The day of the trial came and all the people gathered around to hear what the king's sentence would be. The poor man and the rich man stood opposite each other. The vizier opened his mouth and said to the rich man, "We have decided that you may cut from the flesh of the poor man, *but* you may not cut one gram more or one gram less from it, only the agreed upon 100 grams. But if you cut more or less, then your sentence will be to die."

And the rich man announced without hesitation, "I will give up any rights to the poor man's flesh." And he left the house very angrily.

The king was shocked at his advisor's wisdom and asked him to tell him how he came upon this solution when he himself, the king, was wiser than his advisor and, yet, couldn't think of such a wise solution. The vizier told the king all that had happened to him on his long journey and how the solution came to him as he was watching a children's game. The king asked that this wise child be brought before him. When the child arrived, he was very scared and pale, shaking as he was brought before the king. And the king suddenly asked him, "Would you agree to be my son from now on?"

The child agreed and went to tell his parents and then came back to the king's palace. Many years passed and the child grew up in the king's house. And when he arrived at the age of marriage, he asked the king to find him a wife. But the king claimed, "You must go out and find your wife, on your own."

Then the young boy wandered around the city but he didn't find anyone he liked and who fulfilled his requirements for a wife. He went further and further until he arrived at a dark forest. As he was wandering around in the forest, he suddenly saw an old man who had a great bundle of branches on his back and who was walking very slowly. And the king's son asked him, "Will you invite me into your house today?"

"Why do you laugh at an old man like me?" answered the old man. "For you see my house is tumble-down and old and about to fall down and nowhere near suitable for the son of a king, like you."

The king's son continued to try to persuade the old man until the old man agreed to host him. As he went into the rundown house, he saw, in a corner of the room, a beautiful young girl. And he said to her, "Take this money and go out and buy a chicken for dinner." The young girl took the money, brought back a chicken and cooked it, and brought it to the table. The king's son divided the chicken to the people who were eating. He gave the head of the chicken to the old father. He gave the legs to the mother. The daughter received the wings. The best part of the chicken, all the rest in other words, he gave himself. At the end of the meal the king's son went out for a walk. The father expressed his shock at the way the chicken was divided. But his daughter explained it to him. "You, father, received the head of the chicken because you are the head of the family. Mother received the legs because it is a sign that she is the stable one at home and holds us together. And I received the wings because very soon I will fly away from here with that young man." Very soon after, the king's son married the daughter of the old man and woman.

This was a great disappointment to the vizier because he too had a daughter whom he wanted to marry to the king's son. And one day the vizier said to the king, "Your son has made a very serious mistake in marrying the young woman who is not suitable for him."

When he heard this, the king became angry at his son and didn't speak with him. When the king's son's wife heard about this, she asked one of the welders to make her a golden shoe. On the queen's birthday, the bride brought it to her as a gift. The king got angry and asked, "Why have you brought only one shoe? Are you laughing at me and at my wife, the queen?"

And the prince's wife answered, "According to the vizier, I heard that the queen has only one foot."

And the king called for the vizier and asked him, "Why did you say that the queen had only one foot?"

The vizier denied everything and then the king's wife explained, "What is this similar to? This is similar to the story that he told about me. And it is similar to what he said about our son's wife. They are both total lies."

The king ordered that the vizier be taken out and put to death. Ever since then, the queen and the king, their son and his wife lived happily ever after without any arguments.

End of Story Note

IFA 4839 in *Min Ha-Mabua*, collected by Yonatan Dani'eli from his mother Simkhah, from Iranian Kurdistan (Marcus).
Variant of IFA 9321 in *A Tale for Each Month 1972* (Cheichel-Hechal).
Tale Types: AT 920 *E (IFA) (The king learns to judge according to a children's game in his courtyard where the clever boy delivers a true judgment); AT 926 C & *D (IFA) (Cases solved in a manner worthy of King Solomon) and AT 890 II (A pound of flesh); AT 875 (Clever peasant girl); AT 1153 (Wise carving of the fowl).
Motifs: J1161.2 (Pound of flesh: literal pleading frees man from pound-of-flesh contract); H601 (Wise carving of fowl); J120 (Wisdom learned from children).

There are many variants of this tale with parallels recorded from Tunisia, Syria, Yemen, Israel-Sephardi, Iraqi Kurdistan, Persia, Morocco, and Afghanistan. One of the variants, IFA 3928 from Morocco ("The Cruel Creditor and the Judge's Wise Daughter" in Dov Noy's *Moroccan Jewish Folktales*), also involves the "pound of flesh." However, this tale revolves around tale type AT 890 where it is a clever young princess who disguises herself as a male lawyer, argues the case in the same way, and thereby saves the young man (K1825.2).

The clever carving of a fowl has captured the folk imagination and this motif is found embedded in well over twenty other stories, including IFA 1714, "He That Diggeth a Pit Shall Fall Therein," included in *Faithful Gardens* (Noy). In this version, a Jew brings a roasted rooster to the King, who orders him to divide it. The Jew gives the head to the King, the wings to his children, and the feet to the ministers. For another variant of the carving of a fowl, see "The Clever Will" in my *Jewish Stories One Generation Tells Another*.

According to folklorist Otto Schnitzler, in his annotations to the tale in *TEM 1972*, "Our central motif (J1161.2) can be found in one of the best known collections in Europe from the Middle Ages, *Gesta Romanorum* (Tales of the Romans), from the beginning of the fourteenth century. It got there from the *Dolofatos* of the twelfth century (cf. Zvi Sofer, *Das Urteil des Schemjaka*, diss., Goettingen 1965, p. 109). This motif's origins may be in one of the rules of the Twelve Tablets of Roman Law. According to the rule, the creditor who did not receive what was owed to him, may cut a part of the body of the debtor, the weight in meat that would be equal to the amount of the debt."

—PS

18

The King's Daughter
and the Choice of Her Heart

There was once a king who had only one daughter and he loved her more than anything in the world. The king's daughter grew up to be a beautiful and wise young woman who had a good heart. Everyone who saw her, loved her.

One day, when they were alone, the king said to his daughter, "You are now grown up, my daughter. God has given you great beauty and wisdom and understanding and a good heart. The time has come for you to marry. There are many fine young men from near and far who wish to take you for a wife. Let your heart choose. Your happiness will also be in my heart."

The young princess thought for a long moment, and then said, "You are right, my father the King. You deserve the happiness that you ask for. So I will do as you say. Even though there are many young men who are handsome and wise, who wear princely crowns and are of noble souls, my soul is looking for love—love of the world and love of another heart. I will search for my love only among the young men of this city. I will sit on the balcony of our palace and you will order that all the young men of the city come before me. When I look at a certain young man, and my heart begins to flutter, I will know that he will be my fated one and I will be his wife."

The king, who had never refused his daughter anything, did not even begin to question her plan. He called to his vizier and ordered him to fulfill his daughter's request. The next day, proclamations were read around the city. On that appointed day, all the young men gathered with hope in their hearts to be chosen by the princess. They had washed carefully, wore beautifully made clothes, and looked handsome. The line was long. At the right time, the princess appeared on the balcony of the palace. She, too, was beautifully dressed and her face was shining with beauty. A lot of people crowded in toward the palace to see what was going to happen. A sign was given. The line of young men began to move. Every young man who passed before the princess raised his eyes to her, and then passed by.

All of a sudden, the princess clapped her hands. This was the sign that the young man who was passing by had caused her heart to flutter. Immediately the king's people went to that young man and took him with them. The crowd dispersed very happily shouting, "Long live the king's son-in-law." All the young men were about to go their separate ways. But at that moment, the princess raised her hand and there was quiet throughout the crowd. And she spoke, "Please do not go before the last young man has passed before me." The ceremonial line continued. And soon again the princess clapped her hands and another young man was chosen and taken to the king's palace. And, even before the last young man had passed by, again the princess picked a third young man. Finally the ceremony was finished and the crowd dispersed as all the young men had passed by.

The next day, the three young men were brought before the princess so that she could choose one of them. She raised her eyes to the first one and her soul was filled with light and her heart begin to pound very heavily. But when she looked at the second one, she was absolutely surprised at his beauty and strong body and all of her began to quiver. But when she looked at the third one, she lost all control. Not only did he have a beautiful face and strong body, but his eyes showed a good heart and great wisdom. The eyes of the princess began to move from one to the other and she did not know which one she wanted. She was embarrassed and confused and excited. She went to her father and said, "Father, my heart loves all three and I want to marry all three."

"That is not possible," cried the king angrily. "Has it ever been heard in the world that a young woman should marry three men? Never. I will not be made a fool of in the eyes of my people. If you do not have the wisdom to choose one of these three, the king's court will decide." The king's court was brought in. Everybody listened with great surprise to her request and they refused it, saying it was against the laws of the kingdom. However, the king's court presented a plan as to how to put these three young men to a test. The three young men would be sent by the king to the sea country. Each of them was then to bring from there a valuable gift for the princess. And according to these presents, they would judge the love each one had for the princess. This suggestion was accepted by the king and the princess and by the three young men as well. They were each given a great bag of gold, put on a ship, and they sailed to the sea country.

After a few days, they got to a great city and stayed at a hotel to rest. On the next day, they talked among themselves and agreed to separate. Each one would go in a different direction and meet again at the hotel in thirty days in order to return together.

The first young man turned north and at the end of his trip he arrived at a beautiful city. The streets were wide and on both sides of the street were palaces surrounded by beautiful gardens. He went along with the other people in the town to the center of the city where there was a market. It was full of everything anyone would ever want. In the street of the welders there were many beautiful things in their windows, distinctive jewelry, pots, sundry tools made out of silver and gold, and a whole necklace of pearls and diamonds that showed off light and all the colors of the rainbow. The young man said to himself, "A thing like this would surely be found in a king's treasury and it would certainly not surprise the princess." And he continued on his way wandering along the marketplace. One day he found himself standing in front of one of the stores. This store was full of mirrors of all different shapes and sizes, and all of them shiny. And there, on the wall, he saw a small woman's hand mirror. It was studded with lovely stones that caught the light. All the other mirrors seemed to be darker next to the splendid brightness of this one. The young man went to see it closer when the merchant approached and said, "This is not a regular mirror. It is a magic mirror and its price is very high. If you put your hand on it and ask to see something that is very far away, anywhere in the world, then your request will be fulfilled in the blink of an eye."

"What could be more valuable than this in the world?" said the young man to himself. "The princess will, of course, like this present because, through it, she will be able to see what happens in all corners of the world." The young man paid the merchant the high price of the mirror and he went on his way.

The second young man turned south. He also went to many cities and many marketplaces, but he didn't see anything except ordinary objects that could be found anywhere in the world. Day followed day and he continued searching for a suitable gift for the princess. He said to himself, "I have not found anything in these shops, which are full of lovely things. I will try my luck in the flea markets. Maybe there, by chance, I will find something ancient or antique and maybe something unique and valuable that cannot be found anywhere else." He went to the flea market and he saw things made out of clay, iron, and rugs and junk without end. At one store he saw there was a crowd and the merchant was calling out, "The price of this rug may be surprisingly high but it is very very ancient. I assure you that this is not just any rug, for it has a secret power. Whoever sits on this rug and asks it to bring him to any place in the world, he will have this request fulfilled in the blink of an eye." And the eyes of the young man opened wide and he thought to himself, "This is a wonderful and valuable gift that nothing can equal. The princess can sit on this rug and be able to fly to any place in the world. What is better than this?" The young man paid the high price and the merchant gave him the rug. Then the second young man went on his way.

The third young man went west. He also walked around from city to city and went to many marketplaces. He saw many things but everything that he saw he was sure the princess could get for herself. There was nothing there that would spark her attention. Time kept passing and he still had not found anything for the princess. It was almost the end of the month and he was in despair of ever finding anything that could be better than the other two young men would find. And he did not want to go back with empty hands.

On the way back to the hotel, he passed by a fruit and vegetable market. He saw the wonderful abundance of all the fruits of the seasons. He went to one of the stores and saw a whole pile of red and gold apples. Then his eyes fell on an apple that looked especially fresh and shiny. He took it and asked for the price. But the vegetable seller said to him, "Young man, you may have any other apple in the store, but not this one. You cannot pay its price. This is not a regular apple, but a magic apple, because whoever puts his mouth on this apple and takes a bite will be healed from any sickness or can even come back to life in the blink of an eye." The young man didn't say a word, but paid the high price and put the apple in his pocket and went on his way. In his heart, he was certain that there was nothing more valuable than life.

The three young men met once again on the day they had decided. Each one told his story and was very proud of the gift he had bought. "If it is really possible to see distances and faraway places in my mirror, come, my friends, let us see what the princess is doing right now."

The young man took out the mirror and passed his hand over it and, miraculously, they saw the princess. But what they saw was a frightening scene. The princess was lying sick in her bed and the king and all the servants and doctors were all around her. And they could see by the expressions of people's faces who stood around her bed that there was no hope. Without saying anything, the second young man took out his rug and spread it out on the floor. The three young men sat on it and the second young man asked that they be brought to the princess. In a blink of an eye his request was fulfilled. As soon as they had arrived, the third young man took out his apple and, without hesitation, put it to the princess's lips. And everyone looked embarrassed and shocked by what this young man was doing. Suddenly, the princess began to breathe again and the color came back to her cheeks and she opened her eyes. She looked at the three young men and then fell into a healthy sleep, with a smile on her face.

The king asked all the young men to come before him. He thanked them for their gifts that they had used to save the princess from death. He promised them that the king's court would come together to hear their stories and they would decide which of the three gifts is the most valuable. And the king's court reconvened. The king and his daughter also attended and listened carefully as the young men told their stories.

The first young man held up his mirror and said, "This is a magic mirror and it is the most valuable because if it wasn't for my mirror, we would not have known about the princess's illness and the other gifts would not have helped."

The second young man claimed, as he held his rug, "Even though that mirror is very valuable, what help would it have been for us to have seen the princess without my rug, because without it, we would not have been able to come here in the blink of an eye. Therefore, *my* gift is the most valuable."

"There is no doubt," said the third young man, "that your gifts of the mirror and the rug helped in saving the life of the princess, but think for a moment and let us see what would have happened if we had seen her, and we would have gotten to the dying princess, but I didn't have my life-giving apple with me. Only that is the thing that brought the princess back to life. And, therefore, this gift is the most valuable."

The other young men tried again and again to convince the king's court about the value of their gifts.

At that moment the king's daughter stood up and went directly to the third young man and held out her hand to him. All those in the room knew that this was the princess's decision. They called out, "Long live the king's son-in-law." And the message was sent out to all the people in the country. The princess and the choice of her heart had celebrations for many many days as was befitting royalty. The couple lived for many happy years.

And we should also be remembered by God and given many happy years. *L'khaim*!

End of Story Note

IFA 10091 from *The Golden Feather*, Story #5, recorded by Moshe Attias from memory, from Greece (Noy).

Tale Types: AT 653 A (The Rarest Thing in the World); AT 653B (The Suitors Restore the Maiden to Life); AT 590 (Resuscitation by Magic Apple).

Motifs: T68.1 (The rarest thing in the world); T92.0.1 (Girl promised to three different suitors; because she is unable to settle the dispute); H346 (Princess given to man who can heal her); D1323.15 (Telescope that shows what is happening in the world); D1520.18 (Carpet which transports one at will): D1520.19 (Magic transportation by carpet); D1500.1.5 (Magic healing apple); E106 (Apple which heals); H621.2 (Girl rescued by skillful companions: to whom does she belong?); Z16 (Dispute as to who is to marry princess); T92.0.1, T92.14 (Suitors restore maiden to life); F660.1 (Brothers acquire extraordinary skill. Return home and are tested); T68 (Princess offered as prize); Q94 (Reward for cure).

This type of cumulative tale flourishes in the folklore of every nation. Stories like "Anansi the Spider" (Africa), "The Skillful Brothers" (Albania), and "Tales of a Parrot" (Afghanistan) are prime examples of the genre. There are such stories in Japan, Germany, and Italy; in Grimm's fairytales and in *The Arabian Nights*. The many Jewish versions in the Israel Folktale Archives are uniquely Jewish, because the kernel of these stories is the talmudic teaching that the greatest mitzvah is performed by the person who gives of him/herself—or who gives up something of his/her own. Only such a person deserves the reward, in this case, to marry the princess. As Dov Noy has pointed out, this, then, is the criterion for choosing one's life partner and friend.

The story involves three elements: a magic glass or mirror (or telescope), a magic carpet (or airplane), and a magic healing potion or fruit, usually an apple. There is an Egyptian variant, IFA 5118 ("The Telescope, the Aeroplane, and the Wonderful Remedy") in *Faithful Guardians* (Noy); "Who Cured the Princess?" in *Folktales of Israel* (Noy); a Yemenite version, "The Mute Princess," in *Elijah's Violin* (Schwartz); as well as the story, "The Magic Pomegranate," along with my commentary, in my *Jewish Stories One Generation Tells Another*.

—PS

19

According to the Two Witnesses

Once there was a Jewish merchant who would travel from town to town and take with him many different things: money, clothes, and much more. And he would always take his donkey and walk with the donkey from town to town and sell his merchandise. Then he would return to his own town.

On one trip, on the route that he always traveled, through a certain forest, he sat down to rest in the shade of a great tree. All of a sudden, a robber came and threatened him with a knife. "Give me all that you have or I will kill you."

The merchant pleaded, "I have a wife and children. I am their only support. Have pity on me. Take all my merchandise and my money and anything you want, just leave me my life."

But the robber replied, "I will take your merchandise and your money and your life. You better start praying before I kill you." And the Jew raised his head to the heavens and prayed. At the same time, a white bird was flying in the sky. The Jew saw it and then said to the robber, "I have no witnesses that you will kill me but God and that bird." The robber laughed, "What? How can a bird be my witness?" The robber killed the Jew and left his body without burying it and took all his possessions and went on his way.

By chance, there was another Jew there, hiding between the branches of another high tree. And when the robber came to the place, the Jew heard all the threats and all that was said between the robber and the other Jew. He couldn't help this other Jew at the time of his trouble because he was afraid that the robber would kill him too.

After the robber had gone on his way, the second Jew got down from the tree, began to cry as he dug a hole in the ground, and buried the murdered Jew, praying for him and his soul.

The Jew who witnessed the murder went back to his town with a heavy heart. He immediately went to the rabbi and told him the whole story. When the rabbi heard the whole story, he said to the man, "Come back tomorrow and you will receive an answer on the matter of the story you have just told me."

The next day, the Jew who had witnessed the murder, still filled with sadness, returned to the rabbi to hear his response. The rabbi said, "When forty days have passed, the robber will be hanged on the same tree under which the Jew was buried." At the same time, the witness heard what the rabbi said but he didn't believe what the rabbi had foretold.

Meanwhile, weeks passed and all of a sudden the witness saw the murderer sitting in the king's carriage. He recognized him immediately and was surprised that the murderer could be traveling in the king's carriage. He began to ask, "Who is that man?" And he was told, "That is the head of the government, the vizier of the king."

Then the Jew realized that the murderer was the king's vizier and he became even sadder than before. He told his friend everything, how he was a witness to a murder and how he saw who the murderer was, and he asked himself, "How can the same man be a murderer and a vizier? If the murderer was given the post of vizier, then where is justice?" After another week passed, the Jew heard that this murdering vizier was going to marry the king's daughter. Because he knew that this would be an occasion of great happiness for the murderer, the Jew's heart became sadder and sadder. His sadness grew and grew until he just sat in his house and did not go outside.

One day, he heard that the wedding was to take place on a certain day that was close to the forty days that the rabbi had mentioned. The Jewish witness said to himself, "Now we are finished. Nothing has happened to avenge the Jew's murder as the rabbi had promised. This murderer is going to marry the king's daughter and he will govern all the land, and after that he will probably become king."

On the wedding night, the king had a great banquet and invited the people in his court, including his advisors. The murderer sat on the right of the king and was very happy. Platters of food were brought to the guests. Then a plate with a white bird that had been grilled was brought to the table. And the vizier, seeing the white bird, remembered what the murdered Jew had said and began to laugh. And the king asked him, "Why are you laughing?" The vizier said, "I saw this white bird and began to laugh." The king was surprised and asked, "Why did this white bird make you laugh? I want to know the reason for your laughter."

The vizier realized that he would now have to explain so he replied, "When I saw the bird, I remembered something that happened forty days ago." The king pressed him, "I want to hear the story, the whole truth."

Then the vizier had to tell the king about how he murdered the Jew and had left him there without burial under the tree. The king was very hurt and reminded him about what is written in *The Book of Samuel I*, ". . . and his anger was kindled greatly" (Samuel I, 2:6).

The king ordered that the murderer be imprisoned, even though it was his wedding. The whole town was embarrassed as it is written in *The Book of Esther*, ". . . but the city was perplexed" (Esther, 3:16).

Then the king said, "We have one witness and that is this bird. But we have need of another witness so that we can try this murderer for that is how it is written: 'At the mouth of two witnesses, . . . shall he that is to die be put to death; . . .'" (Deuteronomy 17:6).

And the king ordered that it be announced in the city that whoever saw the murder should come and be a witness. And the Jew who had been a witness to the murder sat with a heavy heart all the time in his house and he didn't go out, not even on the wedding night to the king's palace. All of a sudden he heard a knock on the door and his friend, to whom he had told the whole story, came in. The friend asked him, "Why are you sitting here? Haven't you heard that the wedding has been canceled and that the vizier has been imprisoned?"

And the Jew who had witnessed the murder, said, "Have you come to laugh at me?" The friend said, "Everything I am telling you is the truth. The king has ordered that anyone who can be a witness against the murderer should come to the palace and speak." The Jew got up, went to the king, and told him what he had witnessed. He revealed all that he had seen and the place of the tree and the grave. He even revealed to the king that the murderer's watch had been buried with the Jew in his grave. He continued, saying, "I make sure that every time I pass by there I visit the grave. I have also seen how all the birds that eat the berries from this tree would fall dead."

The king ordered that everyone must go to this place and verify the report of this witness. And if it is true what he said, then he would indeed be a true second witness. The king's servants went to look for the place. When they returned they announced, "We have found that everything this Jew has said is indeed the truth."

The king then ordered that the murderer be hung on the tree under which the Jew was buried. And the Jew who had been a witness to the murder was no longer sad. He was very grateful for the just punishment for the man who had murdered the Jew. He was also now consoled because everything the rabbi had predicted had come true.

End of Story Note

IFA 10, 435 from *A Tale for Each Month 1974–75*, Story #16, collected by Shelomo Laba from Abraham Gabay, from Iraq (Noy).

Tale Types: AT 960 (The Sun Brings All to Light); AT 780 (The Singing Bone).

Motifs: D1715 (Murderer repeats last words of dying man); N271.1 (Crime is brought to light).

There are twenty-six IFA parallels from Morocco, Syria, Eretz Yisrael, Yemen, Iraqi Kurdistan, Iraq, Persia, Afghanistan, Romania, Poland, and Russia. The motif where a bird is called to be a witness to a murder and the laughter of the murderer brings about his capture is common to this version and to three parallels from Russia, Persia, and Afghanistan. The main motif in this tale, *Me'igra ram livira amikta* from *Hagiga* 5b ("From a roof so high to a pit as deep"), points up the irony of the man who has achieved such a high rank and, because of his crime, falls so low. This is indeed a cautionary tale.

The theme of non-human witnesses occurs in other folktales. In "The Promised Betrothal" in my *Jewish Stories One Generation Tells Another*, there are three witnesses to the pledge of the young man to marry the woman: a weasel, a well, and the stars. (See also my introduction to the story, which also mentions other variants.)

—PS

20

The Camel's Wife

There was once a barren woman who prayed for a child all the time. One day this woman was sitting on her house steps when she saw a stranger on the street coming closer to her. She got up from her place and invited the man into her house. The stranger went inside, washed and ate, and rested. When he was about to leave, he said to the woman, "I see that you do not have any children. If you go to the desert and walk for three days, you will come to a deep well. If you drink of its water, you will give birth to a baby."

What would she not do in order to have a child, so she did not question what the man had told her to do. The woman went to the desert and walked for three days and there she found the well. Although the water was dirty, she drank from the water and returned to her home. After nine months she gave birth to a baby, but it was born in the form of a camel. The woman kept the baby at the house with her. The camel grew and one day it said, "Mother, it is time for me to marry. Go to the king's house and ask for his daughter for your son."

The camel's mother replied, "But I don't have any beautiful clothes to wear to the palace."

"Don't worry, mother. That is not a problem. Go to the cave over there and repeat three times, 'The camel is dead; the camel is alive.' *Met hakamal; chai hakamal.*"

So what did the mother do? She went to the cave and said three times, "The camel is dead; the camel is alive. *Met hakamal; chai hakamal.*"

Voices answered her, "*Khas v'ha leela*—it should never be. Oi va voi!" And they gave her beautiful clothes.

The camel's mother put on the clothes and went to the palace. When she was brought before the king, she asked the king for his daughter to marry her son. The king answered, "I will agree to this marriage, but first your son must obtain three things for me: one, a carpet that would seat all of the king's army but, when it is rolled up, it would be able to fit into the shell of a nut; two, a bunch of grapes that the whole king's army could eat, but some grapes would still remain in the cluster; and three, a watermelon whose rind is made from gold and whose pits are precious stones. If your son does not fulfill my request," warned the king, "I will have him killed."

The woman returned to her son and told him all that the king had said. The camel replied, "Don't worry, mother, to obtain these objects is not a problem. Go back to the cave and say three times, 'The camel is dead; the camel is alive.' Then ask for the carpet."

The mother went to the cave, repeated the saying, and requested the carpet. When she received the carpet, she brought it to the king's palace.

The next day, the camel's mother went again to the cave, repeated the saying, and asked for the bunch of grapes. When she received the grapes, she brought them to the king.

On the third day, the camel's mother went to the cave, repeated the saying, and asked for the watermelon. When she received it, she gave it, too, to the king.

The king now had no choice but to agree to the marriage between his daughter and this woman's son because, after all, the woman's son had fulfilled all of his requests.

The wedding was held with royal ceremony and celebration. The people who accompanied the bride brought her to the house of the groom. When they all left, the camel-groom came to her room and said, "I have a secret to tell you. I am not a camel but a man. But if you reveal my secret, you will never see me again." When the camel finished speaking, he took off his fur and there, before the bride, stood a handsome young man. The bride was amazed—and very happy. And so they were married.

One day, a war broke out in the country. The king's daughter asked her husband to help her father. The camel went out to war and, in the battle, was wounded in his leg. Seeing the wound, the king gave his son-in-law a handkerchief for wrapping around the wound. Not long after, the king's army won the war and there was a great victory party in the palace. The bride, the king's youngest daughter, came to the party along with her three sisters whose husbands had also fought in the war.

At this party, the older sisters wanted to hurt their youngest sister's feelings by saying to her, "Your husband is a camel so he should have stayed at home and not fought in the war and certainly not come to the party. But our husbands fought in this war and deserved to come to the party." The youngest daughter became very upset and enraged and, in her anger, revealed to them that her husband was really a man. "And not only that, but when his leg was wounded, the king gave him his own handkerchief to use as a bandage."

"Go home and burn the fur and skin of your camel-husband," they told her. That night the bride burned her husband's camel skin and fur, as her sisters had advised her to do. When the husband smelled the burning, he understood what she was doing and said to her, "You will not find me until you come after me walking with an iron walking stick in your hand and iron clogs on your feet."

As soon as he finished speaking, the husband turned into a dove and flew to the heavens.

The bride went back to her father and told him, "My sisters have goaded me into burning my husband's fur."

And the king said to his daughter, "I will build you a bath house and everyone who comes to wash there will have to tell you their life story and what was unusual in their life."

One day, a woman came to the bath house who told this story. "I have three girls that weave string that they sell in the market. One day, when the moonlight was very strong, I thought that the dawn had already come. So I took the thread and went out to the market. On my way there I saw a camel and a beetle. I followed them to a cave. When the cave opened, they went inside and I went in after them. There I saw, in the cave, an oven. In it was bread that was baking itself. And someone was yelling:

> *Ho tanoor cham tachve et yada kee ain ha'adon ohev ota.*
> Burn her hand oh oven hot
> Because the master loves her not

Burn her hand oh oven hot
Because the master wants her not

Then the mother arrived at the place to eat, and again she heard the same voice calling out the same words.

Ho seer, ho seer cham tachve et yada kee ain ha'adon ohev ota,
kee ain ha'adon rotze ota.

Suddenly three doves came to this place. They brought a golden tablecloth and they opened it and said,

Ho bait, ho bait bache bechee tamroorim al ba'alat hamizrakot al
ba'alat hatzmidim
House oh house, cry bitter tears
For him who owns the necklace
For him who owns the fountain
House oh house, cry bitter tears
For the master lost forever
For the master in the mountain.

And all the walls of the house began to cry." Then the guest washed in the bath house and left the place.

The king's daughter followed this woman to her house and slept there. The next day the woman gave her a walking stick made of iron and iron clogs for her feet. She also asked the woman to show her the way.

The king's daughter finally saw the camel and the beetle and she went after them. She followed them for days until they arrived at the cave. They went into the cave and she went into the cave too. There she saw all the things the woman had described to her. When she arrived at the oven, she heard the voice say,

O tanoor cham, al tachve et yada,
kee ha'adon hoo ohev ota,
kee ha'adon hoo rotze ota.
Don't burn her hand oh oven hot
For the master loves her a lot

Don't burn her hand oh oven hot
For the master wants her a lot.

And when she came to the pot, she heard the voice saying the same words.

Ho seer, ho seer cham, al tachve et yada,
kee ha'adon ohev ota,
kee ha'adon hoo rotze ota.

And then three doves came to the place. They brought out the golden tablecloth and they opened it up and said,

Ho bait, ho bait, ma'aley pee hatzchok
el ba'alat hatzmidim ve hamizrakot.
House oh house that smiles and laughs
For him who owns the necklace
For him who owns the fountain
House oh house that smiles and laughs
For the master found and rescued in the cave deep
in the mountain.

The king's daughter had stayed hidden the whole time watching. Then the dove asked her to come out of her hiding place. She came out slowly but when she saw her husband, she ran to him, dropping her iron clogs and her walking stick on the way. Ever since then the couple lived happily ever after.

And the king's daughter gave the bath house to the woman who had helped her find her husband again.

End of Story Note

IFA 11,987 from *A Tale for Each Month 1978*, Story #12, collected by Aviva Shemesh from her mother, Marcel, from Iraq (Noy).

Tale Types: AT 425* Q (IFA) (The abandoned wife because of the breaking of a tabu by her bewitched husband, finds him, with the help of a boy or a woman, when he is mourning for her); AT 425 I, II, III, IV, V (The Search for the Lost Husband).

Motifs: D621.1 (Animal by day; man by night); B640.1 (Marriage to beast by day and man by night); S215.1 (Girl promises herself to animal suitor); L54.1 (Youngest daughter agrees to marry monster; later the sisters are jealous); C932 (Loss of wife/husband for breaking tabu); C757.1 (Tabu: destroying animal skin of enchanted person too soon); C421 (Tabu: revealing secret of supernatural husband); H1385.4 (Quest for vanished husband); H1125 (Task: wandering till iron shoes are worn out); M202.1 (Promise to be fulfilled when iron shoes wear out); H1233.1.1 (Old woman helps on quest); H1010 (Impossible tasks).

There are eleven parallels of this Jewish oikotype in the Israel Folktale Archives, such as the Moroccan variant, "The Bull's Head and the King's Daughter" (IFA 5787). However, there are over two dozen stories recorded in the Israel Folktale Archives of AT 425 (The Search for the Lost Husband) and its subtypes.

This is a transformation love story of "Beauty and the Beast" motif (D735.1). There are a number of such stories where the hero is born in the form of an animal, most often as a snake, such as "The Snake Son" and "The Fisherman's Daughter" in my *Jewish Stories One Generation Tells Another*. In an Elijah story, it is the heroine who is born with the face of a beast. See "Her Wisdom Is Her Beauty" in my *Tales of Elijah the Prophet*.

The Hebrew rhymed dialogue has been interpreted in English by Roslyn Bresnick-Perry.

—PS

21

Two Friends

There was once a very rich man who was not a follower of the rabbi, the Gaon from Berditshev. But since he was from the same town as the great Rabbi, he said to himself, "Even though I don't believe in the rabbi, I will go in to see what his power is and what draws so many people to him." He went in with a number of other people. The rabbi's secretary gave each one a piece of paper on which to write his requests.

One asked for children because he didn't have any; another asked that his children be healthy; another asked for a great business success and to earn a lot of money; and so on. But when the rich man went in, he hadn't written anything on the paper. He just gave the Rabbi a donation. "What are your requests?" asked the Rabbi. "I don't have any. I do not need anything. I have a wife, children, riches, respect, and honor. Since I am from the same town as you, I just wanted to greet you, Rabbi," answered the rich man.

Then the rabbi replied, "Since you have no requests nor anything to say, I will tell you a story." And this is the story the rabbi told him.

There were once two friends who loved each other very much. They grew up together and got married to young women from the town, but one couple moved to another town. The friends would write to each other—at first every week—and then every month. Finally they wrote less and less frequently until they stopped writing. After all, each became busy with his own work and his own life.

It happened that one of the friends became poor and he owed a lot of money. There came a time that if he didn't pay the debt, he would go to prison. Then he remembered his friend who had his own successful business and so he traveled to that distant town to see him. His friend welcomed him and then, without a moment's hesitation, the friend turned to his secretary and said, "Make up a list so that half of what I have will belong to my friend." Then the poor friend returned home and paid off all his debts.

As it happened, a short while later, the rich friend became poor. And when he had no more money even for bread to feed his family, his wife reminded him of his friend. So he traveled to his friend's town. But when he arrived at his house, there was a guard in front of his friend's house, and he said to the guard, "Go tell the master of the house that I have come." But when his friend, the now-rich friend heard this, he said, "Who is this? I don't know any such person. Tell him to go away."

When the friend heard this reply, he became ill and could not return home. And he died. And when he died, suddenly in heaven there was a great commotion. The angels had decided there had to be a trial in heaven. But when the poor man's soul reached heaven, he asked, "How is it possible to have a trial?"

The angels in heaven said, "That man who had become rich must die."

"What?" questioned the man, "That friend must die because of me? I don't want that. I will suffer more and more and more but my friend must not die on my account."

Then the angels said to him, "In that case, if that is how you feel, then you must be born again."

So the man who died was born again, and he grew up and became head of a family. And he was very poor. And he began to ask for charity from people. He had to go to his friend. He knew where he lived. His friend was religious and lived just outside of the city. He had even built a synagogue there.

Now this poor man was also a Talmud chakham—so he went to the Beit Knesset. Everyone was sitting there and each one wanted to invite this poor Talmud chakham to his home as a guest for dinner, for Shabbos. But then the owner of the synagogue, the rich man, came in and he invited the poor man for dinner.

At the rich man's house, they served him fish. And the poor man talked Torah. They served him soup, and the poor man talked more Torah. Then they gave him meat and other good things. When he finished eating, he bid them shalom and left the house. But since he had always been so poor and had never eaten such rich good food, and so much at one time, he fell ill and fainted on the stairs.

When the rich man saw this, he started to cry and wring his hands. This was the second time this had happened. The first time a man had died and now a man had fainted. What would the rabbi say? What would the rabbi think of him? When the man came out of his faint, the rich man pleaded with him to give him a good recommendation in heaven. That he was sorry that because of him a man had died. (Of course he didn't know that this was this same friend who had already died. Only the poor man who had fainted knew what had happened previously and of their relationship.)

Then the man opened his eyes and said to the rich man, "Go and tell your family that you are leaving—even tell them that you are going as far as America. And when you go from the house, get on your wagon and go to the city. Then get off your wagon and a man will be there waiting for you."

The man did everything as he was told. He rode to the city on his horse and wagon. There he found the man waiting for him who took the rich man's good clothes. And as soon as he did, the rich man became old, wrinkled and dirty, and bent-over. He wore the clothes of a poor man. Then he was told that he should go to a certain place to live. This was the law that he must follow. And he went to this place. There he had to eat the food meant only for the dog who stood next to the entrance of the house. And when the owners, who were wealthy, saw this old beggar eat the dog's food, they began to give him food of his own. Then the maid asked him one day, "Who are you? Where will you sleep?" And he answered, "I will sleep here, near the fence." The woman felt sorry for him and kept the door open so he could feel some warmth from the house and gave him a sack to sleep in next to the dog. Slowly he got used to this.

Now, the man's family began to worry about what had happened to the rich man. He had left the house mysteriously one day and did not return nor did he ever send any word to them. It was as though he had just disappeared. Meanwhile the family began to feed this poor man and treated him like a pet. But really this rich family was none other than *this* man's own family, but, of course, he did not know that. Nor did they recognize him. And this continued for a year; two years passed and they had gotten used to the fact that the master of the house was not returning home.

When this man's punishment time was over, he got back on the horse, went to the city, received his good clothes back, and resumed his physical appearance and returned home. Everyone was happy to see him. It was unbelievable. After a while, the family wanted to know what had happened to that poor beggar who had been living in their yard.

"Father, we had someone here who was very poor but he made us happy and we played with him."

After a big meal, the father went into the next room and there the other poor man appeared. But when the rest of the family knocked on the door to come in, the poor man disappeared. Then the father realized who the poor man was. He began to weep, realized his terrible sin, and was finally forgiven in heaven.

After the rabbi told the story, it was time to eat and the rabbi invited the rich man for dinner.

End of Story Note

IFA 18,164 collected by Hadara Sela from Hinda Scheinfarber from Poland. This story was never published.

Tale Type: Elements of AT 470 (Friends in Life and Death).

Motifs: M253 (Friends in life and death); **H1558** (Tests of friendship).

Levi Yitzhak of Berditshev (1740–1809), one of the hasidic masters, was also known as Levi Yitzhak the Merciful. He always pleaded for Divine mercy for the Jewish people. Born in Galicia, he became one of the best-loved *zaddikim* who stressed the element of joy in Hasidism and good that is in man. There are many legends told about him.

One of the stories told about him gives us a brushstroke glimpse into the kind of person Levi Yitzhak was: "Levi-Yitzhak admired King Solomon, the wisest of our sovereigns. Why? Because, according to the Midrash, he mastered all languages? Because he knew how to speak to birds? No. Because he understood the language of madmen" (Wiesel, *Souls on Fire*, 105).

Another powerful story takes place on Yom Kippur when Levi Yitzhak asked a poor illiterate tailor, "Since you couldn't read the prayers, what did you say to God?" And the tailor tells the rabbi how he spoke to God about his sins, which were quite small: how he failed at times to return a piece of leftover cloth, how he ate non-kosher food at times, etc. And then the tailor continues, "Now take Yourself, God! Just examine Your own sins: You have robbed mothers of their babies, and have left helpless babies orphans. So You see that Your sins are much more serious than mine. I'll tell You what, God! Let's make a deal! You forgive me and I'll forgive You."

"Ah, you foolish man!" cried Rabbi Levi Yitzhak. "You let God off too easily! Just think! You were in an excellent position to make Him redeem the whole Jewish people!" (Ausubel, *A Treasury of Jewish Folklore*, 160).

These brief stories give us a flavor and feeling of Levi Yitzhak the Merciful.

For another story of Levi Yitzhak, see "What Made Rabbi Yitzhak Change His Behavior" in this collection.

—*PS*

22

The Maggid of Dubno

The Maggid of Dubno was a storyteller. Whenever he was approaching a certain town for a visit, the news would travel so quickly that within a few minutes everyone in the community would have already heard that the Dubner Maggid was about to arrive. The men knew that the Maggid would deliver a good sermon in the synagogue, peppered with parables they could understand and think about all week long. The women knew they would hear the stories from their husbands. And the children knew they would hear the stories twice—once as their fathers would tell it to their mothers, usually at the Shabbos table—and then when their mothers would tell the same stories to them.

"So you'll learn something, listen." That's how the mother would always begin the story.

The Maggid was famous because whenever he was supposed to answer a question, he told a story instead. And often the stories were filled with humor and silly characters. The children didn't understand what they could learn from these stories, but they certainly laughed— and remembered them—from year to year.

One Shabbos afternoon, the Maggid was walking along the riverbank with one of his students. A young man, running up to them, and in a challenging voice shouted, "I hear that you tell good stories—stories that make people have faith. Well I don't believe in God anymore and I've lost my faith. Try out your skills on me and see if you can get me to believe after all."

The Maggid smiled and answered: If you will give me a moment, I *will* tell you a story.

Once there was a village. And who lived there? Simple people. One day a stranger came to that village and saw a group of men standing around a tiny flame in a forge and they were blowing very hard trying to fan this flame into a roaring fire.

The stranger looked amused and, after a while, said, "Don't you have a pair of bellows?"

"Bellows! *What* are *bellows?*" they asked. "We've never heard of those things."

"Bellows help to make a fire without all your breath."

So the stranger made a pair of bellows for the villagers and then continued on his travels.

A few weeks later, the stranger passed through the same village.

As soon as the people saw him, they came running after him, laughing and jeering. "You and your *bellows!* What right did you have to make fun of us!"

"What do you mean?" replied the stranger.

"Those bellows you gave us don't work. They don't make a fire at all! We tried and tried. You fooled us, that's all."

"Perhaps there is something wrong with them. Let me examine them," the stranger said. And he looked at them carefully, but they seemed to be in good working order. After a few moments he said, "Let me see how you have been using them."

The villagers agreed and handed the bellows to the most prominent member of the group, Yankel. And Yankel began to work the bellows with both hands, pushing and pulling the handles until he was tired and stopped.

"See, they don't work. Do you see a fire?" he asked in a scoffing voice.

"No, but where is your hot coal?" asked the Maggid.

"What? You mean we still need to have a hot coal to start the fire?"

"Oh yes. Without the hot coal, all you can produce with the bellows is a strong stream of air. Nothing more." answered the stranger.

The Maggid turned to the young man and said, "So you see, my friend, I can tell good stories that stir the heart. But only if the "hot coal" burns there with the love of God and a feeling for our faith. But once that ember cools, then even the best of my stories cannot bring the feelings back."

And the student and the Maggid continued their walk.

One day the student approached the Maggid and asked, "How do you always succeed in getting even the stingiest people to give charity?"

"Well, as a matter of fact, I am about to visit a wealthy scholar and to ask him for a big donation to help the poor and the orphans. Come with me and you'll see for yourself how I do it," answered the Maggid.

And so the two of them set off for this encounter.

As they approached a mansion, the student shook his head and said to the Maggid, "I have heard about this man. Although he is a great scholar and one of the wealthiest, he has the tightest fists. Why should you waste your time here?"

But the Maggid only smiled and kept walking, saying, "Listen well, my student."

The Maggid knocked on the door and asked to see the master. And when the scholar came to the door, he greeted the Maggid and the student warmly. But when the Maggid announced why he had come, the scholar immediately began to tell them how busy he was studying *Vayyikra* 19 and that they would have to return another day.

When the Maggid heard this, he began to discuss verses 9–10, in particular, which deal with consideration for the poor, and adding commentary and quotations. The scholar, in response, added his own interpretations and other sources.

Seeing that all he was getting was a lecture, the Maggid turned his discussion to telling of parables. But the scholar matched him with other talmudic stories.

Realizing that he was not accomplishing what he had hoped for, the Maggid finally interrupted and said, "Let me tell you a brief parable."

Many years ago a young man had set sail to see something of the world before he would settle down in his quiet town. On his way home, he stopped at an island. The people there were very friendly and welcomed the young guest. That night, they made a banquet in his honor. He was so delighted with their ways, he wanted to repay them for their hospitality. They seemed to have everything they needed, except for one thing. He had noticed at the dinner that they did not have onions. In fact they had never heard of onions. And so, as a reward, the young man brought a huge bag full of onions from the ship, and showed them how to plant them and how to cook with them. And that night they ate a delicious meal cooked with onions. The people there were so grateful for this gift of onions that they gave their guest a bagful of silver coins. And the young man returned home.

When he arrived home, he went to visit a neighbor and told him of his adventures, including his good fortune on the island. This neighbor was a scheming young man and he decided to find out what else those islanders lacked. He questioned the young man carefully. Then he finally decided to bring them garlic. He stored sacks of those little garlic bulbs on a boat and set off for that island. And yes, the people welcomed him in the same way, with a banquet. When he brought them sacks of garlic as a gift, the people were delighted to learn of this pungent bulb. And then they prepared another meal seasoned with garlic.

"As a parting gift," they told the neighbor, "we will give you our most precious possession."

The neighbor grinned, hardly able to wait to carry the sacks of silver onto the boat. Impatiently he watched the people place the bulging sacks in front of him. And when he opened them, one after another, he saw that they were all filled with onions.

"*Onions!*" he shouted in exasperation. "But you gave my friend silver. What good are they? I can't buy anything with onions."

With that, the Maggid turned to the wealthy scholar and added, "And so you see, trading discussions and stories is very fine. But this does not provide the poor and the orphans with food and clothes. What I need in this case is money."

Hearing that, the scholar went into the house and returned with a open handful of gold coins.

On another day, the student was walking with the Maggid and asked, "Why aren't lectures and sermons enough to explain a point of law or a lesson? Why do we need stories and parables? Why not give just a sermon without your stories? What do they really add to a sermon?"

The Maggid smiled and said, "How can I not combine parable with sermon when stories are as necessary as . . ." The Maggid stopped for a moment, and then added, "Wait, let me tell you a *moshol*."

A wealthy man married his daughter to a poor innocent scholar. This young man had studied in a yeshiva all his life and never worked for a living. The wealthy man, as was the custom, agreed to support the young couple so that the young husband could continue the study of Torah.

But the wheel turned and the wealthy father lost all his money. The young scholar was now forced to go out to make a living, for the first time.

With the permission of his father-in-law, the scholar took his wife's dowry, which had been put aside, and decided to become a businessman. The plan was for him to buy merchandise cheaply and resell it at a profit.

Before the young husband left for his first business venture, the father-in-law said to him: "You have never been involved in business and have only spent your time with books. So I will give you some advice. Do not buy everything that is offered, because, after all, there are many scoundrels out there waiting for a naive person to come along so that they can get rid of damaged goods. So listen and remember. Before you buy, examine the object carefully to make sure there are no holes or faults. If you see anything that is not right, do not buy." And then the father-in-law gave him a list of what to buy: a samovar, a teapot, a set of cups and saucers, and a few strainers.

The young scholar-turned-merchant purchased everything and returned home. His father-in-law examined what the young man had bought, approving the purchases. But then he said, "But I don't see any strainers."

"Of course not," answered the young man proudly. "You told me not to buy anything with holes. When I saw the strainers they offered to sell me, I saw immediately that they were no good since there were none without holes."

The father-in-law threw his hands up and replied, "No! No! No! Some things must have holes in them in order to be useful. How else can you separate the tea leaves from the tea, the coarse from the fine, the useless from the useful? A strainer without holes would be just a pan, not a strainer after all."

After that story, the Maggid added, "So now you can see how a story illustrates a point better than any lecture or explanation. A story, the most beautiful way to teach, stays with you much much longer than any lecture. I hope you see now that a sermon without a story is as valuable as a strainer without holes."

As the Maggid was leaving the *shul* one Shabbos, a young student ran over to him and shouted, "How do I know that you are telling the truth, Rabbi, when you tell us so many of your parables. They are just stories and Judaism is based on truth. Why don't you just teach us directly by telling us what we should or should not do? You hide every lesson in a story and then cover it with more stories! Stories just get in the way of the straight truth."

The Maggid turned from his companions, interrupting the discussion, and said to the young student, "As long as you are talking about parables, then give me just a moment and let me tell you one more parable. Perhaps then you will understand why story is so necessary."

Bare Truth was walking down the street one day. And wherever Truth went, naked and undressed, people turned away, ignoring, and even worse, rejecting Truth. Poor Truth. What could he do. No one wanted to look at him or give him a chance.

Then one day, Truth was walking down a side street when he met his friend, Parable. Parable was dressed in magnificent embroidered colorful clothes, with shiny sequins, and feathers.

"Truth, tell me what is wrong? I see by the way you are walking that you are not holding your head up high, as you should."

"Oh Parable, my friend, how can I hold my head up when people reject me and don't want to look me in the eye. My heart is so heavy. But you, Parable, what do you do to get so much attention and people crowding around you?"

"Well, Truth, I don't know how to tell you this, but—look at yourself. You are not much to look at. You are naked and plain. And no one wants to meet Truth face-to-face. Here!" And without saying another word, Parable took off her cape and hat and put them on Truth.

And suddenly Truth, dressed in Parable's garments, looked so attractive!

From that time on, wherever Truth went, wearing his new magnificent clothes, people welcomed him and listened carefully to every word.

Completing this parable, the Maggid turned to the young student, saying, "When I tell my parables, I do not want to hide truth or distort the lessons of Judaism. But rather I hope that truth will find its way into your heart through the parable because then it is more attractive and appealing to listen to a story than just to the bare truth. And you will remember the story always."

The Maggid knew that when the students came with him as he would collect for charity or deliver his sermons, they would learn many stories from him. The Maggid always hoped that the students would continue telling his stories. One day, after many years, one of his students asked, "Rabbi, I have noticed that you always answer a question with a story. And since you are asked so many questions—and preach so many sermons—and collect, often from the same people year after year, for so many charities, you need a great many different stories. How do you know so many stories? And how do you choose the stories to tell that are so perfect for the subject?"

The Maggid smiled and answered, "Let me answer your questions with a story."

A long long time ago a nobleman sent his young son to the military academy to learn how to shoot. After five years, the young man was returning home, riding his horse. His uniform was covered with medals. As he passed through a small village, he saw, on the side of a barn, a hundred circles drawn in chalk and in the center of each circle was a bullet hole.

Stopping his horse, he called out, "Who is this amazing marksman who can shoot a hundred perfect bull's-eyes. I must meet him."

Just then a young child came up to the man on the horse and said, in a matter-of-fact voice, "Oh that's Narele, he's the town fool."

"I don't care what he is! Anyone who can shoot a hundred bull's-eyes must have won every gold medal in the world. Even I can't do that! I *must* meet him!"

"No, no, you don't understand," replied the child, "Narele doesn't draw the circle first and then shoot. First he shoots, and then he draws the circle."

"And that's the way it is with me," concluded the Maggid. "I don't just happen to have these perfect stories to fit the subject that is being discussed. First I read many stories. I listen to many stories. I keep those stories in my head. Then when I find a story I especially like and need to tell, I introduce the subject for which I have the perfect story."

And so it is with all storytellers!
Let's continue our walks with the Maggid of Dubno!

End of Story Note

The Maggid of Dubno, Rabbi Jacob Kranz (1741–1804), developed the parable, the *moshol*, as a primary teaching tool. Called "the Jewish Aesop," he imitated the aggada and Midrash by combining lessons from the Bible and its commentaries with the folktales of the people he met on his travels through Poland and Germany.

A parable, referred to as a *moshol*, is similar to the fable and does, in fact, belong to the same genre. The purpose of a Jewish parable is to illuminate a verse or passage of Torah or to clarify a Jewish value or tradition. A Jewish parable differs from the universal parable in that it is composed of two parts: a *nimshal* and a *moshol*. The *nimshal* is the frame: a question that is set up at the beginning followed by a connection at the end that serves as a direct response to the question first posed. The *nimshal* teaches us what we can learn from the *moshol* and how to apply that lesson. The *moshol*, the story-example in the center of the parable, is the tale inside the *nimshal*, a statement of the lesson or its application. Parables are fascinating and delightful, transmitting knowledge and inspiring understanding in a delightful and creative way and always in the language of the people.

In this story, I have strung together five parables, with commentary that would lead up to five *mosholim*, like exquisite pearls on a golden string. These parables were part of the Dubner Maggid's repertoire. They can be found in Heinemann's *The Maggid of Dubno and His Parables*.

One of the best known is the onion/garlic story (#2), attributed to the Dubner Maggid as well as to the authorship of a poem with the same theme by the Hebrew poet Chaim Nachman Bialik. There are also many variants in the Israel Folktale Archives from Egypt, Iraq, and Iran. Other versions can be found in *Lessons from Our Living Past* (edited by Jules Harlow) as "The Duke of Onions and the Duke of Garlic" and in *A Coat for the Moon* by Howard Schwartz and Barbara Rush as "The Rusty Plate."

The Truth and Parable story is a favorite among storytellers and I have heard many versions of this parable used to make the point of why we must tell stories. Truth reaches us through a story in a beautiful way and we can, thus, face the truth. Story is the coating of the "philosophic pill."

The last of the tales (#5) is "The Bull's-Eye," which has become my signature story since I often tell it as I open my storytelling programs. It is the opening story in my *Jewish Stories One Generation Tells Another.*

What I love about these parables is their use of humor; the surprise turn at the end of the *moshol.* When we laugh, we can begin to gain a perspective and learn a new way of looking at or acting in a situation. How wise the Dubner Maggid was to teach through parable.

So give me a moment, and I'll tell you a story . . .

—PS

23

The Fulfilled Dream

Once there lived in Syria a very old man who had sons and daughters, grandsons and granddaughters, great-grandsons and great-granddaughters. One day the man got up and turned to all his descendants and said to them, "Let us go up to Zion, Yerushalayim, the holy city." And the sons and the daughters of this rich man looked at him in surprise and shock and said to him, "How can we go up to Zion, my father, for every other place where Jews lived, they do not have a real home. But we live here, thank God, with everything good. What do we lack here now? You have worked all your life and now you want us to lose everything we have here. You know that we cannot go out of this country with any of our money or any of our possessions because the entire way is filled with thieves and robbers. No, we cannot leave this country without giving all of our possessions to the people on the way to the place where we want to go. What will happen when we get to Zion if we have nothing there. We do not even have a country there."

But the rich father was stubborn and claimed, "In my dreams, Rabbi Meir Baal haNes, the miracle doer, appeared and said to me, 'You must go up to Zion because that is where your place is.'"

When the sons of the family heard these things from the old man, who was 106 years old, everyone got up, gathered their wives and their children, and packed all their belongings. Everything they could take, they took. Whatever they could not take, they left, and they went out on their way. And on the route that the family rode through, there were many thieves and robbers. However, they did not have any choice but to pay the ransom in order to pass. Their main hope was that they should arrive healthy.

And indeed when they arrived in Zion, the family did not have anything left. They immediately went up to the grave of Rabbi Meir Baal haNes, the master of miracles, in Tiberias. Then everyone looked for a place to sleep in Tiberias, in a house or in a hotel. But the head of the family announced, "My place is near the grave underneath the stars. Here I will sleep and that is what will be." And no matter how much they begged, nothing helped. After all, they did not want to let their old father sleep outside. But he was stubborn and he stayed to sleep in that place next to the grave. In his dream, Rabbi Meir appeared again and said to him, "You are a good man. And what you were ordered to do, you did. Tell me now, what do you lack and I will help you."

And the old man said, "Rabbi Meir, I gave all my possessions as ransom in order to pass through and to come to Zion. Now we do not have anything."

And Rabbi Meir answered, "Go buy a piece of garlic and plant it. From this you will have all your support." And again the old man did as Rabbi Meir had told him to. He bought some garlic and he planted it on a small piece of land that was near his house. When the garlic grew, a blessing was given to everyone and it did not have an ending. Everyone who picked the garlic and sold it, always received money. And more and more garlic grew.

The old man sold the garlic and he became very rich. And he was a man who was happy with his lot. He also gave a lot of charity. And where did he keep his money? He kept it inside his leaning stick. Nobody knew how much money he had and where this fortune was.

When this man returned his soul to the Creator, at the age of 135 years, the stick broke because it could not stand the sadness of the death of its owner. In this way, the family recovered all the treasure of their father.

And the family remained in Zion and lived with great happiness.

End of Story Note

IFA 8244 from *A Tale for Each Month 1968–69*, Story #17, collected by Ziona Cohen from her father, Abraham Mordekhay Mizrahi from Turkish Kurdistan (Cheichel-Hechal).

Motifs: D1812.3.3 (The prophetic dream); K1641.8.*1 (Holy grave brings itself from the diaspora to Eretz Yisrael); and N521 (The treasure in stick).

As Abraham Mordekhay Mizrahi said, at the time of his telling, "It is important to note that this story is true and speaks of a man who wanted to get to Jerusalem and die in the Holy City." Dreams have a prophetic power, especially when Elijah the Prophet appears in a dream. In this story, we have another performer of miracles who appears to the rich father in Syria, Rabbi Meir Baal HaNes (Rabbi Meir the Miracle Worker). He was given that name on account of the miracles ascribed to him in aggadic literature. For more about Rabbi Meir, see the note to "The Leopard and the Fox" in this collection.

The "*aliyah* dream," to ascend to the Land of Israel, prescribes the future of the dreamer and everyone in his family (and sometimes even the people of an entire community). Following the establishment of the State of Israel (1948) and the War of Independence (1948–1949), there followed a great "Ingathering of the Exiles," people coming from many lands in waves. This gave rise to the creation of many "ascension legends," whose heroes are ordered (usually by dream) to lead the family/community to Israel.

Edna Cheichel-Hechal reports in her annotations: "In a Yemenite memorat-legend (IFA 839) the 'Ascension-dream' is dreamt on the same night by elders of various communities. On the following morning the narrator meets an old stranger with a shining face (Elijah the Prophet?), who smiles and utters three Hebrew words: *Et dodim higiah* (the time of love has come; cf. Song of Songs 2:12: 'The time of singing has come,' and Ezekiel 15:8: 'Thy time was the time of love'). As these words were the slogan, expected for generations as a prophetic omen, all knew that the time of redemption had come and preparations started for the move Home" (*A Tale for Each Month 1968–69*).

A dream played a decisive role in allowing Moroccan Jews to leave their country and make *aliyah*. In the 1950s, King Hassan II had a dream in which his dead father appeared and told him "to let the chickens out of the coop." The baffled king invited a rabbi to the palace to interpret this dream. The rabbi told him the meaning of the dream—that the King's father wanted him to let the Jews emigrate from Morocco to Israel. As a result, the Jews were free to leave their country. Given the freedom to emigrate, a great many of the Jewish community left in that first wave of *aliyah*.

Dreams serve as a catalyst for a story-within-a-story in many folktales. See "The Exchanged Letters," "A Neighbor in Paradise," and "Can Fate Be Changed?" in this collection. See also "The Dream Interpreter" and "The Dream and the Treasure" in my *Jewish Stories One Generation Tells Another*.

Wordplay is often interwoven in the Hebrew tales, as it is here. In the dream there is the suggestion that the old man plant garlic for a livelihood. The Hebrew word for garlic is *shum* and it is a play on the words *shum davar*, which means "nothing," to point up the lack of importance of this vegetable, which will be the source of wealth (not nothing) for the family.

—PS

24

The Poor People and Their Shares

In the town of Yassy, which is in Rumania, there lived a rich Jewish banker, Yacov von Noyshaf. It was his custom, as was the custom for many rich people, to give out money as charity on one day a week in his office. This rich banker appointed a clerk to do this special job of distributing the charity.

Once, on Purim, a poor man from a faraway place happened to be in this town. When the clerk gave him the regular amount for charity, the poor man refused it saying, "I have come especially to receive a bigger amount of money."

The clerk answered him, "The amount is not up to me." So the poor man demanded permission to see the banker himself.

The banker received this poor man, heard his claim, and gave him a larger amount as charity. But this beggar also refused this amount saying, "It is still not enough."

The banker got very angry, "I don't owe you anything. I give out charity to beggars in the amount I want."

And the beggar asked the banker to allow him to tell him a story.

And the banker agreed, and this is the poor man's story.

In the days of Haman the evil one, when the Jews saw that their ending was near because of the terrible pronouncements of Haman, they announced a fast, prayer, and giving of charity. Among other things, the rich people decided to give out all their possessions to the poor people and this is what they did. And when the pronouncements, the terrible punishments and sentences were canceled, the poor people began to worry about what they had received. They said, "Why should we have all these material

161

possessions? We don't know how to take care of them. We don't know how to deal with them. We don't know anything about being merchants or salesmen. The more possessions, the more worries you have. We should give them back to the rich people." And so when the poor people came to the rich people—that is, the formerly rich—to return their money and all their possessions, the rich people didn't want to take them back. They told the poor, "What we gave you is yours." The truth is that they also knew the secret of "The more possessions, the more worry."

And then the poor people explained to the rich, "We don't know anything about business. We will eat everything. We will waste all the money. Then we will again have to come to you for handouts and charity. But then you won't have anything to give us. We don't want to get used to a better life just to have it all end and be taken away from us."

And the rich people heard the claims of the righteous poor and agreed to take back their money and possessions, but on one condition, saying, "We will continue to deal with business and be merchants, but you must come to us every year, on Purim, the day they rescinded the terrible proclamation, and we will give you your share. Since the possessions that are in our hands are really yours, we are going to just keep them for you and pay you every year."

And that is the way it has happened for all these many years.

When the poor man had finished his story, he turned to the banker and asked him, "And now, sir banker, what do you think? Do you think that you are giving me something of yours or something that is simply a percentage of my own possessions that are with you as a type of deposit?"

And since the banker liked this story, he gave the poor man with a generous hand as he was asked to give.

End of Story Note

IFA 170 from *Seven Folktales*, Story #1, collected by Miriam Yeshiva from her mother, from Rumania (Noy).
Motifs: P160 (Beggars); V400 (Charity); J1330 (Repartee concerning beggars); J1580 (Practical retorts connected with alms giving); A1599.15 (Origin of begging); H594 (Enigmas concerning begging).

Charity (*tzedakah*) is central to the Jewish way of life. Charity is one of the three foundations of the world (*Avot* 1:2). The Talmud delineates the importance and rationale for giving charity (as well as the punishments for those who do not). (See *Baba Bathra* 10a, 10b, and 11a and Midrash Rabbah, Leviticus 34:10–11.) The Talmud also offers this explanation for how the Jews "inherited" poverty: "What is the meaning of the verse: 'Behold I have refined thee but not as silver; I have tried thee in the furnace of affliction?' It teaches that the Holy One, blessed be He, went through all the good qualities in order to give [them] to Israel, and He found only poverty" (*Hagiga* 9b). The philosopher Maimonides enumerated eight levels of giving charity, the highest being to help the needy person support himself in some occupation.

There are many occasions in Jewish life, including the *yahrzeit* of a person, or the celebration of a life-cycle event, when the giving of charity in that person's memory, or honor, is an especially meritorious way to remember that person. Helping those less fortunate than ourselves is one of the greatest mitzvot. As it is written: "Charity saves from death" (Proverbs 10:2). On holidays, such as Purim, there is the tradition of giving *mishloakh manot*, the giving of fruits and hamantaschen to friends as well as money to the poor (see *Esther* 9:22). The origin of giving charity, as well as the origins of certain customs, create etiological stories (A1599.15: "origin of begging"). This story belongs to this category.

Since the giving of charity is such an important part of our Jewish lives, it follows that there have to be many in need of that charity, thus the reason for many beggars in our world who help us fulfill this mitzvah of giving charity. As a result, there are many folktales with this theme. Many of the stories revolve about the cleverness of the beggars, who especially use imaginative arguments to convince the rich man to give an even greater handout, as in this story.

What we have in the Jewish oral tradition, then, are a multitude of humorous stories with impudent characters known as *schnorrers*, beggars, and tricksters, such as Hershele Ostropolier and Joha. Ausubel captures the characteristics of the *schnorrer* well: "He [the schnorrer] disdained to stretch out his hand for alms like an ordinary beggar. He did not solicit aid—he demanded it. . . . Since he was obliged to live by his wits he, understandably enough, developed all the facile improvisations of an adventurer . . . Next to his adroitness in fleecing the philanthropic sheep was his *chutzpah*, his unmitigated impudence. He would terrorize his prey by the sheer daring of his importunities, leaving him both speechless and wilted, with no desire to continue the unequal combat . . . One also had to be trigger-intelligent, imaginative, persuasive . . ." (Ausubel, *A Treasury of Jewish Folklore*, p. 267).

But we do not have just one kind of Jewish beggar type. On one hand, there is the famous "beggar" for charity, Rabbi Yaakov Kranz, the Maggid of Dubno, who used wit and story to good effect. However, he would not ask for money for himself, as regular beggars would, but rather give it to needy people or raise money for a worthy cause. The Dubner Maggid's most effective method of persuasion was through the use of ingenious parables. Whenever he would encounter a wealthy miser who offered excuses in place of a donation, he would ask him an intriguing question. Then, within the same breath, say "Give me just another moment to tell you a parable." (See "The Maggid of Dubno" in this collection.)

On the other hand, the chutzpadic trickster/beggars, such as Hershele Ostropolier and Joha, who raised money for themselves alone, used words like arrows that always hit their mark in order to divert and persuade the rich man. In this way, the beggar's aim, to teach the greedy person a lesson and sometimes also get a free meal thrown into the deal, would also be accomplished. (See "How to Sell a Menorah!" in my *Eight Tales for Eight Nights* and "Going Along with Joha" in my *Chosen Tales*.)

The character of the beggar becomes a folk clown and is represented in many jokes and humorous anecdotes. See the section on "Droll Characters" in *A Treasury of Jewish Folklore*. This story, "The Poor People and Their Shares," can be classified as a humorous story.

—*PS*

25

The Yemenite King
and His Jewish Advisor

There was once a Yemenite king and Zehariah the Jew was his chief advisor. Zehariah was the head of all the king's lands and all his wealth. Because Zehariah managed everything with great success, the king loved him and preferred him above all his other advisors. His other advisors became very jealous and looked for a way to shame Zehariah in the eyes of the king.

One day the head of all the advisors turned to the king and asked him for the reason for his favoring of Zehariah the Jew. "There is no discrimination. Zehariah is simply the smartest of all of you," answered the king.

"Is it possible," said the head of the advisors, "that you would let me ask Zehariah three questions, and, if he knows the answers to these questions, we will receive him with love."

"Very well," answered the king. "But now you must tell me what those questions are that you plan to ask Zehariah."

"The first question is," said the advisor, "What is the speed of a bird? The second question is, What is fatter than a pig? And the third question is, What is sweeter than honey?"

"Good," exclaimed the king, "and now call Zehariah."

The vizier went out to the court and called Zehariah to come to the king's palace. Then the king asked his advisors to sit near him while he asked Zehariah the three questions. The king said to him, "Zehariah, I will give you three days to find the answers. And if you cannot give answers that would satisfy the advisor, your fate will be in his hands."

With his head bowed, Zehariah returned to his house, closed the door to his room, and refused to leave, not even to eat or drink. His wife was very troubled by his behavior so she called Hannah, their wise and beloved daughter, to talk with her father. Hannah came and asked her father to open the door because she wanted to speak with him. Zehariah opened the door and told her everything that had happened. When Hannah learned the reason for his behavior, she began to laugh a great laugh.

"Why are you laughing at me?" asked the father "A day has already passed and I have not yet begun to solve the first question."

"I will tell you the answers to these questions, father, and you will also laugh," replied the daughter. "First come to eat and drink. Afterwards I will tell you all the answers and you will tell them to the king himself, even before the three days the king has given you."

Zehariah ate and drank and then his daughter told him, "Father, the answer to the first question is that the speed of a bird is the speed of the eye. The second question is that the earth is fatter than a pig. And the third is that what is sweeter than honey is the soul of a person."

Zehariah returned to the king's palace and told them that he was prepared to answer the king's questions.

When the king heard the answers that Zehariah gave, he was very surprised. Not only did he find those answers to be wise, but so, too, did those advisors who hated Zehariah. "There is no question that someone gave you those answers," said the king. "If you don't tell me immediately who gave you those answers, I will order that you be hanged by your neck until you die."

Zehariah was very afraid and said, "My only daughter Hannah, she is the one who told me those answers."

"I see that you have a very wise daughter. And if her beauty is as her wisdom, it will be good. And now go back home and bring your daughter to my palace, but she should come satisfied from food and not satisfied, dressed and undressed, riding and not riding."

Zehariah returned home, again with his head lowered. Hannah was waiting very impatiently for her father's return and immediately saw that he was troubled, that perhaps the answers did not please the king. When she asked about this, he replied, "No, the opposite is true. The king liked your answers and his advisors, too, liked your answers very much. But I have now an even bigger trouble." And Zehariah told his daughter about the king's wishes.

"Don't worry," answered his daughter. "With the help of God we will get through this as well."

During the three days, Hannah didn't eat anything. But on the third day, before leaving to go to the king's palace, she ate a few sesame seeds. Then she unrobed and wrapped herself in a silken dress that was very flowing and transparent. Then she got on a sheep and she rode to the palace with her feet dragging on the ground.

The king was sitting on the balcony of his palace and when he saw the rider, he immediately understood that this was Zehariah's daughter. He ordered his servants to bring her to him and asked her, "Have you eaten and are you satisfied from your food?"

Hannah then told the king what she had done and what she had eaten.

"It is very wise what you have done," said the king. "And I have no need to ask anymore. I see how you answered my other two riddles. You are a very wise woman and deserve to be queen. But there is one condition I will set, that you should never get involved in my kingly judgments."

Did she agree to this condition? Yes, she agreed.

"If that is the case, then today you will become my queen." And the king held a great banquet and she was declared the queen.

One day, a man was walking on the road and he was carrying a great and heavy package on his back. As he was walking, a wagon passed him and he asked the owner permission to get on the wagon and ride. However, the owner of the wagon refused and continued riding. But then, when, after a short distance, the wagon driver saw from a distance how difficult it was for this man to continue walking with that heavy burden, he called him and told him to get on the wagon. Of course the man did not hesitate and immediately got onto the wagon.

When they got close to the capital city of this country, the female donkey that was pulling the wagon gave birth to a baby donkey that then died. The owner of the wagon began to shout, "This man who put all this extra weight and burden on my wagon is guilty of causing my donkey to give birth to a dead baby." And he immediately demanded that the man pay for all damage that he had caused him because of this.

But the rider said, with great distress, "I was walking and when you saw me, you called me to get on the wagon. Therefore, I shouldn't have to pay you any kind of penalty."

By this time, many of the people in the town gathered around and the police came and took them to the king for his judgment. The king heard both their claims and gave his judgment: "The rider with his heavy burden is obligated to pay for the damage." He tried to argue that he didn't have money to pay the fine. But all the claims and all the arguments of this poor man—and he was very poor—didn't help.

As the man left the palace, one of the servants of the palace, who had heard the case, went to the man and told him, "Perhaps you should bring your case to the queen because she, in all her wisdom, will know how to advise you in this terrible situation."

This man then went to find the queen. He poured out all his troubles to the queen. Taking great pity on him, she said, "Listen, tomorrow the king is about to go out with his ministers around him. On the way, they must pass by a certain river, on the outskirts of this city, that everyone knows has no fish. Go and buy a fishing pole and go to the river and start fishing. The king will be shocked and he will ask you, "How do you expect to catch fish in a river that has no fish?" And then you must tell him, without fear, "What I am doing is as logical as your judgment was, to make a poor man like me give payment to a very wealthy man, an owner of a wagon, for some damage that was certainly not caused by me."

And the man obeyed the queen and did as she told him to do. And when he saw the king and his entourage coming toward him, he began to fish with great energy. When the king and his ministers saw this, they said to each other, "This man must be crazy." But when the king got closer to the man, he couldn't contain his curiosity and asked him what he was doing because surely he knew that there were no fish in that river.

"My actions are as logical as your judgment," replied the poor man, "to cause a poor man to pay a wealthy man damages that were surely not caused by him."

And the king understood this clue and released the man from paying the fine. But when he returned home, he called the queen and asked her the reason why she broke her agreement between them. She knew that she was not permitted to get involved in any of his kingly judgments.

"I couldn't stand the injustice because the poor man came to me and cried and told me about all his troubles and debts; I had to help him."

"But this does not change the fact that you have broken an agreement we made. You will have to return to your father's house. But first you may take with you the most valuable thing you would like."

"Oh king, please let me hold a great banquet before we part."

The king agreed. At the great banquet, the queen made sure that the king would be served the strongest wine. And when he fell asleep at the table, she ordered her servants to take him and bring him to her father's house. And after the king had slept a number of hours, he woke up and asked Hannah, in shock, "Where am I?"

"Oh my king, you are in my father's house."

"How did this happen?" asked the king.

"It's all very simple," answered Hannah. "You told me that I could take the most valuable thing in your house and I took it."

"There is no one who deserves more than you to be queen," said the king. "I ask your forgiveness."

The king and the queen returned together to the palace and they lived happily ever after in wealth and wisdom until the end of their days.

End of Story Note

IFA 6699 from *Faithful Guardians*, Story #8, collected from Sasson Shamur, from Yemen (Noy).

Tale Types: AT 875 (The Clever Peasant Girl); **AT 875 IV** (The Dearest Possession).

Motifs: J1111 (Clever girl); **H561.1** (Clever peasant girl asked riddles by king); **H561.1.1.1** (Clever daughter construes enigmatic sayings); **H632** (Riddle: what is the swiftest? Eye); **H653.1** (What is the fattest? Earth); **H633** (Riddle: what is sweetest? Sleep); **H1053** (Task: coming neither riding nor walking); **H1054** (Task: Coming neither naked nor clad); **H1063** (Task: coming neither hungry nor satiated).

This is one of the most popular folktales in the world, including among Jewish groups, and has been collected from China to Western Europe. Familiar universal versions include "Clever Manka" and "Clever Gretchen" as well as "The Maiden Wiser Than the Tzar."

In Jewish versions, the last episode of this story can be found in the *midrashim* on the Talmud (*Pesikta*). The story, IFA 9254, found in *A Tale for Each Month 1971* (Noy), consists only of "The Dearest Possession" motif, which is the core midrashic story. The general frame of "The Clever Peasant Girl" tale type is also the structure of "The Emir, the Jewish Counselor, and the Sheep" in this collection.

Also see my commentary and another version of this story, "The Innkeeper's Wise Daughter," in my *Jewish Stories One Generation Tells Another* and my recorded version on the CD *The Minstrel and the Storyteller*.

—*PS*

26

Money Comes and Money Goes
But a Skill Stays with You Forever

There was once a young man who was lazy and not very serious about his studies. All he wanted to do was play games. One day, his mother suggested that he learn a skill that could help him not only earn a good living, but make him feel useful because he would be helping people. "Why do I need a skill? What good is a skill?"

The patient mother said simply, "Let me tell you a story."

A young and handsome king wanted to know what was going on in his capital city. So what did he do? He went on a trip to the outskirts of his city. When he didn't find anything that interested him, he started back to the palace. But then he looked around him and he saw that he was standing outside of a beautiful large house and around it was a beautiful flower garden, which was filled with the most fragrant perfumes. As the king got closer to the house, he saw sitting on the porch three people—an older couple and a beautiful young woman. She was probably their daughter, he thought to himself. The king asked them, "May I sit with you and rest for a while?" "Of course," they answered, and they invited him to sit with them on their porch. Sitting there, the young woman served the king some coffee. As he was drinking, they began to have a conversation. They first asked their guest where he came from and what were his requests.

The king answered, "I came to buy jewels and diamonds because that is my business." As he was talking, the king noticed the young woman was listening very attentively. This gave the king courage and self-assurance. When the parents went into the house for a while, he turned to the woman and asked, "Would you marry me for you are very beautiful and I like you very much."

"I will not marry anyone who does not have a skill. Money comes and money goes, but a skill will stay with you forever. That skill will stay with that person and he will never know a day of hunger."

And the king decided that he would go and learn a skill. "But promise to wait for me and not marry anyone else."

The young woman promised to wait for him and the king went back to his palace. He invited expert rug weavers to come to the palace. He gave them a great amount of money and asked them to teach him the skill of rug weaving. The rug weaver agreed for he was a true artist. When the king felt that he knew enough about rug weaving, he told this to his loved one and she invited him to her house.

When the king received the invitation, he left immediately to go to his beloved. On the way he became very thirsty so he went to a cafe and had a cup of coffee. But when he went to pay, he was suddenly thrown into a dark cellar. He looked for some way to get out or for some help. Suddenly he heard a terrible voice ordering him, "Don't move! Any try you make to escape will end with your death. Only if you give us some ransom will you be freed."

"I have no money," answered the prisoner. "But it is known that I can weave rugs, which is a very skilled profession. You can sell my rugs and receive a great deal of money."

"I agree," answered the voice, "on condition that you start your work right away. I will put you in a small room and there I will bring you food and all the materials you will need. You will do nothing but weave your rugs."

And the prisoner was brought to a room on the side of the cellar and food was brought to him and all the materials for the rug weaving. He began to weave a rug, and, after one month, he had woven a rug of such beauty that had never been seen before. One of his jailers took the rug and went to sell it to one of the known merchants. The merchant saw that it was a very well-made rug and began negotiations about the price. But, in the meantime, the merchant noticed that among the flowers and designs of the rug there was a message in the rug. It was a desperate message and it was written in very small letters. It said, "The king is in trouble. The sellers of these rugs have imprisoned him."

After the negotiations were finished, the merchant took the rug and went to the police. The police immediately imprisoned the seller of the rug. In the beginning, he lied and said that he knew nothing about the king and where he could be found. But after threatening him with hanging from the nearest tree, the man told the police everything and brought them to where the king was imprisoned. The police hung the owner of the cafe. The king was freed and he married the young woman who was so wise.

At the time of the wedding celebration, the king told the story of what had happened to him. And when he had ended his story, the king added the wisdom he had learned, "Money comes, and money goes, but a skill will stay with you forever. And because of this skill I was saved from a sure death."

At the end of the story, the wise mother turned to her son and said, "So you can see from this story how a skill will always stay with you—and can also save you from certain trouble."

End of Story Notes

IFA 5610 from *Faithful Guardians,* Story #1, collected by Moshe Haimovits from David Cohen, from Tunisia (Noy).

Tale type: AT 888A* (The Basket-maker).

This tale type, identified in the IFA as "Handicraft saves from death," has also been labeled as "The Value of a Profession" in another folklore resource. There are many IFA variants from Tunisia, Persian Kurdistan, Iraq, Persia, Afghanistan, Bukhara, Poland, Rumania, and Russia. A variant can also be found in Irish folklore. See variants IFA 1625 b and IFA 4838. In the first variant, the king learns embroidery; in the second a young man learns to make a rug. Sometimes the craft involves basket making. However, in all the stories, the message that saves a life is woven into the cloth/rug/basket.

There is a very different story in which weaving of cloth also saves a life. By recognizing a particular woven cloth of an unusual design, the king successfully identifies his children and saves the Queen. See "Children of the King" in my *Jewish Stories One Generation Tells Another.*

The advice of the title was handed down to me by my mother. Having internalized this message, I decided to frame the story by using it and telling the folktale as a teaching tale. Perhaps her sage advice came from the Talmud: "R. Judah ben Ilai also said: Anyone who does not teach his son a trade is as though he taught him to be a brigand; . ." (*Kiddushin* 29a).

—PS

27

There Is No Justice in the World

A man was walking a long distance on a very hot day. After a time, the man grew very tired. On his way he saw a whole group of stones. He sat on one of them to rest.

All of a sudden, he heard a voice from underneath the stones. "Help me come out of here for the rocks are pressing on me."

The man's heart filled with pity. He got up, picked up the stone, and from beneath the stone out came a snake and it ran away. The man didn't think about it very much and he continued on his way.

After a short time, he lay down to rest. He felt something cold around his neck. When he looked, he saw a snake was wound around it. He asked the snake, "What do you want?" The snake answered, "I want to strangle you."

"But I saved your life, and now you want to repay a good deed with a bad deed?" asked the man.

And the snake replied, "There is no justice in this world."

The man said, "You must not judge alone. Come, we will go out on our way and we will find someone who will judge between us. And if he says that you must strangle me, then you will do it. And if not, then you will let me go."

They went on their way and they met a horse that was standing and eating grass. The man went up to the horse and told him the whole matter and he asked, "Now tell me, please, judge between us." And the horse said to the snake, "Strangle him. There is no truth among people. When I was a small horse, they took care of me and treated me well. All the children played with me. But when I grew up, they worked me. I was good for my master. And now when I cannot plow the ground anymore, they don't give me food. I must come here to eat this bitter grass."

The man said, "It is possible that you had a bad master. But there are also good people in the world who would not treat you this way. Come, let us continue on our way and maybe we'll find another animal who will have a different opinion about people. So the three of them continued, the man, the snake, and the horse.

They met a dog that was very big, digging in the ground, looking for food. And the three of them went up to the dog and told him everything that had happened. The dog answered with the same answer that the horse had given. "Strangle the man. When I was young, people took good care of me and loved me. But I grew up and got bigger. They connected me with a chain to their house and I took care of their sheep. I barked at anyone who got close. Now that I am old and I can't bark very loud any longer or can't run very far, they have thrown me out. Therefore I must look in this field for bodies of mice to eat. Is there truth, justice and honesty in the world? Strangle the man!"

And the man said, "It could be that the dog had terrible masters, the same as for the horse. They were not very fair. Come, let's go to the forest. There we will find animals that did not serve man. Maybe we will hear something different from them."

The snake refused to hear this suggestion. But the man said, "Do not be in such a hurry to kill me for you will be able to kill me in the end anyway." So they continued until they met a fox on the way.

The man said to the fox, with the snake still around his neck, "Two judges have already judged between me and the snake. Now I want you also to be a judge." And the fox said, "How can I judge this case when I have not seen where it all began. Come, let us go back to the same place where everything took place. Only after I have seen how everything happened, then I can give you a judgment." When they arrived at that place, the fox said to the man, "Now lift up the rock and show me how everything happened." And to the snake, the fox said, "Now I want to see you go back to the place where you were lying so I can see exactly how the situation was."

And the snake did as the fox suggested. Then the fox turned to the man and said, "Leave him there underneath the stone." And this is what the man did. The snake stayed under the rock and he suffocated.

The man went on his way, happily and with a light heart with the fox accompanying him. As they were walking, the fox turned and said, "I have saved your life. Now I want you to pay me for saving it."

The man asked, "How can I pay you?" And the fox answered, "I don't need a lot. Just a chicken everyday will be enough for me."

The man agreed, "I will do that gladly. The payment of a chicken will not hurt me." And the fox went back to the forest.

The man continued on his way until he arrived at his house and told his wife and his sons all that had happened to him. Everyone in his house was very happy. His wife said, "Yes, we have sixty chickens. Every day, I will fulfill the fox's request."

That night, they heard the whining and screaming of the fox in their garden. The woman said to her husband, "Do you hear? The fox is taking all of our chickens that we have promised him." So they sent one of their children to tie up one chicken, and to bring it to the fox. And this is what they did every day.

One day, the wife said to her husband, "We had sixty chickens. But the fox has eaten them all. Now we have only one chicken left for us. What shall we do?"

"Take the ax and kill the fox. We will then have a good piece of fur that we can sell and we will be able to save the last chicken."

That night, the man hid in his garden. When the fox came, as was his custom every day in order to receive his chicken, the man cut off the fox's head at the neck.

And from this, we can see, that indeed there is no justice in the world.

End of Story Note

IFA 8004 from *A Tale for Each Month 1968–69*, Story #2, collected by Dinah Behar from Wolf Sosenski, from White Russia (Cheichel-Hechal). **Tale Types: AT 155** (The Ungrateful Serpent Returned to Captivity); End of story involves tale type AT 154 III (The Man Goes for the Geese but Instead Brings Dogs Back in his Bag, K235. The dogs chase the fox to his hole.)
Motifs: W154.2.1 (Rescued animal threatens rescuer); J1172.3.2 (Animals judge against man because he always acts ungratefully to them); W154 (However, that is the way of the world).

A variant, IFA 5319 from Iraqi Kurdistan, "There Is No Pity in Man's Heart," is found in *Min Ha-Mabua*, Story #32 (Marcus).

This is an international tale told in many countries including China, Russia, Sicily, Italy, Argentina, West Indies, Brazil, Denmark, Ireland, France, Spain, and Finland. It is one of the most popular animal stories in Israeli literature, written and oral. For example, there are many Jewish parallels from Morocco, Tunisia, Libya, Yemen, Egypt, Iraq, Bukhara, and Romania. Often the animals involved are varied. In a Moroccan variant, there is a lion instead of a snake. In Egypt, there is a snake, a woodcutter, a donkey, and a fox. In a Romanian version, there is a snake, a man, a wolf, a horse, and children.

According to the folkloristic annotation, it is possible to believe that the teller received this story from a non-Jewish source mainly because the judge is not King Solomon as is usually the case in Jewish versions.

The question of truth and justice continues to intrigue us and we keep exploring it through our folktales, especially animal tales. When we read stories such as this one, we need to ask ourselves, how would we act. What is justice? What is truth? There is great wisdom to be mined in this story.

See also "Ungrateful Men" in this collection.

—PS

28

Can Fate Be Changed?

There was once a king who lived very happily and he was also very wealthy. He had a slave whose face was disfigured and his body was heavily scarred. He lived in the palace and he was very faithful and devoted. One day the king said to his son, "When I die, you must leave the slave in the palace and do not send him away." And the king's son promised his father to keep his pledge and to do as he asked.

After some time, the king died. His son was crowned in his place. Then the young king married a woman and they had a daughter. The daughter grew up and she was a beautiful young girl and was also very wise. On one of the nights, the dead king appeared to his son in a dream and ordered him, "You must go and give your daughter to the scarred slave as a wife."

In the morning, the young king woke up, shocked, and told all his ministers what he had dreamed. They advised him, "Not far from our city there is an old and wise man. There is no one like him in understanding the matters of luck and fate. Send a messenger to ask him 'Can one's fate be changed?'" And the king called for his scarred slave, gave him some food for the way, and ordered him, "Go and look for the man who is unlike any other in understanding the matters of luck and fate. When you get to him, ask him, 'Can one's fate be changed?'"

The scarred slave went out on his way. Suddenly he heard a voice calling. He looked around but he didn't see a living soul so he continued on his way. But again he heard the voice. He still did not see anyone. But when he heard the voice a third time, he saw that the voice was coming from the branches of a tree. Then he understood that it was the tree that was talking to him.

"I am a reincarnation," said the tree to the slave, "and my leaves are medicine. Any sick person who smells my leaves will be healed."

So the slave picked a few of the leaves and continued on his way. Then he arrived at a spring. When he got closer to it, he slipped and fell into the water. When he emerged from the spring, his skin had turned smooth. He had turned into a handsome young man. When seeing this, he decided to go back to his country. As he got closer to the king's palace, he heard a crying voice. When he asked what the meaning of this was, he was told, "Our king is ill and his illness is fatal." The slave asked to see the king. When he went inside, he brought the leaves to the king's nose. The king only had to smell the leaves and he turned completely healthy.

The king did not know how to reward this young man who had cured him. He asked his daughter, "Would you agree to marry him?" The king's daughter agreed to her father's suggestion and the wedding was held. The couple lived very happily and peacefully.

Only one thing puzzled the princess. Her husband very often repeated this sentence, "There is no fate or luck that can be changed."

When she told this to her father, the king called for his son-in-law and asked him what the meaning of it was. And the young man answered, "I am the slave whom you sent to that wise man to find out matters about fate and to ask him if fate can be changed. And this is your answer that I have brought to you. Fate cannot be changed." And he told the king all that had happened to him.

Now the king finally had the answer to his question. And the king was happy that he had received help from heaven in order to fulfill his father's request in the dream. He held a great banquet for all the people in the city to celebrate the found wisdom.

End of Story Note

IFA 6177 from *A Tale for Each Month 1964*, Story #3, collected by Jacob Zemer-Tov from his mother Juliet from Baghdad (Kagan).

Tale Types: AT 930 (The Prophecy); AT 460B (The Journey in Search of Fortune)

Motifs: T22.2 (Predestined wife); M312.1 (Prophecy; Wealthy marriage for poor boy); N370 (Vain attempts to escape fulfillment of prophecy); D1860 (Magic beautification); H1210.2 (Quest assigned by King); D1812.33 (Dreams that reveal the future); D1500.1.4 (Magic healing leaves); D2161.3 (Magic cure of physical defect).

The title question is often treated in folk literature as it is a question we wrestle with in our human condition. In this story, too, there is a prophetic dream as in the story "The Fulfilled Dream." But this dream is a request by the dead father of the king to marry his daughter to a particular slave. This prompts the quest for finding the wise man who can answer the eternal question, can one's fate be changed? There are also the elements of healing leaves and water that transform the physical appearance, as in a number of other stories. See "The Wonderful Healing Leaves" in this collection and "Her Wisdom Is Her Beauty" in my *Tales of Elijah the Prophet*. Also see "The Mute Princess" in Howard Schwartz's *Elijah's Violin*.

There are many variants of this tale in the Israel Folktale Archives from Yemen, Persia, Iraq, Afghanistan, Morocco, and Israeli Arabs.

An interesting Iraqi story containing elements of AT 930 and motif K511 is IFA 335, "With God's Will All Is Possible," in Dov Noy's *Folktales of Israel* (#49). In the end, the king finally accepts what the title declares and concludes with the insight that he has learned, "There is no escape from fate."

—PS

29

The Prince of the East
and the Princess of the West

In one of the Eastern countries lived a young prince who loved to read stories. Day and night he would sit and read all alone and he would be very interested to read of kings and princes and about their lives and their adventures.

One day he read a story of a princess from one of the Western countries. She was very wise, she was very good, and she was so very beautiful that she was a marvel to look at. But she never wanted to marry anyone, even if this person would sit by her door day and night, or even if he was one of the noblest and richest people in the world. She did not want to get married. Now this princess was very kind and very gentle and very delicate in her ways and her words. And so everyone who saw her loved her. And everytime someone loved her, he would want her and swear to himself that he would marry her no matter what. But everyone who went to the king to ask for her hand in marriage, would receive the same answer: "You should know, my son, that even if you want to be in my house, you must be strong in every way to stand all the trials you must win. If you lose any of the contests against my daughter, you will die as that is your punishment for losing. And until now there has not been one person who can best my daughter. Thirty-nine handsome young men who were strong and brave and were willing to try anything in order to get her hand in marriage have lost their lives."

And even though the king warned the different people who had come to ask for his daughter's hand in marriage, this Eastern prince decided to try his luck. He turned to his father to ask permission to marry the princess of the West. The king was amused by his son's request but he also thought that his son wanted to mock him so he said, "You do not have to go on with all your stories and legends and mock me and your mother in trying to go find your luck. Stay here with us as my day of death is coming closer and you will have to succeed me on the throne."

"No Father, I do not mock you with my request to try my luck. For I will marry this princess who is the smartest of all the princesses in the world."

Even though the son tried to convince his father more and more that he should let him seek this young woman, his father continued to disapprove. However, the son argued so much until the father could not stop him from going. And so the king finally agreed but he felt as though he would never see his son again.

All the preparations were made and the son started on his way in a kingly procession, accompanied by slaves and soldiers and knights.

In the afternoon, the prince decided to rest a bit. All of a sudden, he heard a faint voice in the distance calling out for help, and crying bitterly. He quickly ran toward it. In front of him he saw a frightening scene that caused him to have such pity. Coiled around an old tree was a snake. And above the snake was a bird's nest with seven chicks. In one moment the newly born baby birds would be eaten by the cruel snake. Without hesitation, the prince hit the head of the snake repeatedly until the snake fell dead. And before this prince could turn around, he saw the mother bird returning to the nest and said to the prince, "My dear man, you have proven your good heart. Tell me, where do you come from and where are you going? Tell me and I will help you if you need me."

The prince told the bird about his goals and the bird said, "It is written that someone who has saved one life, it is as if he saved the whole world. And you have performed the mitzvah of saving seven lives. Therefore, you deserve some sort of payment for this good deed. Now listen to what I have to say and follow my advice. When you meet the princess, stay with her alone and suggest a competition. The first person who can force the other person to answer a question will be the winner of the competition. But if the person who does not answer, no matter how great the temptation, that person, the one who stays quiet, will win the competition. When the princess agrees to the contest, turn to the lamp and ask the lamp to tell you a story. Then you will see how things follow after that. Now go in peace and may you have success."

The King's son parted from the bird and continued on his way until he arrived at the princess's castle. And there he asked the king if he could try his luck in competition with the princess. The king tried to stop him and even brought him to a room where the heads of all the other suitors who had tried and failed were put.

But the king saw that this young man was determined in his ways and so the king told him the conditions for the competitions. Finally the king said, "You must know that you will die if you do not defeat the princess." The prince accepted this condition.

The evening of the competition arrived. The prince of the East and the princess of the West sat together in a room. As they ate of the different foods that were served, the prince suggested to the princess a competition exactly in the way the bird had told him. The princess agreed.

Then the prince turned to the lamp and said, "Tell me, my wonderful lamp, tell me a story so I won't be bored." All of the sudden the bird's voice was heard and she spoke from within the lamp. "That's what it shall be, that's what it shall be, dear prince of the East. I will tell you a story and here is the beginning of the story."

Many years ago three men met by chance on a road near a town. They had been riding from the morning til the evening and towards the night they ate their meal. When they had finished eating, they stayed overnight in the town until the morning. In the morning the men decided they would continue on their way together. Because of dangers of the night, they decided to sleep in shifts, each taking turns guarding the other two who would be sleeping.

The first one who was to stay awake was a carpenter. In order not to be bored, he gathered different pieces of wood around him and he carved them into a beautiful statue. At the end of his shift, he awoke the second man and told him that it was his time to guard. Then the carpenter went to sleep.

The second one was a tailor by profession. He sat for awhile looking around to see how he could occupy his time. Suddenly his eyes fell on the statue. It was a beautiful work of art. So the tailor took pieces of cloth he had in his bag and made a beautiful gown for the statue. When it was his time to sleep, he woke the third man and told him to stand guard.

This third man was a pious man. When he saw the statue with the gown, he decided he would breathe the breath of life into it. The specific name of God was on his lips and right before him, the statue became a beautiful young woman.

When everyone was awake, they all became surprised by what they saw. Now all three wanted to marry this beautiful young maiden.

And now the bird-lamp turned to the prince and asked, "Who do you think should marry the young girl?"

"Well, of course, the carpenter is the one who should marry her because he is the one who made her," answered the prince.

"You are wrong," said the bird-lamp. "The tailor is the one who should marry her because he is the one who dressed her naked form."

Meanwhile the princess listened the whole time to the story and didn't say one word. But when she heard what the bird-lamp and the prince were saying, she could not stop herself and said in a loud voice, "The two of you are not correct. Neither the carpenter nor the tailor deserves to marry her. Only the third one deserves to marry her because he was the one who breathed life into the wooden statue. Without the breath of life how would it be possible to marry the young woman?"

So the princess failed this trial because she was forced to talk. According to the conditions set beforehand, she now had to marry the prince. But she didn't want to marry him and said to him, "Even though I failed, I would still like to try my strength again."

While the prince sat in his room alone, the bird came to him at the window, but this time she was in the form of a young woman. Again she told him how to act with the princess, while the rules of the competition were to be the same as the night before.

During the meal, the princess suddenly turned to the lamp and said, "Lamp, o lamp, tell me a story." There was no voice, no answer. Again the princess turned to the lamp and said, "Lamp, o lamp tell me a story. I've spent my entire childhood with you in the room. I have told you all my stories and touched you with my own hands and always protected you, dear lamp. Lamp, o lamp tell me a story." And there was still no answer from the lamp. The princess sat down quietly.

The prince laughed softly and turned to the chair in which he had been sitting and said, "Chair, tell me a story. Tell me an interesting story so that I will not be bored."

And the bird opened her mouth from behind the chair and started to speak.

"Dear prince of the East, the story that I will tell begins this way.

There was once a rich merchant, Suliman was his name. He had one son. The son did not have any learning, he was not very smart, and he was certainly not very handsome. And everyone who saw him turned their face away so they would not be disgusted by his appearance. And the father was embarrassed by his ugly dirty son, especially when he went to deal with the other merchants. In fact the other merchants did not take this merchant seriously and sent him away because of that son. One day the merchant Suliman decided to send away his son Ibrahim. When he suggested this to his wife, his wife was upset, because what mother would agree to be separated from her child, no matter what. In the end, Suliman decided on a plan to send his son away with a beautiful hat in which were three jewels of different sizes. In that way, their son could live decently rather than as an animal eating garbage. One day, the mother got up in the morning and told one of the servants to take her son and leave him in a faraway place so that he wouldn't be able to find his way home.

That morning, when Ibrahim woke up, he found himself lying on a sheet in a place he did not know but with the hat and the jewels next to him. In the beginning, he did not understand what was done. Then slowly, after he looked around and walked around, he understood that he would have to wander from place to place in the world. With no other choice before him, he gathered his belongings and he went on his way. And as luck would have it, the young man met a gardener with a good heart who accepted him in his home on the condition that he work with him in his garden. And Ibrahim accepted this offer and stayed with the gardener.

One day the daughter of the king saw the man working in the garden and noticed one of the jewels in the crown of his hat. The glitter of the small stone so dazzled her vision for a moment that she wanted this jewel. And so what did she do? She sent her servant-girl to ask for it from the owner. When the young girl went to Ibrahim and asked for one of the smaller stones from the crown, the young man agreed to give it up on condition that he see the face of the princess. When the girl went back to the princess to tell her what the young man had asked in exchange for the stone, the princess agreed readily. She went to the window and through the window the princess showed her face to the young man. But during the time she was there, the princess noticed a second stone in the crown and wanted this one too. In return for the second jewel the young man asked for a kiss. This time the princess also agreed and, after the kiss, the princess noticed that the young man's face had changed and he was looking more attractive. After a little time, the princess noticed the third and largest stone in the hat and she wanted this one as well and she asked for it. But this time the young man asked for marriage. The princess agreed to marry the young man because of his good heart and the nice way he acted toward her while she was in his garden, which was across from the garden of the king—and also because of his beauty. In fact, the young man had become quite handsome. After a time, the young man married the princess and there were many celebrations. The couple lived very happily and they had many sons and daughters.

"This is the story, dear prince," finished the bird-chair. "Now you must reveal your thoughts. Did the young man achieve his success because of his mother, his father, or the gardener?"

"In my opinion, it was his father who helped him achieve greatness because he threw him out of the house," answered the prince.

"No," answered the chair, "you are not right. It was his mother who changed his fate because she gave him the hat with the three jewels. If it were not for the jewels, the princess would not have married him."

"Both of you are wrong," answered the princess suddenly. "The gardener is the one who brought good luck to the young man. If it were not for the gardener who brought him to his house, he would never have met up with the young princess and he would not have achieved greatness."

This is the way the princess again failed by speaking out. She now really had to marry the prince because she had failed to win the contest again. However, even after the beautiful wedding, she was never sorry that she had married the young man. In fact the opposite is true. She was very grateful for her fate because her husband was good and wise and kind and he continued telling wondrous stories.

End of Story Note

IFA 1221 collected by Elana Zohar Cohen from her mother Flora Cohen from Egypt. This story has not appeared in published form.
Tale Type: AT 945 Part II (The Wooden Doll: a. A mute princess is offered to the man who can make her speak; b. The gardener tells his dog (a picture) in her presence of a woodcarver who made a wooden doll, a tailor who clothed her, and himself who gave her the power of speech: to whom shall she belong?; c. The princess breaks silence.)
Motifs: H343 (Suitor test: bringing mute princess to speak); F1023 (Creation of person by cooperation of skillful men; D435.1.1 (Transformation: statue comes to life); H621 (Skillful companions create woman: to whom does she belong?; F954.2.1 (Mute princess is brought to speech by tale ending with a question to be solved); Z16.1 (Tales ending with a question).

In this frame story, the prince, who seeks to marry the wise mute princess, receives advice from a bird whose life he saved as to how to make the princess speak, and thus win her hand in marriage. There are a number of stories where birds give good counsel (Motif: K604, "The three teachings of the bird") such as "The Bird's Wisdom" in my *Jewish Stories One Generation Tells Another*. However, in this story, the advice is a direct reward for performing a good deed from a grateful animal, the storyteller-bird.

The saying about someone who has saved one life has saved the whole world is found in the Talmud: "The reason Adam was created alone in the world is to teach you that whoever destroys a single soul, Scripture imputes it to him as though he had destroyed the entire world; and whoever keeps alive a single soul, Scripture imputes it to him as though he had preserved the entire world" (Babylonian Talmud *Sanhedrin* 37a; Jerusalem Talmud *Sanhedrin* 4:12, 22b in Bialik and Ravnitsky, *The Book of Legends*, 682:385). There is also a talmudic story about a man, called Benjamin the Righteous, who was in charge of a charity fund. When a woman came to appeal for funds for her seven children, there were no available funds left. However, the righteous man provided them with money from his own pocket. For this charitable act of saving lives, he was rewarded with twenty-two extra years of life. (*Bava Batra* 11a)

The first of the inner stories is a popular one in Jewish folklore as it is in India, Greece, Africa, Turkey, and Indonesia; and a variant can be found in *The Thousand and One Nights*. There is a variant in this collection: see "The Princess Who Would Not Speak." Also see "The Mute Princess" in *Elijah's Violin* (Schwartz) and "The Princess Who Refused to Talk" in *Jewish Folktales* (Sadeh).

—PS

30

Queen Hatam and King Tye

A dervish went from place to place with his walking stick and his backpack and every place that he went, he would sing. In this way, he supported himself by accepting money from his listeners. Once, on his way, he saw a broken-down hut and he went in to rest. There, inside this hut, sat another dervish who was a relative of Queen Hatam, and he was reciting prayers.

"Hello to you, my brother," called out the dervish-guest. "I am a wandering dervish. Could you let me rest here in your hut? I am very weary from my travels."

"Of course," answered the dervish who was the resident of the hut. "Please sit and we will spend some time together in prayer and in talk."

And the wandering dervish sat down on the ground, with his legs crossed, next to his host. He began to tell him, the way he would tell a good friend, about how he had started wandering through the whole world. With great attention the resident dervish listened to what had happened to the wandering dervish as he served him bread and onion in order to revive his hungry soul. The wandering dervish asked his host, "Tell me, how is it that you are part of such a powerful and noble family—a relative of Queen Hatam—and yet you suffer such poverty living in this hut? Why don't you turn to the queen for help? Perhaps she would put an end to your suffering in this life?"

"What you say is true," answered the host. "My queen relative is very noble and good-hearted, but it is better to be supported from the work of your own hands than live off the generous heart of Hatam."

And during this friendly conversation, the wandering dervish asked the host, "What do you know about the way of life of our praised queen?"

And the host said, "Queen Hatam has a wonderful hotel that sits on top of a beautiful mountain, surrounded by beautiful gardens. There are four gates, one for each direction of each wind and everyone who goes there receives amazing hospitality. Each guest is served wonderful food on a golden plate. The guest can eat all he wants and then, after three days, this golden plate is given to that guest when he must leave."

The wandering dervish decided that he would go to Hatam to find out for himself if these things were really true. After many months of wandering, he arrived at this wonderful hotel of Hatam. Immediately they welcomed him and gave him delicious food on a golden plate. The dervish ate with great relish and he warmed his heart with all the drink that was also offered. When he left the hotel after the allotted three days, they gave him the golden plate as a gift. The wandering dervish refused to accept this expensive dish because he wasn't used to eating off golden plates. But the host forced him to accept the gift. The dervish thought to himself, "If Queen Hatam is so rich, how much richer must be King Tye for he is the governor of all the surrounding lands. I will go to the king and find out what he has. I will also find out where he comes from and what kind of a man he is."

After many years of wandering, he came to the kingdom of King Tye. However, to his misfortune, he did not find the king in his capital city, because the king happened to be on a trip in one of the distant cities with his entire entourage. And when the wandering dervish arrived at the king's camp in this faraway city, he found the king taking care of a sick donkey. This donkey had a terrible wound on his back. So what did the dervish do? He began to sing in his clear ringing voice. However, the king did not pay attention to him but rather kept on taking care of the donkey. Then the dervish went to the tent of the king's daughter and asked for a drink of water for his parched throat. After he drank, he went on his way.

Only after King Tye let the donkey go out from its stall, he saw that the wound was healed. He turned to his daughter and asked, "Where did the dervish go, the one who sang such beautiful tunes?" She answered, "He asked me for a cup of water to quench his thirst and he went on his way." She pointed in the direction in which he had gone. King Tye got on his horse and caught up with the dervish. "Because of my attention to the injured donkey, I wasn't able to turn and speak with you. Now tell me what is your wish and I will fulfill it."

The dervish told King Tye about Queen Hatam and about her great riches and her beautiful hotel, how every guest there gets generous servings of food on a golden plate and that, after three days, the guest is presented with that gold plate as a gift. Tye couldn't believe what he heard. He turned to the dervish and said, "Man of this message, if what you say is true, I will give you my beautiful daughter to marry and you will govern, in my place, over the kingdom of Tye." He sealed the promise with his ring. He immediately dressed himself as a dervish, and the disguised king and the dervish set out to meet Queen Hatam.

When they arrived at the great hotel with the four gates, the king saw what the dervish had said was indeed true. Both guests were given a gold plate heaped with delicious food. As they left the hotel at the end of three days, they received the gold plate as a gift, just the way the dervish had described it to the king. And King Tye turned to the dervish and said, "Everything you have told me about Queen Hatam is true. And as I promised you, my daughter will marry you and be your wife. After the wedding, you will sit on my throne and govern the whole kingdom for all your days. However, before I send you to my beautiful daughter, sit in my tent, which is near the palace of Hatam the Queen, and sing your sweetest songs. If the Queen asks you about your wish, answer her, "Even if you had a mountain of gold, unless you worked to get more, there would still come a time when the gold would end. Dear Queen, how can you keep on giving each of your guests a golden gift?"

According to the King's request, the dervish went and sat in the tent that was near the Queen's palace and began to sing with a ringing clear voice—until Hatam noticed him.

Hatam approached him and asked him what he wanted. The dervish asked her, "Even if you had in your possession a mountain of gold, this gold would come to an end if you didn't work. Dear Queen, how can you keep giving each of your guests a golden gift?"

Queen Hatam answered him, "At a certain place, many hours from here, a young man comes out every day just before evening. One of his cheeks is red, the other is white. He sings in a beautiful and sweet voice that charms me to no end. Then he plays a beautiful tune on his flute.

And after he plays his flute, he breaks out into tears and cries bitterly. Afterwards he leaves. If you can tell me the secrets of his heart, I will tell you the secrets of mine."

When the dervish returned to King Tye with Queen Hatam's answer, Tye sent the dervish with a letter for his daughter instructing her that she must marry the dervish and put him on the royal throne. Tye himself, dressed as a dervish, decided to go and find this young man with one red cheek and one white cheek. Before evening he got to this beautiful place where there were many flowers and fresh running waters. All of a sudden, this young man with soulful eyes sat down on a rock next to the stream and began to sing with a beautiful voice. After the song, he took out his flute and played the same song all over again. There was a sense of joy and peacefulness everywhere. But then, all of a sudden, the young man broke out into tears, a bitter weeping. When he got up and was about to leave, Tye approached him and said to him in a gentle voice,

> Young man who sings with so much charm
> What makes you cry? Who wishes you harm?
> Open your heart and tell me why
> You stop your song, and start to cry?
> *Na'ar yafetoar elem naim kol*
> *Galeh et li bekha li saper li ha kol*
> *Ma heviyeha l'vehe nehaim*
> *Aharey shir ha sheharnin v'hiksim*

The young man answered with great anger and bitterness, "Leave me alone please. Far away from here sits an old woman and she washes two white head scarves over and over, and, after that, she puts them in mud and goes back and washes them all over again. She does this every day from morning to night. If you can tell me her secrets, I will then tell you mine."

The next day Tye got up very early and turned toward the direction where the old woman lived. After a long walk through the mountains and the valleys, he got to the running river in the valley and there he saw the old woman sitting on the edge of the river and washing and soaking the two white head scarves. He saw how as soon as they had been washed sparkling white, she then put them back into the mud near the river.

After that she washed them again in the clear water of the river. This she did time after time. Washing them and muddying them . . . washing and muddying . . . washing and muddying.

Tye turned to her and sweetly said, "Please tell me, gentle old woman, why are you making the scarves dirty and then washing them clean again?"

The old woman looked angrily at Tye and said, "A short distance from here, there is a great city surrounded by a fortress. In one of the houses lives an old man. He makes saddles and, on every saddle, he paints a beautiful picture. Everyone who sees these pictures wants one. When his work is done, he brings them to the market to sell. Many people want to buy these saddles—they fight to buy them, bidding higher and higher. But the minute the bid reaches 100 tomans for one saddle, the old man stops the bidding. Just as he is about to give it to that bidder, he takes the saddle in his hand and the old man breaks it up into little pieces. If you can tell me his secret, I will tell you mine."

Immediately Tye went to that city, and went directly to the main marketplace. And what did he see? The old man was there offering to sell the saddle that he had beautifully sewn and painted. Many people were bidding against each other to buy this expensive saddle. Everyone raised the price of the bid until it reached 100 tomans. The minute it reached that price, the old man took the saddle in his hands and broke it up into a million pieces. Tye ran after him, asking him, "I would like to know, respected old man, why do you want to break this saddle into pieces? You have put in much effort and now it is in so many little pieces."

"Go away from here," screamed the old man in anger. "You came to find out my secret, dervish. But a certain distance from here, there is a little bridge that stretches across the river and this bridge is used as a service crossing. Near the bridge sits a poor man and he holds out his hand to everyone who comes and goes. Before evening, his son comes to him and the beggar gives him money for only one day's food for his family. The rest of the money that this beggar has collected from all the passers-by is thrown into the river. If you can tell me his secret, I will tell you mine."

So Tye went in the direction of the bridge, and after a long time he arrived there. Next to the bridge was a poor man, who was singing in a voice that was sad. He was holding out his hand to all the passers-by. Tye put some silver coins into his hand and sat a certain distance from him to rest and observe. When the sun was about to set, the beggar's son appeared and this poor man gave him some money for food for all of his family. Then the poor man threw all the rest of the change he had collected that day into the river and left.

Tye turned to him and said, "Tell me, poor old man, why do you throw all your beggings into the river? This is your earnings from a whole day." And the poor man scolded him for interfering in his business and said, "In a certain town that is on the edge of the sea lives a rich merchant. When he comes home every evening he dresses up his dog with very fancy clothes, sits him on his lap and plays with him. His servant serves the man a plate full of meat and chicken. He eats it and feeds his dog too, all the while kissing and petting his dog. He collects the bones and goes to his beautiful wife who is imprisoned in a metal cage. He whips her and throws the bones at her. If you will succeed in telling me his secret, then I will tell you mine."

During the night Tye slept on a pile of straw. The next day he got up early and started walking with his cane and backpack along the mountains and the valleys until he arrived in the town that sat on the edge of the sea. He asked all the passers-by about this rich merchant, but no one could tell him where to find this man. Just before evening, as he was walking along the streets of the city, he heard the barking of a dog from one of the houses and the screaming of a woman. He opened the door of the courtyard and his eyes discovered a terrible sight. A beautiful woman was sitting in a metal cage and a man was standing near her whipping her and throwing chicken bones at her. The dervish-king approached him and said to the man with great anger, "What kind of heart do you have to whip a soft and beautiful woman with such pleasure? What joy do you have in imprisoning and humiliating her in this way? Don't your eyes see that I am a godly dervish. You should be ashamed and embarrassed at your terrible deed."

"Poor dervish," answered the rich merchant. "You have come to find out my secret. Well, a long distance from here, among the mountains, there is a city. All the residents of this city, young and old, wear black clothes. If you can find out the reason for this custom, I will tell you my secret."

Tye gripped his walking stick and he put his pack on his back and he went out to find the city between the mountains. After wandering many many days, he came to the place he was looking for. Just as the merchant had said, he found all the people of the city wearing black. He also changed his vest and clothes to black clothing and walked among them for a day. From here to there, from time to time, he met an old blind man who was holding out his hand to passers-by as a beggar. Tye gave him a few coins, and whispered in his ear and asked, "Tell me, old man, why are all the people wearing black? Is every day here a day of mourning to you?"

As soon as Tye asked this question, the blind old man got very angry and, in anger, he held out his two hands in order to grab the questioning person, as though catching a fish. Tye ran away from the old man and didn't ask any more questions. Since it was Friday, all the people in the city went out for a walk, as was their custom. They all got together in one place in order to receive visitors. Tye followed them and waited very expectantly to see who was coming. All of a sudden, in a distance, they saw a man riding on a cow coming toward them. To his astonishment, Tye saw that the rider and his cow were wearing black and in the hand of the rider was a black mirror. As the rider in black approached the residents of the city, all the people, as one, fell on their faces in prayer and begging. Then all those people began to cry at once, as in one voice. All of a sudden, in anger, the rider of the cow threw the mirror to the ground. He turned his back on the people and he went away. What did the people of the city do? They went back to the heart of the city and continued their usual activities.

Tye followed the man who was riding on the cow. All of a sudden, the rider stood up, turned around, and said, very angrily, "Why have you followed me? Who are you? Go away immediately or else your own death will be on your head." And Tye turned, as though he were leaving, and the rider of the cow rode on. However, the dervish-Tye continued carefully to follow the rider. The rider went into a dark and foggy cave. He removed a heavy stone from the mouth of the well and he was about to go down some steps into this deep well in the ground. Here again the rider spotted the dervish-king and he said again angrily, "Come after me and you will be my food for this evening." And the rider descended the stone steps.

With great courage and determined to find out the secrets of all these people, Tye followed him down the many secret steps into the depths of the earth until he came upon the rider. He saw that they were surrounded by beautiful flowers and fields and trees. All these gardens surrounded beautiful homes that belonged to ghosts and demons. The rider took out his sword and put it on the head of Tye. Tye said, "Please have pity on me. I am a king and the governor of many lands and all I wanted to do was to find out the secrets of many people. That is what has brought me here." And Tye told the rider everything that he had found. At the end he added, "Tell me, righteous person, tell me what I need to know. If I succeed in solving all these riddles, please give me my life in return. But if my answer does not satisfy your knowledge, you may end my life with your sharp sword."

Tye's words softened the heart of the rider. He agreed to tell Tye all his history.

My father Constantine the king and my mother were barren. Everyday she would hold out her hand to the God above and ask Him to give her the fruit of her womb. On one of those days, when a dervish came to the kingdom, the barren queen asked for his advice and asked him to pray for her. The dervish said to her, "I am willing to do what you ask, but when the child is seven years old, you must promise to give him to me for instruction." And the king and queen agreed to his request. The dervish gave them two apples, one for the king and one for the queen, and he promised them that very soon the queen would give birth to a son. And it was indeed so. The queen became pregnant and, in time, she gave birth to a son.

After seven years, the dervish came back to the queen, who is my mother, and took me from the royal house and brought me here. Everyday I would go out for a walk. One day I heard the voice of a girl. I turned in every direction to see who was speaking. Suddenly I saw a skull sitting on the ground and it called to me and said, "Hear me, son of the king, you are imprisoned in a place where there is no way out. Here you will be eaten, you will be the meal for this dervish. He is not a dervish but rather a monster in disguise as a dervish." And I began to shake out of fear and I began to ask the skull, "Tell me, creature of this earth, how can I get out of my bitter fate? Guide me with your advice and save me from the teeth of the monster."

And the skull turned to me and said softly, "Listen to me, sweet child, the dervish will take you to a great kitchen and there will be a pot filled with water and a fire beneath it. With his magic he will make the water and the fire disappear before your eyes. If he tells you to bring water, answer him that you are too small and that you do not have it in your power to fulfill his order. If he tells you to lift up the cover of the pot, answer that you would like him to show you how to do it. So if he lifts up the cover of the pot, quickly lift up both his legs and push him into the pot and cover him with the cover. And in the pot the dervish will find his death.

"Above his waist there is a key ring with seven keys. Take the key ring and go into the castle and open a different door with each key. In the seventh hall, in the seventh room, you will find a cage hung from the ceiling. In this cage there will be a book. Take it and go down into the center of the garden and you will find a pole surrounded by water. Get on top of it and carve a circle in the center. Sit in the circle and read the book. All of sudden, a whole army of demons will appear. Be brave and do not be afraid of them because their blood is in your hands. After they disappear, they will appear again for a second and for a third time. But if you don't show any kind of fear, and keep reading the book until you are finished, they will make you king of this place and give you the king's daughter to marry."

So I did everything the skull told me to do. I also married the king's daughter. But one day, my wife and I had an argument, a small argument, and I slapped her cheek. My mother-in-law got very angry at me and turned her daughter into a wagon and herself into a cow. And this was the cow that I was riding. The people were wearing black because they were asking my mother-in-law to return to her original form and to return her daughter into what she was before. And now if you will succeed in returning them to their original form, all's the better. If not, then your blood is on your own head.

Tye asked the rider for a certain kind of rice, some oil, and other foods. After he prepared a wonderful meal, he sat down next to the cow and the wagon. As long as the food was cooking on the stove, Tye didn't stop singing in a pleading voice:

> Oh gentle queen come back to me
> Come back, come back, as once you were
> Pity this powerful king who must see
> Return oh daughter of kings, once more

Come back, come back in your own dear form
Pity this king who is so forlorn.
Shuvi shuvi malka adina
Shuvi shuvi malka ledmudteykh
Khusi al melekh ram v'neesah
Shuvi shuvi bat melech yafah
Shuvi bat melekh k'blee et muteykh
Khusi ha melekh ram v'neesah

The entreaties of Tye and his song were so powerful they softened the heart of the cow and she transformed herself into her original form, a gentle and sweet woman. And also her daughter shed the form of the wagon and she returned to her womanly appearance as the king's daughter. As long as the king's daughter was in the form of the wagon, the demons and ghosts refused to serve this cow rider. But as soon as his wife returned to her original form, all the demons came in great numbers and surrounded the king's throne and served him as they had in the past. The king laughed with joy because his beloved wife was now returned to him and he embraced her with great joy.

After that he turned to Tye and said to him very fondly, "Now tell me, king of flesh and blood, what is your wish and I will help you attain it." And Tye told him of all the things he had found on his long journey. He asked him to reveal to him all the secrets of the people he had met on his way. But the king told him he could not do this. But the king agreed to send three of the demons who would protect him and save him from all danger in his travels. But the demons chosen to accompany Tye protested, "Oh no, it would be terrible to go with someone who is of flesh and blood. Let us give him hairs from our head instead. If he should need our help, let him burn one of these hairs and we will appear to help him." So the demons gave Tye some hairs from their heads and he was sent on his way in peace.

First Tye arrived at the town where they were all wearing black. He told them that the queen was no longer in the form of a cow and that the daughter of the king was no longer a wagon. As soon as the people heard the news, they all took off their black clothing and instead put on green clothes. Then Tye left this city. However, some of the townspeople didn't consider him trustworthy and didn't believe him. So what did they do? They caught him and were about to kill him. Tye said, "Have pity on me because I am a king of a very vast land. Wait until Friday and, if what I say is not true, then you can do with me what you want."

So the people of the city imprisoned Tye in the prison and waited impatiently for Friday. That day the king appeared riding his horse, gave them the news of the return of his wife and mother-in-law, and ordered all the people of the place to change their clothes from black to green clothing. All the people were happy for their king. During their rejoicing, they freed Tye from his imprisonment and sent him on the way with great respect.

Tye asked one of the elders of the city for an official document from the city that he had actually been in their town and had fulfilled their wish.

When he arrived at the merchant's place, he said, "Listen, my brother, I am the dervish that was at your place many years ago. You said then that if I tell you the secret about the people who wear black in the town that sits between the mountains, then you will tell me your secrets." Then he showed him the official paper.

The merchant was very surprised to see this paper and said,

Many have gone this very way.
Yet none have returned, what more can I say—
I will tell all my secrets to the one who succeeds
And returns unharmed who completes the deed.
Rabim halkhu b'derekh zu
al khloz ahu akhloz meemena
et saper kol sitrei lidi
la mishazakhal lazor meemena

"I loved my wife very much," he continued, "and I guarded her like I guard my own eye. One day a dervish appeared at my house and told me, 'Your wife has forty lovers. Every night when you fall asleep, they take her and have parties. Then before you wake up, the lovers return her to your bed and you do not even know that she had been gone. Let me, dear merchant, sleep in your house, and when they come to revel, I will wake you up from your sleep and then you'll know my words are true.' I listened to the dervish and I hid him in a secret corner of my house. He was right. The strangers came to take my wife when I was in a deep sleep, and immediately the dervish woke me up, as he had promised. I went out with my dog to see where the strangers lived to save my wife from their terrible "tortures." When they felt my presence, they wanted to beat me and kill me, but my loyal dog bit them with his sharp teeth and saved me from their hands. I went home very confused. Only right before morning did my cheating wife return. That night my love for her changed and, because of her actions, I locked her up in the cage. I put her jewels on my loyal dog and that is also why I give the good pieces of meat to my dog and I throw only the bones to my wife."

Tye was shocked at the beautiful woman's deeds but he begged the merchant to forgive his wife because she had already been punished enough. And with kind words, he succeeded in bringing the two together until they forgave each other. He also took an official letter from the merchant stating that he had been at his house and fulfilled his mission there.

Tye continued on his way to the poor beggar who sat near the bridge. Tye found him in the same place as at the first meeting and said to him, kindly, "Dear brother, I am the dervish who wanted to know your secrets. Now I will tell you the secret of the merchant you sent me to." And Tye told him all the secrets of the merchant and showed him his letter.

The poor man, surprised at the successful mission of Tye, said to him with admiration,

> Many have gone this very way
> Yet none have returned, what more can I say—
> I will tell all my secrets to the one who succeeds
> And returns unharmed who completes the deed.

We were once two brothers. Our father was a rich merchant. After his death, we shared equally what he had left in his will. While I lost all my money on gambling and entertainments, my brother got richer from day to day. In my difficulty, I turned to my brother for help. He gave generously all that I asked and he comforted me in my troubles. His wife also comforted me in a very kind way. One day a terrible rage came over me and I decided to kill my brother and his wife in order to get all their riches. I said it and I did it and I received all their riches. But again I wasted everything.

Finally I realized that even great riches cannot satisfy the heart. They create only illusion. That is the reason I hold out my hand to beg every day. Then I give all that I need for the daily running of my house to my son and the rest I throw into the river.

After listening to his story, Tye took a letter from him saying that he had fulfilled all that the poor man had sent him to do.

Tye then turned to find the saddle maker again. After some years of wandering, he met him and said to him, "I am the dervish who asked you to tell me why you always break all your beautiful saddles into little pieces and you gave me a very difficult mission. But I have fulfilled it successfully." Tye told him all that he found out about the rich merchant that sits in the city on the sea and gave him the letter. He also told him about the poor man who puts out his hand by the bridge. The saddlemaker was surprised at the courage of this man and said to him,

> Many have gone this very way,
> Yet none here returned, what more can I say—
> I will tell all my secrets to the one who succeeds
> And returns unharmed who completes the deed.

The saddlemaker, with a great sigh, began to tell his story.

I once had a son and a daughter. They were beautiful, as beautiful can be. And once, while they were playing by the side of the well, they were kidnapped by demons. Ever since then I draw their figures on my saddle and I go to the market to see if there is someone who can comfort me in my troubles. And when I don't find anyone, I break my handiwork and get out of there as quickly as possible.

Tye immediately took one of the hairs that were in his hand and, in the blink of an eye, the three demons appeared to help him. Tye demanded that they return to this poor father his son and his daughter and that the demons shouldn't bother this family any longer. The demons immediately brought the son and the daughter and presented them to their father. The father hugged his children with great happiness. He gave Tye a letter that affirmed that he had succeeded in his mission and sent him respectfully on his way.

Tye took his walking stick in his hand and made his long way back to the old woman. He showed her the letter from the saddlemaker and demanded she tell him her secret.

The old woman said to him:

> Many have gone this very way,
> Yet none have returned, what more can I say—
> I will tell all my secrets to the one who succeeds
> And returns unharmed who completes the deed.

Once I sat at the side of the river to rest from my work. All of a sudden, a beautiful girl, one of the daughters of the demon, appeared and said to me, "Oh good old woman, would you adopt me as your daughter?" "Of course," I said to her happily. And she said to me, "In that case, I will announce that you will be my mother and that you will guard me loyally. I will lie down and put my head on your knees and you must promise me not to put my head on the ground and place another girl's head on your knees." I promised to fulfill this condition as much as I could with all my strength. A while later, another girl appeared, and she was also the daughter of the demon. She was even more beautiful than the first and she asked, "Would you, old woman, adopt me to be your daughter?" "Yes," I told her happily. "And then you should put the head of that one on the ground and put my head on your knees." Her beauty blinded me and I forgot about my promise to the first girl. So I fulfilled the will of the second demon daughter. "O you cheating old woman," cried the second one angrily. "I see that you are not loyal to my sister, so you will not be loyal to me as well." And in the blink of an eye the two of them disappeared. Since that time they have not appeared to me again. My worry has been so great that every day I cry and I wash these two head scarves and then I make them dirty again and then I wash them again. This I do from morning to night without rest, without rest.

Tye pulled out the second hair from his hand and immediately the three demons appeared before him. Tye asked for them to bring the two girls to their poor mother and he made peace between them. Then he took a letter from the woman saying that his mission was successfully accomplished.

After that he turned on his way to find the young boy who had one red cheek and one white cheek. After some time Tye reached him and showed him the old woman's letter saying, "I am the dervish who asked to know your secret. I have successfully fulfilled all my missions that were given to me. Now you must also tell me your secret."

With great shock, the boy looked at the brave dervish and said:

> Many have gone this very way,
> Yet none have returned, what more can I say—
> I will tell all my secrets to the one who succeeds
> And returns unharmed who completes the deed.

One early morning I sat on top of a beautiful hill and I was singing. All of a sudden there appeared one of the most beautiful daughters of the demons. She listened very attentively to my songs and to my playing. When the sun set, with her very delicate hands she gave me a treasure and then she disappeared. This is what this beautiful girl did every day. One day, my songs put her to sleep. When she woke, she asked me to put her head on my knee, but she warned me not even to try to kiss her. But her eyes charmed me and her beauty attracted me so that I was driven out of my mind. I then put my lips on her two red cheeks and I gave her two kisses. Immediately the young girl got up very angrily. She slapped one of my cheeks and bit the other and she disappeared without ever coming back. Ever since then I have one cheek that is red and one that is white. From a broken heart, I sing every evening with a sad voice and I play a sad song on my flute. When I cannot hold in my sadness any longer, then I break out into tears.

Tye immediately took out and burned the third hair. Immediately the three demons appeared and Tye ordered them to bring the beautiful young girl to this sad young man. When she arrived, Tye made peace between the couple and the young girl promised to visit the young man on the hill every evening and listen to his songs. With a grateful heart, the young man gave Tye a letter stating that he had succeeded in his mission. Tye left them happily.

Tye took his walking stick and his backpack on his shoulder and finally returned to the place he most wanted to go, to the palace of Queen Hatam. He went to the queen and told her all that he had found during these many years. He then gave her, as if a great gift, the letter from the young man with the one red cheek and one white cheek. The queen took the letter from his hand, and, with her voice filled with respect, said,

> Many have gone this very way,
> Yet none have returned, what more can I say—
> I will tell all my secrets to the one who succeeds
> And returns unharmed who completes the deed.

Listen to me, brave dervish. My father was a king who ruled over many countries. Every year, from all the corners of the world, people sent him great beautiful and expensive gifts. He had many servants and, among these servants who did his bidding, there was a woman servant who kept a male monkey near her. The monkey fell in love with this servant and she became pregnant and she bore him a piece of fatty meat, which resembled the tail of the sheep. When my father was cooking this certain food, he put a little piece of this meat into it and fed it to the woman. The servant only had to taste a bit of this food and immediately turned into a great lump of gold. My father built a great hotel and it attracted many guests. To every guest who stayed there my father gave a generous helping of this pilaf. Then this person would also turn into a lump of gold. That is what my father used to do all the years of his life. And he collected a treasure of gold. But he always hid this fat meat so I would not see it. One day, I found this meat and I put a little piece in his food. He ate only a little bit of it and immediately fell to the ground and turned into a gigantic lump of gold. I made a vow that I would never enjoy any of the gold and I would always give it away to the guests who came to the hotel.

She brought Tye to the big tunnel that was near the palace and it was full of golden bodies, so many that you couldn't even count. "All these golden bodies were once humans who had tasted the food with the fatty meat. The guests who come here are the families of those who have lost their lives. As a gift to them in order to make up for their loss, I give each one a golden plate." At the end of the story, Hatam asked the dervish-king about what he had found and what he had gone through.

Tye told her his story.

I was once a king of a great land and I sat on a great throne. However, I gave it all up because of you. Now, for many years, I have searched for the way to find out your secrets.

And Queen Hatam answered him,

> You've given up your throne for me
> I will refuse my own for thee
> A royal throne now waits for you
> As husband and wife we'll live life through.
> *Veetarta al keeskha b'glalee*
> *Gam anee evater biglakha al kis'ee*
> *M'ata teshev al kisei malkhutee*
> *Eheyeh isht'kha v'al ta ba'alee.*

And Tye and Hatam were married and they ruled together with justice and honesty. With great respect and affection, they were often called by the name HatamTye.

End of Story Note

IFA 7154 from *With Elders Is Wisdom*, Story #14, collected by Hanina Mizrahi from Akababa Levi, from Iran.

Tale Types: AT 852*B (IFA); AT 567 III (Transformation of the Wife); AT 461A I. (The Questions); AT 465A (The Quest for the Unknown).

Motifs: H941 (Cumulative tasks—Second assigned so that first can be done); Z20 (Cumulative tale—tales arranged in chain); P331 (Refusal to receive proffered help until a series of stories has been told); H580 (Enigmatic statements).

The opening narrative serves as a frame for the inserted tales. In order to learn why the Queen offers such fabulous hospitality, the hero is sent by her to get another person's story, and then, in turn, is sent to another and another to get that one's story. Finally he hears, consecutively, stories of seven persons. This is a cumulative tale that, in the end, unites the two royal characters in marriage. This is truly an amazing story with multiple stories within a story frame.

The recurring rhyming Hebrew stanzas found throughout the story were cast into a poetic English by Roslyn Bresnick-Perry.

For an Afghanistan variant of this intertwining-stories tale, see IFA 8294, "The King Who Wanted to Know the Fisherman's Daughter's Story," in my *Jewish Stories One Generation Tells Another.*

—*PS*

31

The Twelve Sons of the Emir

There was once a very old Emir who had twelve sons. The Emir took an oath that he would only marry his sons to twelve sisters. The Emir looked for a long time for twelve sisters for his sons, but he never succeeded in finding what he was searching for. One day, a poet came to him and told him about an Emir who lived very very far away and had twelve daughters.

The old Emir mounted his horse and rode to the Emir who was the father of the twelve daughters. The two Emirs agreed between them about the marriage of their twelve children.

The twelve brothers married the twelve sisters, but their happiness did not last a long time. The day after the wedding, the brothers were found dead and their wives were shrieking and crying. Nobody knew the reason for their deaths. When the father heard about this great tragedy, he went out of his mind. The father began to wander from place to place and wandered for many many years. At the end, he came to a village where he was a guest of the head of the village. When this head of the village heard the tragic story of the wandering Emir, he wanted to comfort him and he told him many stories.

And this is one of the stories he told:

There was an Emir who had an only daughter whom he loved very much. And she loved her father in the same way. They had a female horse and only the daughter knew how to ride her. One night the Emir got up in the middle of the night and wanted to ride on the horse. He didn't tell his daughter about this beforehand. The horse began to neigh. The daughter heard the neighing horse and thought that there were thieves stealing the horse. So what did she do? She quickly ran to the pen of the horse, took out her sword and hit the man who was there. The man fell, bleeding, drowning in his own blood. In the morning, the daughter went to tell her father about what had happened during the night. And suddenly she realized she had killed her own beloved father. In spite of everything, she did not go crazy. Her soul remained whole. And now she is a princess ruling in place of her father.

So with the help of these many comforting stories, the head of the village succeeded in calming down the wandering Emir and returning him to his place, to his throne, and to the rest of his family. When the old Emir returned to his palace, to his great happiness, he found twelve young boys instead of his twelve sons. For these were the sons of his sons.

Until the end of his days, the Emir remained peaceful and content. And when the Emir went to his grave and his soul was restored to God, he was returned with a light heart.

End of Story Note

IFA 184 from *Druse Folktales* as heard by Salman Falah in Kefar Sami'a. **Tale Type: AT 844*A** (IFA) (Search for a sorrowless home). There are fifteen IFA variations including from Morocco, Tunisia, Libya, Egypt, Syria, Israel, Kurdistan, Iraqi Kurdistan, Israel-Sephardi, Persia, Afghanistan, and Rumania.

This type is a subtype of AT844 ("The Luck-bringing Shirt") as in "The Happy Man's Shirt," the Italian folktale in *Italian Folktales* by Italo Calvino, which was originally a Greek tale. A similar story is from Saudi Arabia, "The Beduin's Gazelle," in Inea Bushnaq's *Arab Folktales*. The plot revolves around a Beduin who has found his son dead. In order to soften the shock for his wife, he asks her to find a cauldron that has never been used for a meal of sorrow in order to cook the gazelle he has brought home. The wife goes from tent to tent looking for such a pot. When she cannot find such a pot, she then realizes that everyone has tasted their share of sorrow. This time it is her turn. (Motif: H1394 "Quest for person who has not known sorrow.")

As the Midrash says (*Devarim Rabbah*): "Every trouble that is to a single person is a real trouble, but every trouble that is not to a single person is not a trouble"; in other words, the more who share the trouble, the easier that trouble is to bear. And often the most therapeutic and effective way for us to share sorrow is through stories that help to give us a perspective and a restored faith. It is also the human voice talking and telling a story that reaches us in a profound and non-threatening way so we are open to relate to the emotion and experiences of the characters. Walter Benjamin writes in *The Storyteller*: "The storyteller takes what he tells from experience—his own or that reported by others, and he in turn makes it the experience of those who are listening to his tale." See "A Story of Consolation" in this collection.

This story comes from a collection of thirty selected Druse Folktales that are found in the Israel Folktale Archives. The Israeli Druse are a religious sect, distinct in many ways from their Muslim neighbors. They had broken away from Shiite Islam in the eleventh century. There are about eighty-five thousand in Israel, while others live in nearby Arab countries. In some ways, the Druse have become assimilated into Israel's national life and have become known for their loyalty to the state. They have been drafted into the Israeli army since the 1950s and also have taken seats in the Knesset. According to Druse theology, a man must strive to do the will of the Creator that is not always understood by the human mind. He must, indeed, totally accept his fate and to receive lovingly good and bad.

In the story, the death of the twelve sons the day after their wedding perhaps expresses fear, memories, and ancient instincts that are connected to the crisis of this pivotal lifecycle event, namely, marriage, which is the only time that directly touches two people equally.

The Israel Folktale Archives, which has collected well over five hundred non-Jewish folktales, are including these non-Jewish tales into the Archives, as Dov Noy writes in the Preface to the book of *Druse Folktales*, ". . . to encourage folkloristic endeavors which lead to the study of the common local roots of Judaism, Christianity and Islam. The hundreds of years of the cultural co-existence of Jews and Arabs come clearly to the foreground in folklore traditions, . . ." (201). Therefore, as we have discovered, there are also Jewish variants of so many of these folktales.

For another story from *Druse Folktales*, see "The Tiger and the Son of the Woodcutter" in this collection.

—PS

32

The Lie That Can Stand on Its Own

There was once a king in one of the old ancient lands and he had a daughter. He loved his daughter so much that he deterred her from marrying all the princes who came as her suitors. It was too difficult for him to be separated from her. The vizier, seeing so many young men who came to ask her hand in marriage, turned to the king and said, "Oh honored respected king, your Majesty, don't give just meaningless answers to the dukes and princes who come to ask for your daughter's hand in marriage, because they may turn against you. Rather you should give them a challenge. You should ask them to tell you a lie, a real lie that has legs, that has never been heard by anyone before. Then you promise them that, only when one of them has succeeded, can that man have your daughter's hand in marriage. Then you will have no problem. You can be sure that a lie like this has never been found before in the world. And this way you will not make enemies of the sons of any other kings."

One day a shepherd came before the king and promised to tell him a lie that could stand on its own, a real lie.

"Is it possible?" asked the king and became very angry. "Is it possible that I should give my daughter to a shepherd?"

And the vizier said to the king, "Just a minute, your Majesty, let him tell you the lie. And afterwards you will be able to get rid of him."

And on the advice of the vizier, the king allowed the shepherd to tell him his lie in front of all the royal court.

And the shepherd came before the king, stood up tall, and before all the elders and ministers of the court, he opened his mouth and said,

For I am a poor shepherd's son who has nothing. In our house there were never any kinds of food except for an egg. With half the egg I went to

212

buy vegetables, and with the other half, flour. I went to the vegetable seller and, at his place, I bought everything I needed for half the price. And the change that I returned, which was half an agura, I received in cash. And when I went to put the egg in his hand, it fell to the floor, and out of it came a rooster with a great big crown. The rooster ran around the market and I ran after it, and I had to jump over things, and it was a great task to try to catch this rooster. I chased it from house to house until I came to a house where the people were threshing rice. Then the rooster started to help these people with the rice threshing. I raised my voice and shouted because this rooster was mine. But the people in the house calmed me down and said, "Let the rooster thrash only five sacks of rice. We will give you some rice as payment and then you can go on your way."

The threshers did this and there was so much rice that the thresher then gave me. But I had a problem because I did not have a sack to put the rice in. And then I thought and I found the solution. I put my hand under the fold of my clothes and I took out of there two fat bugs. I took their skin off and I sewed them together into a sack. I used their insides for string. Then I put the rice into the sack and closed it with the bug's string and I put the bag onto the back of the rooster. And the two of us went walking across the river. Because I was afraid the bag might fall into the water as we crossed the river, I took the rice, grain by grain, across to the other side of the river. After that I rode on the back of the rooster and we crossed the river. Then I collected all the grains of rice and put them back into the sack and closed the sack, put it on the back of the rooster and we returned home. From all the pressure of the heavy bag of rice, there was a wound on the back of the rooster.

My mother said to me, "Quickly go to the market, and with the half of the agura, buy a nut and with this we will cure the wound." So I did what my mother had suggested. With the coin I bought five nuts. Four of them I ate and the fifth I put on the rooster's wound. And to my great surprise, a tall nut tree immediately grew on the back of the rooster. And I climbed up the tree, and to my surprise, I saw a great wide piece of land that was spread out above my head. I went up to it and there I saw that the whole piece of land was planted with good and juicy watermelons. I cut a big watermelon and I put my knife into it. But the knife sank inside. I put my hand into the watermelon, but I could not find my knife. In order to find the knife, I put in both my legs and my whole body. To my surprise, I found there a man who was a camel herder. And the man asked me, "What are you doing here? Who do you have here?" And I said to him, "I came to look for my knife." And the man laughed at me and said, "My camel ran away from me and it is already forty days that I am looking for it here and I haven't found it. You will not be able to find anything here, let alone your knife."

The king laughed. Then the king turned to one of his servants and told him, "Give the shepherd ten *tomans* and tell him to go. Because these lies cannot stand up."

They gave the shepherd ten *tomans* and he went away.

The next day, it was announced in the town that anyone who could tell the kind a lie that could stand up could have the king's daughter for a wife. And when the shepherd heard this announcement, he went to the market, bought ten big barrels with some of his money, and, with the change, he paid seven porters to bring these barrels to the palace.

The next morning the shepherd presented himself before the king himself.

My father was a very rich king and he lent your father, who was poor, seven barrels full of gold coins. I come now to get from you this debt that your father owed to my father. And here are seven barrels that I have brought with me for you to fill up with the gold.

And the king called out very angrily, "It is known that my father and his father and all our ancestors were kings. And your father and your father's father were only poor shepherds. How can you tell such a terrible crude lie that your father lent my father seven barrels full of gold coins? How can this thing be possible!"

And the shepherd answered him with great confidence:

"If what I say is true, then the gold is mine.
And if what I say is a lie,
then your daughter is surely mine."
Im emet dover pi, Hazahav hoo sheli
V'im sheker bapi, Bitkha hi sheli

So the king brought his beautiful daughter to the shepherd because he was obligated to fulfill his promise. The couple lived all their years together happily ever after.

End of Story Note

IFA 7160 from *With Elders Is Wisdom*, Story #20, collected by Hanina Mizrahi from Akababa, from Iranian Kurdistan.

Tale types: AT 1920F (He Who Says "That's a Lie" Must Pay a Fine); AT 1920 (Contest in Lying); AT 1920F*A (IFA) (I. King promises reward for a story of lies; hears many stories, but does not admit that they are lies. II. Hero relates that king's father borrowed from his father a huge amount of money; king denies it and pays the reward.).

Motif: H509.5 (Test: telling skillful lie).

There are many "Tales of Lying" (AT 1875–1889) in international folktales; they are among some of the oldest stories, including some from Europe, Japan, and Turkey. One such tale, from Denmark, is titled "The Princess Who Always Believed What She Heard."

There are also numerous parallels in Jewish folklore. In fact, the tall tale appears as a predominant genre in rabbinic literature. Yassif explains that "Folklorists have classified such stories in international indexes of motifs and story types as 'tales of lying' or as 'comic legends,' indicating the confusion in the categorization of tales of this type as a clear-cut genre" (p. 182, Yassif). (For more about tall tales in the rabbinic literature, see pp. 182–183 and 187–191 in Yassif's *The Hebrew Folktale*.)

The Sephardic oral tradition also features a significant number of tall tales. This story has variants from Iraq and Turkey, and several from Persian Kurdistan. See "The Great Lie" (IFA 342) and "The Tall Tale of the Merchant's Son" (IFA 7) in *Folktales of Israel* (Noy).

Clever wordplay is a favorite element in Jewish stories from every country, but the tall tale involves a lying contest, usually to win a princess. The lies told by the hero, often a simple shepherd or the youngest brother who is considered a fool, must utilize a combination of wild imagination with outrageous actions. See "A Tall Tale" and "The Seven Lies" in my *Jewish Stories One Generation Tells Another*.

The rhyming reply by the shepherd at the end of the story was rendered in poetic English by Roslyn Bresnick-Perry.

—*PS*

33

The Exchanged Letters

In northern Iraq there was a king who had a son who was very successful in every way; he was very handsome, very wise, and very quick-minded. When the son grew up, the king dreamed a dream that his son, the prince, would become wiser than he and would become an even greater leader. But not only that, there would come a day when the king himself would bow down before his son and wash his feet. And the king would go about the palace with great sadness, for many days, because he didn't know the meaning of this dream. The king felt that he was beginning to hate his son. And, therefore, he even began to be bitter about his life and to cause his son a lot of problems. Every since the dream, whenever the son would do things, the father was never satisfied with what he did. Nothing satisfied the king. In the end he would scold his son and call him a failure. In short, there was no end to the troubles the father made for his son.

The prince saw that his father hated him and, for some reason, he was disappointing his father without any reason. And he thought to himself, "What can I do to be successful in my father's eyes?" But he never found the solution. The prince walked alone in the palace and hated by his father.

One evening he asked his mother, "Please prepare some simple clothes, some food for the way, and some money, for I must leave. I cannot live here anymore. I want to leave the palace and to wander in the world until I find my place in it. It is possible that if I will be far away from home, I will be able to understand the reason for my father's anger and direct my life so that what I accomplish will be more successful."

The queen never understood why her husband was always angry with their son and the reason for his hatred toward him. Once she collected her courage and asked the king the reason for his hatred. But the king shut her up quickly and said, "Don't you dare ask me any more about it."

So the prince went on his way, wandered in the forest and in the fields and on roads that were not really roads, until he left the border of his country. He arrived at a faraway foreign country where nobody knew him. So what did he do? Because he had only a very little bit of money in his pocket, a gift from his mother, he went into a hotel, paid for a week in advance, and registered under an assumed name so nobody would know who he was. The young prince was a very handsome young man and very wise, and also very gentle in his language and his manner. Every day he went out to the streets of the city to visit the marketplaces and talk with people. This continued until he was left without even a penny. He didn't have anything left, even to stay another night at the hotel. He didn't have money even for a meal.

So the young man left this city and went to a different city. There he saw a great house that belonged to a very rich sheik. And the young man was told that this sheik was very hospitable to guests and strangers. For three days, any guest could come in and eat and drink and sleep there. But only on the fourth day would the host ask him about his travels. The young man didn't reveal who he was or his reason for his coming. But the sheik understood that he was very polite and educated. The young man asked if the sheik would accept him as a servant in his house. The sheik agreed because he knew that he wouldn't be poorer if he had to pay one more servant, more than the forty that he already had. But he also decided that he would make him his personal servant.

As time went on, he also became the personal servant to the sheik's beautiful only daughter. No other male servant had ever set foot in her room before. And the other more experienced and older servants were very jealous of the young man. They were jealous that the sheik would prefer him over them. So what did they do? They all got together and decided on a plan to make the sheik hate the young man as much as they did so as to cause him to be thrown out of the house. And then they found the way to deceive the sheik. One of them would go to the sheik and tell him, "When the young man brings food to your daughter, and he is in her room, he hugs and kisses her."

When the sheik heard this, he was very very angry. He called all his forty servants to him and everyone of them verified this false statement. So the sheik ordered that wet switches be brought. Then he called the young man. And without even telling him the reason, the sheik ordered that his other servants beat him on the legs. And when the daughter heard about what the sheik was doing, she went to her mother and begged her to ask the father to let the young man go because he was innocent and had never touched her. And even more so, in her heart, she loved the young man with a great love, even though the two of them had never even exchanged a word between them. Then the daughter threatened that she would kill herself if her father did not stop torturing the young man. Her mother went to her husband, the sheik, and spoke to him and told him that the servants were lying and that there was no truth to what they said. The sheik's anger became even greater because all forty servants had been witnesses before him. It couldn't be a lie. So what did he do? He ordered that the soles of this young man's feet would receive even more whips and then he would be thrown out and left in a dark alley. But before they could even do that, the sheik's wife had managed to put some money into the young man's pocket. The young man lay in the street without even being able to move because the soles of his feet were hurt and swollen from all the whippings.

A man passed by the alley riding on a donkey and saw the wounded young man. He understood that the young man was not a simpleton. He didn't ask any questions but just lifted him and placed him on the donkey and brought him to his house. A month passed and two months passed. The young man got better and his wounds healed. He began to stand on his feet again and walk. The young man thanked his patron but didn't tell him anything about himself. When he left the house of his patron, he went to a different city, very far from the city of the sheik.

In this place, he was taken into the army and became a soldier. In a very short time, he became an outstanding and talented officer. Many years did not pass until he was the head of a whole unit of elite soldiers. During the years that passed since he was thrown out of the sheik's house he did not forget the beautiful daughter. And miracle of miracles, every day he loved her more and more, and that was without even seeing her during all those years. Now, as an elite officer, he searched for ways to know what happened to that daughter in his absence. What did he do?

He dressed up as an ordinary soldier and went out to a junction outside of the city and took the one road that led to the sheik's city.

On the way, he met a wandering Bedouin and began to talk. He found out that the Bedouin wandered from city to city. The young man asked him, "If you would be a messenger for me, I will pay you very well." The Bedouin agreed. The officer wrote a letter and put it in an envelope and made the Bedouin swear, "Take this letter only to the hands of the sheik's daughter, and only you must bring me her answer."

What was written in this letter? The young man had written in it how much he still loved her and how he could never forget her. But what did the messenger do? He opened the letter, read it, and wrote a different letter, for this Bedouin knew how to read and write. And what did he write in this letter? "My love, I'm sending you this letter because I want to know how you have gotten along in life. I have married a woman and I have three children. Please send me an answer." And the messenger closed the envelope and went over the border and arrived at the sheik's palace. He stole into the room of the daughter and gave her the letter and asked for an answer if she wanted to give one. He explained to her that he was going back to the country from where he was sent with the letter. The sheik's daughter read the letter and tears came out of her eyes and she wrote an answer. This is what she wrote: "From all my love and missing you, I have never married. But since you have married, I only wish you happiness and health." The sheik's daughter paid the messenger, closed the envelope, and then remained shut up in the room, quiet, not eating or drinking. What did the messenger do? He opened the envelope, took out the letter and, from such an evil heart, he wrote other words. He wrote, as if the princess had answered herself, that she was happy to hear about his marriage and about his children. She had also married and she also had children. That was what the messenger wrote instead.

The Bedouin brought the letter to the officer of the army. When the young man read her letter, his heart was broken. But what could he do? Everyday he thought only about his love. How could she have married someone else in the meantime. The officer kept the letter, but a small doubt entered his heart. He couldn't believe that she wouldn't have waited for him, after she had seen all his pain and suffering because of her, and without any of it being his true fault. The whole time he thought in his heart, "How could she have married another when the whole time I have stayed faithful?" In the end, he decided to look for the Bedouin in order to hear from him all that had happened in the sheik's daughter's room. Simply he had begun not to believe the Bedouin's story. He also didn't believe that this was the sheik's daughter's handwriting. So what did he do?

He ordered the junction be guarded very heavily and ordered his people to stop anyone who tried to pass through and to bring that person to him for questioning. At the same time, the sheik's daughter began not to believe the letter that she had gotten and the story of the Bedouin. So what did she do? One day, she wore the clothes of a simple Arabic Bedouin and wrapped herself in a long cloak and wrapped her head in a kafia so that no one could really see her face. She took some food for the way and a walking stick and went out in the direction of the place where, according to the Bedouin's story, the army soldier had been stationed on his base. She went for a whole week or more on foot until she arrived at the junction. There she didn't know where to turn. In which direction should she go? All of a sudden, she was arrested by a number of armed soldiers. She didn't talk with any of them. The soldiers didn't let her rest but brought her directly to the tent of their commander. It was obvious that everyone thought that this was a simple Arab. The sheik's daughter immediately recognized the young man, even though many years had passed since the first time that they had met. And the young man who had been beaten and tortured by her father, the sheik, had grown up. And she too had grown up. However, the officer, in spite of this, did not recognize the sheik's daughter. "Spy!" shouted the officer. "Who sent you to spy on my army?" And the stranger asked in a very soft voice to speak with the officer of the unit alone and swore that she did not have any guns or even a knife. And when the bodyguards of the officer went out, she asked, "Where are your wife and your children? I came to say 'hello' to your family."

He answered, "I do not have a wife and I do not have any children. I have never married any woman," answered the officer. And the young woman took out the letter that the messenger had brought her. In the meantime, she took off her long coat and the kafia from her head and there stood before the officer the sheik's daughter whom he had thought about all these years. Then the officer took out of his pocket the letter that she had supposedly sent to him. And it was clear to both of them that they had not written those letters and that everything in them was an absolute lie. The sheik's daughter wanted to immediately marry her love, the choice of her heart, but the officer was much more thoughtful.

First of all, he wanted to take revenge on all those who had hurt him in the past. So what did he do? He ordered his army to prepare for a training trip to the sheik's city. He sent his love back to her house under heavy guard. When the young woman arrived back at her house, she told her parents that she had wanted only to go out to see her country. For up to that time, she had never left her palace.

When the officer arrived with his whole unit at the sheik's city, he invited the sheik to come to him and said, "A number of years ago, a young man served in your house and you had certain suspicions according to the testimony of your forty other servants. You should know that that young man was the king's son. And before other important additional things are revealed, I would like now to see those forty servants hung on a tree for the crime that they caused by the torture of that young man. And if not, I will immediately destroy your whole city."

The sheik got very scared and he collected the forty servants to him, and among them was the Bedouin messenger who had taken the letters back and forth, but who had substituted his own letters. And only afterwards did the officer present himself to the sheik and reveal to him, "I am that young man whom you tortured. I am the king's son of a neighboring country who decided to leave his father's castle and travel in the world. That is how I came to you. That is also the reason your daughter has refused to marry anyone up until now and why I have also remained single. And now, after I have returned the debt I owe to those criminals in your home, I have come to ask for your daughter's hand in marriage so that she can be my wife. I hope that you will forgive me for not doing it according to the custom of our world, that is, that my father is not asking you for your daughter to marry his son."

After the sheik agreed to the marriage, the officer told the king and queen, his parents, everything that had happened to him during the past years that he had been absent from their home and town. The king arrived in the sheik's city and he was very sorry about his thoughts and his deeds after he had had that dream. He kissed his son's hand. But the son did not agree that his father should bow before him. Instead, he gave honor to his father and bowed before him and washed his father's feet.

The wedding was held with all the honor and beauty and abundance. And because of this wedding, all the discord that had existed between the king's country and the sheik's country vanished. And every since then everybody has lived happily after in peace and in prosperity.

End of Story Note

IFA 8820 from *A Tale for Each Month 1970*, Story #2, collected by Moshe Bort from Mordecai Asher of Iraqi-Kurdistan (Noy).

Tale Types: AT 517 (The Boy Who Learned Many Things); AT 725 (The Dream); AT 930 (The Prophecy: I.a. It is foretold that a poor boy is to become the king's son-in-law); AT 930 III. Uriah Letter. (a. The king discovers him and sends him with a letter to the queen with instructions to kill him. b. On the way robbers change the letter so that the queen is instructed to give the princess to the boy in marriage); AT 875 (The Clever Peasant Girl); AT 425 (The Search for the Lost Husband)

Motifs: M312 (Prophecy of future greatness for youth); B312.0.1 (Dream of future greatness); D1812.3.3 (Future revealed in dream); K1837 (Disguise of woman in man's clothes); K2100 (Jealousy of servants); K978 (Uriah letter); K511 (Uriah letter changed); K1355 (Altered letter of execution gives princess to hero); Z71.2 (Formulistic number: Forty).

There are many folktales that open with a dream foretelling the future; sometimes it is to tell the king/rabbi that a child will be born; that they can have a choice between a daughter or else a son who will die by his thirteenth birthday (or will have many tragic situations in his youth); or that a son will be born who will be wiser than the parents who will wash his feet when grown. These dilemmas set up the catalytic factor in the story, as the prophecy dream does in this story. In a way, this is a quest story for the young man to discover himself as well as search for his true love.

In the frame story, the king's son is the hero and in the inner story a poor wanderer. This enables the form of the unlikely hero to become great. According to folklorist Dov Noy, in the archetype of this story it is very possible that there had been a hero who was a shepherd, but with the unification of the two stories, "the king's son" is expelled from his high position in the inner story.

There are many variants of this story, including versions from Persia, Yemen, and Tunisia.

The folkloristic annotations by Dov Noy draw parallels between this story and the biblical tale of Joseph. In this story the king has a prophetic dream about bowing to his son who will become a greater leader and washing his feet (similar to the dreams of Joseph but in which his father and the rest of the family would bow to Joseph); the story then shifts to the prince who is forced to leave home (as Joseph was sold by his brothers). After some adventures, the wandering prince becomes of service to strangers (as Joseph is made Pharoah's assistant); the story of the false sex accusation (as Joseph was accused by Potiphar's wife); and finally in the end, there is the fulfillment of the dream as the family is reunited and the prince shows great honor to his father (as Joseph and his family are reunited and he also shows honor to Jacob).

—PS

34

The Neighbor in Paradise

The head rabbi of the Jews in a certain city was a wise and good man who feared God. He was a Torah scholar. The rabbi always wanted to hear about the different members of his community for he wanted to be sure that they would stay on the right path.

Once, in a dream, he asked Elijah the Prophet, "After my death, who will be my neighbor in Paradise?"

And that same night, in a dream, Elijah the Prophet answered him, "Your neighbor in Paradise will be that well-known robber who is now the mayor of such and such town."

The rabbi was puzzled by Elijah's reply. A robber as his neighbor in Paradise? How could that be possible? Was that a just reward? So he went to that town, which was very far away, in order to meet the man who, according to Elijah the Prophet, would be sharing the same bench with him in the Garden of Eden.

As the rabbi was walking along one of the streets of the city, he met a young boy and asked him, "Who is this man who is the mayor of this city? I want to meet him."

The boy replied, "Rabbi, he is the richest man of our town and owns an inn. But you who are such a great and famous rabbi, how is it that you come to speak to such a man who hates justice and rabbis, too?"

"No matter. Show me where he lives." And the rabbi arrived at the inn of the mayor. As he greeted him, the rabbi blessed the mayor with peace. But the mayor did not answer, and so giving the rabbi the impression that he, the mayor, did not want to talk with him. But the rabbi stayed, waiting in his place. After some time, the mayor brought the rabbi into his inn and he showed him to a bedroom. And then, all of a sudden, the mayor said, "Wait a moment. I have something to do and when I finish, I will speak with you." Then the mayor went into the next room and closed the door. When the rabbi looked through the key hole at what the mayor was doing, he saw him praying, wrapped in a *tallit* and *tfillin*. The rabbi now understood that the mayor was really a righteous man who is hiding his true identity, because, for some reason, he didn't want to make known his true deeds.

After more time had passed, the rabbi saw people going into the room of the owner of the inn. They gave the mayor all kinds of accounts of the money he had given to them. And all the money had been given apparently for *tzedakah* and the needy. And the rabbi heard all about the widows who received money for the education of their children, and about Jewish merchants who were saved from bankruptcy, and more and more. And even though these things were said in whispers, the rabbi, who had put his ear to the wall, heard everything.

All of sudden, some servants came to the place and told the mayor that there are 600 young men and young women from near Spain who were caught by thieves. These thieves were asking for a ransom of 2000 dinari for the release of these Jews. The mayor made sure that this money was immediately paid to the thieves and that the kidnapped young people were to be brought to him.

After a few days, they were brought to him and they were beautiful young men and young women. The rich man arranged a place for them in his great courtyard. After they were all settled in the courtyard, he said to them in a harsh voice, pretending to be angry, "From now on you are my workers. I freed you and I paid for you. I have the right to take you out to be killed. But if you listen to what I have to say, I will free you—but only on one condition, that each young man will choose the young woman who will be his wife—and she must consent."

Then he turned to the rabbi and said, "When each young man has chosen the young woman to be his wife, you must make sure that they will have a *chuppah* and marry according to the laws of Moshe and Yisrael." And the rabbi did what the mayor said for he also wished to save prisoners.

That evening they held a splendid wedding celebration with 300 couples and all the guests from the community.

A few days after the weddings, the rich owner of the inn gave every young couple a gift of money so that they could begin their lives together. The rabbi sat the whole time in the mayor's house and watched everything that was happening.

And one night, near midnight, the rabbi heard a knock on the door and the voice of a young woman. And the rabbi listened because he wanted to know what a strange woman alone could ask from the mayor at midnight. And in his heart he was suspicious because he thought something secret was going on between this woman and the mayor. How shocked the rabbi was when he heard what the woman said, "My husband died a few days ago and I have stayed alone, a widow, taking care of many children. I have just put them to bed and to sleep and I have come to you to ask you for help, for a loan so I could support my poor orphaned children."

"Here, take this money," said the mayor as he gave her a whole handful of money. "And this should help you for at least a year. During that time, you must remember your husband. Only at the end of the year you should look for another good person in order to marry so that you will not remain alone, as a widow, until the end of your life."

And when the rabbi heard this, he went into the room of the secret righteous man and said to him, "There is a rumor that you were once a thief and that you act very cruelly to all of God's creatures. But I have now seen that you have actually gone back, *hazarta b'tshuva*, and that you are a righteous man in all your ways. Tell me your story."

And the mayor told the rabbi this story:

> Ever since I was a young child, I was involved only in embezzlement, robbery, and thievery. I had a whole list of sins on my soul. For forty years I did these terrible things.
>
> One day I decided to change my ways, *lahzor b'tshuva*, because I decided in my heart and said to myself, "All these bad things I have done until now have been a mistake. From now on I will work for God and I will work with God and in a straightforward and just way." And I did just that.
>
> So one day I went to the desert and in my pocket I had one gold coin. I called out, "God, I will begin my good deeds from today. And whatever I earn from this gold coin, I will divide into two. One part will be donated to God by helping Jews and other people. The other part I will keep for

me." And then I went back to town and became a merchant of small trifles. Very slowly I began to become rich. My possessions grew.

As I had promised in my oath, I gave one part of my earnings to *tzedakah* for the poor people. And whatever I kept for myself, I invested in business. Whenever I gave money to the poor people, I gave it anonymously, as a secret donation. And I also opened a very large restaurant and built a very beautiful inn. And when the people of the town saw that this Jew was one of the richest in the town, they made me the mayor. Of course none of the residents in the town knew about my good deeds because I would give my gifts to the poor and to the widows and orphans only through messengers. And these messengers were sworn never to reveal who had sent them. So that's how it was with all my business negotiations. I always wore a masked expression as though I were a person who could never perform a good deed.

The rabbi waited until the mayor had finished his story. Then he said, "It will be my good fortune that you will be my neighbor in Paradise after both of our souls find full rest under the shade of the wings of the *shekhinah*. God blesses the man who is righteous in all good deeds for all people."

When the rabbi returned to his town, he was no longer puzzled by Elijah's answer.

And that's how it has been for all these years.

End of Story Note

IFA 9314 from *A Tale for Each Month 1972*, Story #2, collected by Zalman Baharav from Semion Plagashvili from Georgia (Cheichel-Hechal).

Tale Type: AT 809* A (IFA) (The Companion in Paradise)

There are parallels of this story from Morocco, Persia, Israel-Sephardi, and Russia. It is usually the rabbi who wants to know who will be his neighbor in Paradise, although in the Russian version it is the Baal Shem Tov. The "neighbor" is often a butcher, a water drawer, a simple man, a blacksmith, and, in our story, a former robber.

This Jewish oikotype (AT809*A) belongs to the category of religious stories. The international tale type is AT 809* (Rich Man Allowed to Stay in Heaven) The oikotype form is as follows: the righteous man (the rabbi or *talmud chakham*) is told in a dream (through Elijah the Prophet) that his neighbor in heaven will be a simple/ignorant man or a miser, etc. The righteous man is shocked and goes out to search for this man to discover why that person won the right to sit next to him in Paradise. In the end, he discovers that it is due to some good deed or mitzvah that he deserves the place in Paradise. The good deed is usually one or all of the following: ransoming of prisoners, giving a dowry for a poor bride or preparing weddings for poor people, supporting a widow secretly.

This oikotype can exist only in a tradition that believes in the rewards for people in the next world. As the Talmud says: "The reward for a mitzva will be in the next world." (*Kiddushin* 38:72). Many other versions of this Jewish oikotype are found in talmudic-midrashic tales and in medieval literature.

Variants of this story can be found in *Tanhuma B* (Introduction), in Wistinetski (1538), *Yalkut Sippurim Umidrashim* (1923), and in several versions in Moses Gaster's *The Exempla of the Rabbis*. There are a number of versions in the Israel Folktale Archives, including IFA 9518 ("Due to the Ransoming of Prisoners") and IFA 5804 ("Paradise Won in an Hour). See "A Companion in the World-to-Come" in my *Jewish Stories One Generation Tells Another*.

—*PS*

35

Caliph Harun al-Rashid

One day Caliph Harun al-Rashid went out for a visit to walk around the town in the disguise of an ordinary citizen. He brought along with him the head of his government, the vizier Ja'afar. During their walk, in one of the fields, they saw a woman burning wood under a teapot in which the water was boiling. Caliph Harun asked Ja'afar, "Do you hear what the water is singing?" "The water is singing?" asked Ja'afar. "I've never heard such a thing in my life." "Yes, yes," answered Caliph Harun. "I will give you one week for you to bring me the answer to this question, 'What is the water singing?' And if not, then I will have you hung."

At hearing this, Ja'afar, as you can imagine, was a very sad man. He didn't know where to go to solve this puzzle. He told his wife what happened. He began to ask his neighbors and other people he knew—but no one could help him. Three days passed and he still didn't know how to solve this problem. Ja'afar, in great despair, went out as a dervish into the field. He would talk to all the passersby but still no one could help him. The water and food he had taken with him were finished and he was hungry. Four days passed and his despair grew. So what did he do? He started on the path to return to his home. Walking next to him was an old man with a bent back from the heavy pack he was carrying. He asked Ja'afar for help. "Lift me, and I will lift you," answered Ja'afar. "You are such a stupid man," answered the old man. "How can I lift you when I am asking for help with what is on my back? And you want me to lift you up? What people there are in this world. You don't have any kind of sack on your back. How do you want me to help you? Go! Go

away," the old man said. Ja'afar knew then that the old man didn't
understand him or the clue that he had given him. So he continued on
his way, and his desperation grew deeper. As he was listening to the
people on the way, he suddenly heard in the distance a voice crying for
help, "Oi va voy! Help me!" And Ja'afar asked, "What is it? What is
happening?" And the people told him that there was a funeral. Ja'afar
realized that this might be a place to meet many new people, and maybe
he could find someone who was wise. But he wanted to test them before
asking his question. So Ja'afar turned to the people accompanying the
coffin and asked, "Is the old man in the coffin alive or dead?" "Oh you
stupid man," said one of the people passing by in the funeral. "We don't
go to bury a man who is alive. Of course he is dead! What kind of
question is this? It is not appropriate!" And Ja'afar didn't say anything
more and passed by quietly. Then he saw a gardener who was cutting
grass. He asked him if he had cut the grass evenly or not. This gardener
said, "Of course you can see that I am cutting all the grass myself." And
again Ja'afar passed by quietly and he saw another gardener who was
cutting all the grasses and asked him if he had cut or not. And the
gardener replied, "But you already see that I have already cut all the grass
on the side." And again he passed quietly. Now he saw that it was
evening and he became tired and hungry and he was worried that
another day had passed. He stopped at a grove to rest.

Meanwhile, the old man, who was carrying that great sack on his
back, finally arrived at his home. He took his great burden from his
shoulders and he began to sigh, "What kind of people are there in this
world. I'm a tired old man with a sack on my shoulders and there is no
one to take pity on me. Finally when I meet a man in the field, he answers
my request for help with "You lift me and I will lift you" instead of
helping me. He wants me to *lift* him. Isn't it enough that he didn't help
me but he wants me to lift him?"

The old man's daughter heard and understood the meaning of that
answer immediately, because she was very wise. She understood that he
had meant that her father should lift this man spiritually. "Father, that
man was obviously full of worries and wanted you to help him solve his
problems that filled his soul. Therefore, he told you to 'lift' him and he
would lift you. But you didn't understand him," explained the daughter.
"All right," said the father, "then listen to the other stupid questions he

asked without any kind of sense. We were still walking when we heard a wailing voice and we saw a funeral pass by. He asked if the man in the coffin was dead or alive. And then the next person who came up to him scolded him for even saying such a thing when it was obvious that they were burying someone who was dead." And the daughter said, "Wait, I will explain it to you. When a person dies, and he leaves children and a good name, then he is definitely not dead. Every time someone says his name in a good way, he is alive." And the old man began to nod his head and understood, for the first time, how wise his daughter was. And then he continued to ask his daughter, "But what about the grass?" And he told his daughter about that question. "Father, if the grass is cut evenly, then it can grow and live. But if it's cut in clumps, it will not be even and it will clump together and die. Father, that man is probably tired and hungry. Go call him. We are known as people who offer hospitality to guests. Since you were with him, you probably know in which direction he went." And the wise daughter thought to herself that this man is very wise.

"Father, take these eggs and twelve pita breads and tell him, 'Your days are good, your months are good, and also your years are good.'" The old man went to find the traveler, but, on the way, he became hungry so he sat down and ate a few of the eggs. When he arrived in the field where Ja'afar was, he found him lying on the ground under a tree, lost deep in thought. "Friend, dear friend, I went back to my house and told my daughter everything that happened between us on the way and she sent you these eggs and bread and told me to tell you, 'Your days are good, your months are good, and your years are good.'" And Ja'afar took the eggs and began to count. After he had counted he said to the old man, "Tell you daughter, 'Your days, your months, and your years are not good.'" So the old man went back to his house and told the daughter what Ja'afar had said. "Father," she said, "this man was tired and hungry. Did any of the eggs break on the way?" "No, my daughter, but I was hungry and I ate a few on the way." Then the daughter understood and said, "Father, go and ask the man to come to the house." The old man went and invited Ja'afar to come with him. When they arrived, he brought him water to wash and let him eat and rest. Afterward, they began to talk between them. And Ja'afar said to the daughter, "Tell me, did you send your father to tell me 'Your days are good, your months are good, and your years are good?' But I counted the eggs and there were some that were missing." "Yes, sir," answered the daughter. "I asked my father when he came home what was your reply. When you answered that they were not good, I understood that my father ate some of them." And Ja'afar understood that this young woman had to be incredibly wise, especially after her father had told her how she had explained all of his questions. Then she turned to Ja'afar and asked him if he was willing to tell her what was troublesome to him.

So he began to tell her the main problem that was bothering him. "I'm the head of the government for Caliph Harun al-Rashid. And one day we went out disguised in ordinary clothing. We went from place to place. At one place a woman was burning wood underneath the teapot. We could hear the boiling sound of the water. And Caliph Harun turned to me and asked me, "What is the water singing?" And I answered, "The water is singing?" I was shocked and surprised at his question for I never knew that water could sing. But again he asked me if I knew what the water was singing. 'I will give you a week and, at the end of that time, if you bring me the answer, then all will be well. But if you don't, then I will have you hung on the highest tree.' And here I am and five days have already passed but still I have found no answer to this question."

"Yes sir, I will help you," answered the young woman. "Water indeed does sing. It sings songs and talks. It only needs ears to listen to it and all who listen to the water will understand it. And what the waters sing and say I will tell you." Ja'afar sighed and at the same time he got very excited and said, "If you tell me, I will give you half of what I own." "I don't need that," answered the young woman. "Just wait and listen. The water is saying this, 'I water the valley where there are trees and now the trees are burning me.'" And when Ja'afar heard this wise wonderful answer, he didn't know what to say to her or what to give her. He was filled with so much relief and excitement. He gave her all the gold and silver he carried, even the watch he had. And then he returned to the house of Caliph singing on his way.

When the Caliph saw him, he understood that he already had the answer to the question. "Sit down and tell me everything you know. Maybe you should first rest and drink something and afterwards you will tell me. It looks to me as though you have the answer to my question," said Harun al-Rashid. "Yes, sir, I have the answer to the problem you put before me. The water does sing, it sings and it also talks. It says, 'I water the valley where there are many trees and now these trees are burning me." The Caliph was happy with the answer, but he knew that it wasn't Ja'afar himself who solved the problem. "Tell me," said the Caliph, "tell me truthfully, and don't be afraid for I have freed you from this punishment, who gave you the answer." Ja'afar began to tell him everything that happened to him and the Caliph knew that this young woman had to be very wise. He asked that she be brought to him, for he wanted himself to test her.

Ja'afar went to her home and told her what he had told the Caliph about her wisdom. Then he told her that the Caliph wanted to speak with her himself. "The Caliph has told me that he would like to marry you and you will be a queen and live in a palace and you will have servants and be happy." But she refused. "I don't need a palace. I am happy now," answered the young woman. But Ja'afar persisted until she finally agreed, but added, "I will not go immediately to meet the Caliph al-Rashid. I also need a wise husband and so I will ask him three questions first. If he answers these questions, then I will marry him." "Good," said Ja'afar. "Tell me the three questions you want to ask the Caliph and I will ask him for you."

The young woman said, "Here is the first questions. There's a blind man that stands at one end of a bridge. Everyone who passes by him, instead of helping him, gives him a slap on his head and tells him 'It is good for you.' Why is this? The second question: There is a welder who comes every morning and gives out the work schedule to his workers. Every morning his eyes are shiny and bright but every evening they are swollen. Since he never works in the shop, what is the reason for this? The third question: There is a shoemaker who sits beneath the tower of the mosque and he sits there and sews one piece of leather every day instead of working. He looks up at the tower and asks, 'Why? Why is this?' If the king can solve these three questions, then I will marry him."

Ja'afar went to the Caliph Harun al-Rashid and told him everything that happened between him and the young woman. And the Caliph said to Ja'afar, "You have brought me these questions, then go and find me the answers!" Poor Ja'afar! He narrowly gets out of one problem and jumps into another. However, Ja'afar can't refuse the command of the

Caliph. Ja'afar set out on the journey to go from place to place until he would meet that certain blind man.

One day he found the bridge and the blind man who was receiving slaps on the head instead of coins. And, yes, people were telling him, "Good for you! You deserve it!" as they slapped him. He approached the blind man and asked, "Tell me why they hit you and don't help you? And why are you quiet about it?" asked Ja'afar.

"It is true that I deserve it. What else can I say?" answered the blind man.

And Ja'afar thought to himself, "Is there such a man that will say I deserve it about himself?"

The blind man then said, "Come to my house and I will tell you." And Ja'afar went with him. The old man asked his daughter to serve the guest food, but Ja'afar refused saying, "First tell me and afterwards I will eat." "Don't worry, I will tell you for I invited you here to hear my story."

And the blind man started his story.

My mother suffered from me when I was a child and she wanted to get rid of me. But because she couldn't, she gave me to the builder to work. She said to him, "Please do me a favor and take this boy. He will help you." And the builder agreed. And one day this builder received work as a contractor in a field. The builder was successful and he liked me and my work. He then went to my mother and said, "Give me the boy and I will take him with me." So the builder took me, along with ten donkeys that had all our tools and possessions on their backs. After a long trip we got to the place. We ate and we rested and the next morning we started to work. The builder began to dig and as he dug, the shovel got stuck on something metal. When the builder heard the sound, he carefully dug out a metal frame with a slab of marble. On this marble was written: "Whosoever finds this marble will find beneath it *pookh*. But there are two types of this *pookh*. On the right side there is this *pookh* that, if you put it on your eye, you will find a treasure. But if you look on the other side, the person who puts it on his eye will be blind."

The builder put on the eye paint from the right side and what did he see? Gold and diamonds and pearls and all kinds of precious stones and silver. He took the donkeys and filled their sacks. When I asked him what it was, he didn't want to tell me, but I understood: "You don't deserve anything. You are only my worker." "But sir," I said, "I also need money and some of this treasure. All I want is one donkey from all your donkeys." So the builder gave the donkey to me and we continued on our way. But then I again began to ask for more. "What do you want?" asked the builder. Then I told him I wanted half of what he had. "Half for you. Half for me." I demanded. We argued and I threatened him, so he gave me what I asked for.

But after a while, I again made some demands for more. "You are already old, you have seen a lot of life and I am still young." "What do you want?" asked the builder.

Finally, after another argument the builder agreed and said, "Take it all!"

But then I said with suspicion, "What do you have? You wouldn't give me the entire treasure if you didn't have something even better, a special secret."

"Everything I did for you was not enough! Everything I gave you was still not enough! You are still looking for other things. I took the *pookh* from the right side and this revealed there was a treasure. And I knew also what there was on the other side," continued the builder, "if you put the eye paint on your eye from the other side, you would become blind."

"You are lying," I said. "With the other eye paint I will surely find something even better."

"What are you saying? Don't do it. I will ask you not to put it on your eye. Your mother gave you to me to work but also to watch after you and I must return you to her. Take all of it. Take anything you want, but don't put it on your eye."

But I didn't listen and I put the eye paint on my other eye. So I became blind. So don't I deserve it? asked the blind man.

Hearing this story unfold, Ja'afar thought to himself that it was true. How foolish this blind man was after all. Then he turned to him and asked him if he knew about a welder and the blind man told him where the welder could be found in Baghdad. The blind man told him which road to take and Ja'afar took that road and traveled to Baghdad. He found that certain welder who opened up the store in the morning, who fixed the work schedule and then left. And Ja'afar approached him and asked if he could work for him. The welder answered that he had no work right now but to come back the following week. Ja'afar stayed in Baghdad asking about the welder. The following week he went back and was hired. After a time, he and the other workers became friends. One day he began to ask the welder why he opens up his store so fast and his eyes are so bright and sparkling, but in the evening when he returns to close the store, his eyes are red and swollen even though he hasn't worked. The welder said, "I will ask you not to reawaken all the troubles in my heart."

Then they continued to talk about many different subjects. One day the welder invited him to come to his home. Ja'afar went with him and the welder began to tell him his story.

I am, as you have seen, a welder. I sell welding tools and I support my family with this work. When I was younger I got married to a woman from a good family. One day I felt like going to Istanbul. It was the same day the king died. In Istanbul they had a very strange custom in order to appoint a new king. They let a bird fly out and on whose head the bird lands, that person will become the new king. The bird flew and came to my head. But the heads of government didn't agree on my becoming their king. "This is a stranger. How can we make him king. We must let the bird fly again." So they let the bird fly again and once again and many other times, the bird landed only on my head. So I became king of Turkey and I ruled there fourteen years.

During that time I got it into my head to go back to Baghdad to my home and to see my wife. That time there was a wall around the city and there weren't many visitors. But because I came suddenly, no one knew that I was arriving. I found my house open and I went into the house and what did I see? I saw my wife sitting on the bed and next to her a young man talking quietly with her. When I saw this, I grew so jealous that I took out my sword and killed them both without asking for any explanation. As they were lying on the bed bleeding, my wife said to me, "Why did you do this, my husband? You left me pregnant. I did not see you again for fourteen years. This is your son." But it was already too late for I had killed them both, without knowing, without asking. I found myself guilty. So I dug them a grave and every day I go to cry for them at the cemetery. Don't you think I deserve this?

And Ja'afar consoled him and said, "God will help you." Ja'afar asked him "Maybe you know where there is a shoemaker" and explained what he was looking for. "Do you know where he might be?" "Oh," the welder said, "he is in Chalab on such-and-such street." So Ja'afar then went to Chalab, a town in Syria where many Jews live.

In Chalab he found the shoemaker and he saw how he kept working on the same piece of leather. Every so often he would raise his eyes to the tower. "What is this?" Ja'afar asked. The shoemaker invited him to his home and said to him,

> Here you see, I am working as a shoemaker. One day, during my work, a hawk came to me and took me in his wings and flew and flew until we arrived at a great and beautiful palace. The moment we arrived there, there were seven young women who welcomed me. They brought me into the palace and gave me to seven other young women who brought me in to wash. What a beautiful bath it was, as if from heaven. I was refreshed. I felt as if I had a whole new soul. When I got out of the bath, still other young women took me to a dining room and there was all kinds of good food, chicken and pheasant, fruits and vegetables, sweets, and they fed me. I can't even describe to you how good it was for I had never found such a day before. It was marvelous. At night I slept next to forty young women. And you would think I would be happy with my life, but on the fortieth night, the head of these women came and, from the way she moved, I wanted to get closer to her. But as I did, she stopped me and said, "Man, isn't it enough for you, forty young women and forty nights." I saw that she was right so I went back. The second night she came and again I wanted to go to her. But then she said the same thing and so I returned to my room. But on the third night, she really made me crazy. And I again went up to her. This time she said it was enough for me. "Go back to your place." And a great wind came and brought me back. And now all the time I look up and ask, "Why?" Maybe the special wind will come again. But it has never happened.

So Ja'afar collected all the stories and went back to the Caliph. The Caliph was happy to see Ja'afar back. He told him to take many camels and many gifts and to go to the young woman and tell her all the answers and to bring her to the palace. The young woman was happy to hear the stories and agreed to marry the Caliph. And so she went to the Caliph. And he also wanted to show that, even though he was marrying a wise young woman, that this young woman was not wiser than he was. So he asked her three questions before the wedding. And he said to her, "Even though I have brought you to me, I will not marry you until you answer these three questions before the wedding." And she said to him, "Ask them." And the king brought out a jar filled with ninety-nine liters of liquid and closed it and sealed it with wax and his seal and said to her, "I'm about to leave the country but upon my return I want to see that there are 100 liters of water without the seal being broken." The second question, "I have a horse, a female horse. I will take the male horse. But upon my return to this country I want to see that there be a foal that is just like the male horse." And the third question, "I will leave you a virgin. And when I come back, I want to see a child that looks just like me." "Good," she said. And so he left her and went on his way. And she bid him peace and a good trip. He gave her permission to be the ruler in his place.

This young woman was an even better ruler than the Caliph. And she became known for her wisdom and her knowledge. Three months after the Caliph had left, she began to think what she would do to answer and solve these questions. She called the head of government to her and said, "I want 20,000 soldiers here in one hour. And when they came she dressed them all in uniforms of the Sheik of Persia and she also wore clothes of the daughter of the Sheik. She asked the head of the government for an unlimited time away from the palace and she also asked him to fulfill her duties as ruler of the country. She went with all the soldiers until she arrived exactly in front of Caliph Harun al-Rashid. He was very angry and surprised about the situation and didn't know what the matter was. He was afraid and sent messages to the daughter of the Sheik to know if she was coming for peace or for war. She answered that she was coming for peace, and the Caliph was happy. He went to visit her.

After they had drunk coffee, which was the custom, she suggested they play chess. The Caliph asked what they would be playing for? She answered, "The person who wins can ask for anything he or she wants." And the young woman won and the Caliph said, "Now you can ask for your prize, whatever you want you will receive." "I don't want any-thing," she said, "only your seal." Immediately he gave it to her and she went back to her tent. She took the jar with the ninety-nine liters of water and opened it and put in one more liter. Then she resealed it with the king's seal.

After a week, as was customary with royalty, she returned the visit and the Caliph suggested they play chess again. And again she won. This time she asked for his horse. She took his horse and released it with the female horse. After two weeks he went to visit her and asked to play chess once more. And again with the same conditions. This time she lost—on purpose. And this time when he began to look at her, she told him, "Don't be embarrassed. You must ask for anything you want. As we have agreed, whatever you, the winner, asks for I will do." "No, no, we were only joking," he said. "But no, not joking, for the other times you fulfilled my requests. We are royalty and our agreements are agreements. I have given you my word," replied the young woman.

So the Caliph stayed with her a long time until she found that she was going to have a child. She returned the horse and his seal to him, and said, "Now I will ask you one more thing before I leave—a signed paper that says that we have played chess according to these conditions and that we have fulfilled them." She took this paper and went back to the palace.

During the year, the female horse gave birth to a foal that resembled the Caliph's horse. And the young woman gave birth to a son who looked exactly like the Caliph. After four years, the Caliph returned. Everyone came out to welcome him back home. The young woman also came to greet him, but she left her son at home. When they met, they began to talk.

After the Caliph had rested, he began to ask the young woman if she had fulfilled his requests, for, if she had, she could be his wife, according to his conditions and according to law. "Yes, your Highness," and she smiled, "I have done all that you have asked. Here is the jar that you have given me with only ninety-nine liters. Look at the seal, for it is the same seal. It is impossible to duplicate it." He opened up the jar, remeasured the contents, and found that, indeed, there were 100 liters, and not ninety-nine. He was shocked and thought to himself that she must indeed be a demon. But he did not say this out loud. He asked where the female horse was and if there was already a foal. And she said, "Your Highness, over there, in the garden, is the female horse." He went out to look and saw the female horse exactly like he had left it with a foal exactly like the horse that he had taken with him. And then he said to her, "And where is the child?" And she said, "Look, he is playing outside with his nursemaid." When he saw that the boy looked exactly like him, he took out his sword and wanted to kill him. "Where did you get this boy?" And she called out, "From me, your Highness! And from the same person who had given me this document." And she took out the document that he had signed after their chess game and said, "Whoever gave me this document is the father of my son." And the Caliph was very impressed with the wisdom and the cleverness of this young woman. And he said to her, "You are my true wife."

The young woman and the Caliph were married according to the law and custom and they lived in great happiness.

End of Story Notes

IFA 1670 collected by Sima Gabai from Adon Sofer, from Iraq. This story has not appeared in published form.

Tale Types: AT 875 (The Clever Peasant Girl): AT 891 (The Man Who Deserts his Wife and Sets Her the Task of Bearing Him a Child); AT 876 (The Clever Maiden and the Suitors).

Motifs: J1111 (Clever girl); H61.1.1.1 (Clever daughter construes enigmatic sayings); K1814 (Disguised as a courtesan, wife makes love to her husband); H561.1 (Clever peasant girl asked riddles by king); H373 (Bride test: performance of tasks): H580 (Enigmatic statements); H1010 (Impossible tasks); H1050 (Paradoxical tasks); J1545.4 (The exiled wife's dearest possession); H1385.4 (Quest for vanished husband); H171.2 (Bird indicates election of emperor); L165 (Lowly boy becomes king); H586.3 (One traveler to another: Let us carry each other and shorten the way); H586 (Riddling remarks of traveling companion interpreted by girl at end of journey).

This folktale revolves around riddling and imaginative questions asked by the king of his advisor. Only the daughter of a certain old man who has an encounter with the advisor can wisely interpret these riddles and questions. This is similar to many folktales of the "Clever Peasant Girl" tale type, such as "The Dream Interpreter" (where some of the riddles are the same) and "The Innkeeper's Wise Daughter" in my *Jewish Stories One Generation Tells Another* and "The Emir, the Jewish Advisor, and the Sheep" in this collection.

The theme of a bird choosing the king, which is in one of the inner stories, can be found in IFA 280 from Iraq, "A Servant When He Reigns" in *Folktales of Israel* (Noy) and two versions of this tale: "The Bird of Happiness" in *Next Year in Jerusalem* (Schwartz) and "The Reminder" in *Who Knows Ten?* (Cone).

In one of the inner stories about the welder, he explains why his eyes are so red by the end of the day. The story he tells is of arriving home after an absence of many years and finding his wife with a man. In a jealous rage he kills them both, only to discover the man was actually his now-grown son. Compare this impulsive reaction to anger with the advice to "restrain your anger" found in the story "Sleep On It" in *Sefer*

Hasidim (Wistinetski) and this author's mother's version retold in the Introduction of my *Jewish Stories One Generation Tells Another.* See also "Wisdom for Sale" in that same anthology. For a story with many elements of this tale, see "The Emir, the Jewish Advisor, and the Sheep" in this collection.

The name of the Caliph Harun al-Rashid and his vizier Ja'afar appear in "The Tale of the Three Apples" in *The Arabian Nights.* Harun al-Rashid was the caliph of Baghdad in 786–809.

—PS

36

Ungrateful Men

There was once a very rich merchant, a widower, and he had a one and only son who was the main source of his happiness. This son was known for giving respect and honor to other people and he himself was very honored and respected. One day the merchant got very sick and realized that he was coming to the end of his days. Before he died, he called his only son and said to him. "My son, I am about to give my soul back to God and I want to warn you. Don't put any trust in people because most of them are very ungrateful. Instead know that it is possible to give all kinds of help to other animals. And that most of them are very grateful and they will never repay you bad for good." And not long after, the merchant died. The son mourned for a long time. Finally, the son decided to move to another country. He got up from his mourning, sold all of his possessions, and, taking the money with him, he went on his way.

In the desert, he saw a snake that was hurt. Part of his tail had been cut and the snake was suffering terribly from pain. The merchant remembered his father's last words. He quickly went and took out of his sack some bandages and bandaged the snake's wound and went on his way.

And then he saw, not far in the distance, a chicken that was wounded in both of its legs. And from time to time it tried to get up but it would just keep falling and lay in the sand and dust. The merchant's son began very tenderly to take care of this wounded chicken and gave it some of his own bread and stayed until the chicken was able to get up and walk around and even fly.

Then the merchant's son continued on his way until he arrived at a hill that was not too high, a hill of sand. From within it, a person's head stuck out. The merchant's son got out his water jug from his sack and gave this man something to drink. The water immediately revived the man's soul. And, afterward, the merchant's son, with his two hands, began to scrape the sand away from this man's head. And during this work, which was with great effort, he remembered his father's last words. But he didn't stop until he was able to get the man out of the sand. For some time, the man stood there as if he were in shock. But when he came to himself, he began to thank his rescuer and bless him. The merchant's son invited him to eat with him. And during the meal he asked the man how he got to be buried in the sand.

And the man told him, "I was a very rich merchant but evil people tricked me and I went bankrupt. And because of this I had to run away. It was two days after I arrived in this desert when, all of a sudden, a great sand storm started and the sand got in my eyes and blinded me. I fell into this pit and the sand covered me."

"And where are you going?" asked the merchant's son.

"It really doesn't matter to me, as long as I don't go back to that country," answered the man.

"I feel that way too," said the merchant's son. "Let's go together."

"Good," said the man. "I will be your slave all the days of my life. It is, after all, to you that I owe my life."

After two days of walking, the two men came to another country. The merchant's son began to conduct business with some of the money he had and the same man that he had saved was always next to him wherever he worked. The merchant's son lost all his money in his business dealings and it was all very bad. But the sharp eyes of the chicken discovered the situation. The chicken immediately went to tell all this to the snake. And after they talked between them, the two of them decided that they must repay the merchant's son for the good deeds he did for them.

"But how will we do it?" asked the chicken. "I, for instance, know a hiding place of diamonds. And with a very clean conscience, I would give this to the very good person who did those good deeds to help us," said the chicken.

"Good!" judged the snake. "I will bring those diamonds to the man."

So the chicken led the snake to the place where all these diamonds were hidden. In addition, there were many other precious stones. The snake took the biggest diamond and brought it to where the merchant's son lived and placed it next to his bed. When the merchant's son got up in the morning, he saw the diamond. He took it and went with it to a diamond merchant. The diamond merchant immediately wanted to buy it for a large sum of money. And when the merchant's son told him that he would go to a different diamond merchant, since he was not satisfied with the sum, he immediately received an additional amount of money. So he sold the diamond. The merchant's son went home with a light heart, but he could not sleep. "Who is it that could have brought me such a valuable diamond?" he thought. His curiosity grew even more when the next morning he found another big diamond. He decided that the next night he would remain awake so he could see who was bringing him this treasure.

But to no use. He never succeeded in finding out anything.

But, in the meantime, the man, whom the merchant's son had saved from a sure death, began to think, "From where does my master get all this money? The business dealings he had up until now have brought him only great losses." And this man could not sleep either and he decided to ask the merchant's son about it. And when he asked and received only a vague answer, he got very angry at him. So what did he do? He went directly to the king and told him, "I am a servant for a man who has lost all his vast inheritance, and yet, everyday, he gets richer and richer. Doesn't that lead to suspicion about where he gets his money— that his source might be a dishonest one?"

"You are right," announced the king. And he ordered that the merchant's son be imprisoned. The young man was brought before the king and asked about the source of all his money. "I know that all the money you received from your father's inheritance you lost in your failed business dealings."

"I will tell you, my king, that I did not steal this money but it is a blessing from God."

"Be quiet," answered the king. "Who are you trying to tell that you do not know the source of this money, that this is a blessing from God.

Throw him in the jail," commanded the king. "And if you do not tell me the source of your money in three days, I will order that you be hung from the highest tree."

In the meantime, when the snake brought the diamond as was his custom, and he put it on the pillow of the young man, he realized that his good-deed doer was no longer at home. And he went quickly to tell this to the chicken. The two of them began to look for him until they found that the merchant's son was in great trouble and in prison.

"I will teach them a lesson," said the snake. The snake went into the prince's room and wound himself around the prince's neck. The king and the queen almost died from fright when they saw that their son's life was in such danger. They called for the court doctors and their servants, but everybody stood helpless and shaking from fear.

At this moment the chicken came in front of the king and asked him, "Would you really like to see three people die at the same time: the merchant's son, your son and you, yourself? How is it that you are such a just and right king, and yet, how could you commit so terrible a crime? The man whom you threw into the prison did not steal the money. The snake and I remembered a great deed that this man had done for us and we have brought him all this wealth. And the man who told on him is a very greedy man and very ungrateful. You should not have pity on him."

The king immediately ordered that the merchant's son be released and brought to the palace. And when the merchant's son was brought before the king, the snake freed itself from the neck of the king's son. Then, by order of the king, the person who told on the merchant's son was hung. And a sign was hung on him, "For those who tell and are ungrateful, there will never be any hope."

Kayn yehi rotzon. And so may it be.

End of Story Note

IFA 7661 from *Faithful Guardians* collected from Menasheh Mashlad, from Iraq (Noy).

Tale Types: AT 160 (Grateful Animals; Ungrateful Man). The tale type for the frame of this story is AT 910 (Precepts Bought or Given Prove Correct).

Motifs: W154.8 (Grateful animals; ungrateful man); B350 (Grateful animals); K735 (Capture in pitfall).

There are a great many Israel Folktale Archive versions of this story including those from Tunisia, Iraq, and Yemen. The Hebrew title of this animal tale, *B'nai Adam Fuyeh Tova*, actually means that these men *should* be grateful, for they owe something back for what was done.

Also see "There Is No Justice in the World" in this collection.

—*PS*

37

The Jewish Weaver's Wisdom

There was once a king in a faraway land and he had a very stupid assistant. But this assistant succeeded, somehow, in confusing the king. One day he advised, "Your majesty, you would gain a lot of wealth if we order all the inhabitants not to use light in their homes—no candles or oil lamps." The king accepted this advice from his assistant.

But what did one Jewish weaver do? He lit four candles at once instead of the one usual candle he would light in the evening. Hearing of this, the king put on regular clothes one day and went to the weaver and said to him, "Do you know that you are not allowed to light candles at night?" The weaver answered, "But I must work night and day because only then can I earn the sixty *agurot* I need. Twenty *agurot* I pay back a debt that I owe, twenty *agurot* I give as a loan, and with the remaining twenty *agurot* I buy everything that I need to make my living. And in order to earn my sixty *agurot* everyday, I must also work at night."

And the king asked the weaver, "And if I send you a goose, what would you do with it?"

The weaver answered, "I would pluck all its feathers and I would send it back to you alive."

The king patted the weaver's shoulders and said, "Remember only this. Only sell things at an expensive price." The king finished his sentence and left the weaver's house with a smile.

The next day, at dawn, when the assistant arrived at his court, the king said to him, "Go and solve the riddle of the Jewish weaver. He earns sixty *agurot* every day. Twenty of them he returns on a debt that he owes, twenty he lends, and from twenty he makes his living. What does this mean?"

The assistant did not know how to solve this problem and asked the king for twenty-four hours to sit and think. The king agreed and said, "I will even give you forty-eight hours."

After the king had left his house, the Jewish weaver dug a pit, two meters wide, two meters long, and two meters deep. When the assistant came to the Jewish weaver, he asked him, "Tell me, what is the meaning of the things that you told the king yesterday. If I do not know the answer, the king will kill me."

The weaver said, "I will solve what I said only if you fill up this pit with gold." And the assistant begged the weaver to lower the price and began to bargain. But the weaver did not change his price. So the advisor was forced to sell his house and furniture, even his underwear, in order to obtain enough gold to fill the pit dug by the weaver.

After the whole pit was filled with gold, the weaver said to the assistant, "Here is a pencil and a piece of paper and write down the solution. Every day I earn sixty *agurot*. Twenty I owe, twenty I lend, and from twenty I make my living. Now open your eyes and ears. Twenty I give to my parents as a repayment for all the years they had taken care of me. Twenty I give to my son so that when he will get older he will be able to give me back this loan and take care of me, and twenty is saved for me and my family for what we need now."

The assistant told the king this solution to the weaver's riddle. The king was indeed very happy that the weaver had understood his clue about the goose, his assistant, for the weaver had really plucked all his feathers by getting all that he had. The king fired his assistant and invited the very much respected Jewish weaver to be his new assistant. Since then the Jewish weaver and his wife have lived a life of peace with happiness and wealth.

End of Story Note

IFA 7582 from *A Tale for Each Month 1966*, Story #4, collected by Efraim Hanuka from his father Elijahu, from Iraqi Kurdistan (Noy).
Tale Type: AT 921A (The Four Coins).
Motifs: H585.1 (The four coins: King: What do you do with the four coins you earn? Peasant: The first I eat (feed self); the second I put out at interest (give to my children); the third I give back (pay debts); the fourth I throw away (give my wife); H561.6.1 (King and peasant: the plucked fowl); H580 (Enigmatic statements); H585 (Enigmatic conversation of king and peasant).

There are parallels of this variant from Yemen, Iraq, Persian Kurdistan, and Afghanistan. The Jewish versions of this story come from the Midrash *Kohelet Rabbah* 2:17. However, many of the versions of this story in the IFA are more similar to the Jewish versions in the literature of the Middle Ages than the midrashic version.

This story involves riddling. Jews have been intrigued with riddles perhaps because, when we were in danger throughout the centuries, we have had to communicate through cryptic messages. The dictionary defines a riddle as "a question or statement so framed as to exercise one's ingenuity in answering it or discovering its meaning." Riddles have mysterious hidden meaning and require us to analyze them, in order to gain a new perspective, to make new connections in our minds. Sometimes we get locked into set meanings of words and phrases, but riddles can cause us to understand them in ways that stretch the mind and entertain us at the same time.

See "The Plucked Pigeon" in *A Treasury of Jewish Folklore* (Ausubel) and "The Woodcutter's Riddles" in my *Jewish Stories One Generation Tells Another.*

—PS

38

A Remembered Story

One day the Baal Shem Tov said to his *hasidim*, "We are going on a journey today and we need to get to a certain place very quickly." Immediately several of his disciples got into the carriage and they began to ride through the night. When they arrived early the next morning, they saw that the shutters of all the shops and houses in that town were closed. From one of the houses a voice called out, "Rabbi, dear rabbi, don't go any further. Today is a holiday for the Christians and it is forbidden for any Jew to be seen in the town." But the Baal Shem Tov continued riding through the streets.

Finally, he arrived at a house where he had stayed before. The *hasidim* entered the house and immediately the Baal Shem Tov went to one of the windows and opened the shutters. Everyone around him shivered with fear. Bells could be heard from a distance as a crowd began to gather in the open center of the city. In a procession, the Baal Shem Tov saw a bishop arrive with great ceremony, climb the special platform stage, and begin to address the crowd.

The Baal Shem Tov turned to one of his followers, Reb Yaacov, and said, "Do not be afraid of the people or of the day. Go to the square, climb the stairs to the stage, and speak to the bishop in Hebrew and tell him that the Baal Shem Tov has just arrived and he must come right away."

Reb Yaacov did as the Baal Shem Tov had instructed him, even though he was filled with fright. When the bishop heard this request, he whispered to him, "Tell the Baal Shem Tov that I will come after my speech."

The messenger went back and told the Baal Shem Tov what the bishop had said to him. The Besht said, "Go back to the bishop and tell him that he must come now, right away." So Reb Yaacov returned to the bishop with this message. But the bishop replied with the same answer. Then the Besht sent his messenger a third time with the same urgent message. "But, this time, stay with the bishop and return together," the Besht added.

On this third time, the bishop left the stage and immediately went to the house with the messenger. The bishop went into a private room with the Besht and stayed there for two hours. Nobody knew what they spoke about.

Years passed. One day, the Baal Shem Tov said to Reb Yaacov, "Soon your daughter will marry. Since you don't have any money for the dowry and wedding, travel from town to town."

"What will I do in these places?" asked Reb Yaacov.

"You should tell my stories. In that way, you will earn enough money to live on, but you will also be able to save enough money for your daughter's wedding," the Baal Shem Tov told him.

And so, without any more questions, Reb Yaacov, together with his wife, began to travel from place to place telling the stories of the Baal Shem Tov. One day, a man came up to him and said, "Do you know that in a certain town in Italy, there is a wealthy man who pays a lot of money for a story, especially a story about the Baal Shem Tov? You should go there and become a rich man since you know so many of his stories."

After a long journey of many months, Reb Yaacov and his wife arrived at his destination. They found that man who loved stories and were welcomed with great hospitality. Everyone knew that on Shabbos, after each meal, there would be stories of the Baal Shem Tov and everyone was eager to hear them. The host invited the entire community to come for the meals. On erev Shabbos, after the first meal and the singing of z'miros, the host invited Reb Yaacov to tell a story. But when he got up to tell, he realized that he could not remember a single story of the Baal Shem Tov. How is that possible when he had lived and traveled with the Besht for so many years? After all, he knew and had told so many of his stories. He knew of the miraculous events that had taken place during that time. Reb Yaacov tried hard to recall a memory, an image, an action. But he could not. His mind remained empty.

"Perhaps you are tired from the long journey coming here," said the host kindly. "Perhaps tomorrow, on the holy Shabbos, you will remember."

And the next day, after the second meal, Reb Yaacov could not recall the stories. During the Seudah Shlishis, he still could not remember any of the stories. Even when it was motzei Shabbos, even then not a fragment of a story entered his head. And he felt so ashamed.

Finally, he said to the host, "I must have some sort of illness that has erased my memory and caused me to forget all my stories." And the next day, after apologizing to the host, he and his wife got on their wagon and left the city.

When they were just at the border of the city, suddenly Reb Yaacov shouted, "I remember one story. I must go back, but I will tell it to you in case I forget it again. It is the story of the bishop."

When they returned to the mansion, Reb Yaacov ran to find the host and said joyfully, "I remember one story, the story of the Baal Shem Tov and the bishop." And he told him the story. He related everything that the Baal Shem Tov had told him, as the messenger, to say to the bishop, that the bishop was to stop the speech, leave the stage and, instead, go immediately to see the Baal Shem Tov. He told him how the bishop and the Baal Shem Tov had entered into a special room together and talked for two hours. Then Reb Yaacov ended the story and added, "But what they said in that special room, nobody knows."

No sooner had the storyteller spoken those last words, when the host got up, hugged Reb Yaacov, and began to weep. Then, in a grateful voice, he said, "I have been waiting for ten years for this story. You see, I was that bishop. I had left my own faith and started preaching hatred of the Jews and rising to a very powerful position. When the Baal Shem Tov took me into that room, he told me I should repent and return to being a Jew. And if I did so, I would become very wealthy and I would also have many children. And more, I would give a great deal of *tzedakah*, which would help many people and I would receive a lot of poor people as guests in my home. Furthermore, he told me, someday a man would come and tell me my story of what had happened between the Baal Shem Tov and the bishop. Then, and only then, would I be forgiven of my sins. So I immediately left the church and my position as bishop and became a Jew again with my whole heart. And I became rich.

I married and God has blessed me with many children. I study Torah every day. I give charity with a thankful heart and I receive many poor travelers and community people as guests. On Shabbos especially, and on holidays, my table is full. But I have waited all these many years to hear my own story told to me. Now I know my soul has been redeemed."

The messenger then received a great gift of money from the grateful man who had returned to his people.

Reb Yaacov and his wife stayed in that man's home for many weeks because the host wanted to hear more stories of the Besht. Reb Yaacov easily remembered the stories and, from his heart, told all the many stories he knew. And when they left for their home, Reb Yaacov understood why he had been sent by the Besht to become a storyteller.

End of Story Note

Source: *'Adat Tzaddikim*, by M. L. Rodkinson-Frumkin, Lemberg, 1865.

Israel ben Eliezer (1700–1760), of Podolia, became known as the Baal Shem Tov (Master of the Good Name) and was often called by the acronym, the Besht. He founded the hasidic movement by traveling from one town to another preaching his ideas—that all are equal, that purity of heart is superior to study, that joy rather than sadness should dominate one's relationship to God. He taught these ideas especially through stories and song. Thus, the *hasidim* treasure the human voice—the voice that can sing and tell stories. Soon there were many disciples, known as *hasidim*, who accompanied the Besht wherever he traveled. As a result, there was a great resurgence of spiritual Judaism and a revival of the oral tradition of storytelling. After the death of the Baal Shem Tov, his scribe, Rabbi Dov Baer, published *Shivhei ha-Besht*, a volume of legends about the Besht. In English the volume is called *In Praise of the Baal Shem Tov* (Ben-Amos and Mintz). As Howard Schwartz writes: "These texts are a product of the sacred literatures of the Bible, Talmud, Midrash, and Kabbalah, but what is less apparent is the influential role of medieval folklore. For hasidic tales incorporate elements of the narrative similar to those found in folktales, as well as the miracles, enchantments, witches, and demons that are so familiar in folklore and fairy tales. Imposed on this archetypal substructure are figures of angels and spirits, a supernatural aspect of hasidic literature that is found in a great many tales" (*Gates to the New City*, 31). See "The Forgotten Story" in my *Chosen Tales* and in *Gates to the Old City* (Patai).

—*PS*

39

The Wonderful Healing Leaves

There was once a king and a queen and they had three daughters. The king wanted that the three daughters marry three men who had high positions and were rich. And indeed the oldest daughter married a prince and so did the second daughter. But the youngest daughter loved a poor young man and she wanted to marry him. The king and queen were against the marriage and they threw their daughter out of the palace.

The youngest daughter married her love, living in poverty but happily. One day the king went blind and doctors came from all corners of the world to the palace but they could not successfully cure him. Until one day, one doctor came to the palace and said, "There is a very special tree that has leaves on it that can cure the king's blindness." The king called for his two sons-in-law to go out to search for this tree. Because the trip would be very long and very dangerous, the king outfitted his two sons-in-law with two fast horses and great packs of food and said to them, "You will meet three people who will show you the way. It will last seven days." And they went out on their way.

In the meantime, the youngest daughter who had married the poor man heard about what had happened. She decided to ask her mother if she would also let her husband go out to look for the healing leaves. The queen had pity on her daughter and gave her third son-in-law a limping horse and a little bit of food and told him about the details that were needed in order to find the healing leaves.

All of this happened only after her daughter had begged her.

Two weeks after the two older sons-in-law had gone out on their way did the poor son-in-law go on his way on the limping horse. After riding for seven days, the two sons-in-law met with the people that they were told about. These people said to them, "Many people have tried to go into the place where these leaves are found and to pick them. But none of them have been able to return from there." And the sons-in-law were afraid and they decided to stay at the place where they had arrived and not return to the palace. One of them opened up a bakery and the other opened up a kebob shop.

After seven days, the third son-in-law came to the place where they were and went into the stores of his brothers-in-law. He recognized them but they did not recognize him. He ate and slept at their house. The next morning he decided to go to the three people that his mother-in-law, the queen, had told him about. These people were cannibals but they also knew the way to the healing leaves. The young man arrived at the river that was in front of the house of one of the three people. The wife saw the young man and asked him, "How did you come here and why did you come? My husband could eat you."

The young man then told her the reason for his coming. The wife brought him inside the house and she fed him and she hid him under the bed. When her husband came home, he announced, "There is the scent of a man I smell here." And the wife tried to convince him that no man could ever come here. But he forced her to bring the man out from under the bed. When the young man stood up, he said, "First I will tell you my life story and only after that you can do with me whatever you want. You are my host and the controls are in your hands." The young man told all about his life history and after the host heard that the king would kill the young man if he didn't bring him the leaves, he said, "If you are not afraid to die at the hands of the king, why do I need to eat you?" And the host invited the young man to eat and sleep in his house.

The next morning the host said to the young man, "We are three brothers. And now you will go to my second brother. But only my third brother will give you directions to get to the healing leaves that you are looking for."

The young man arrived at the home of the second brother and told him about his meeting with the first brother. The second brother then sent the young man to the third brother.

This brother said to him, "Go for ten meters from my house and you will see a field of knives. Don't be alarmed and say, 'Oh, what beautiful grass! What beautiful flowers!' Then immediately all the knives will turn into flowers and grass. After you pass through the field, you will see a field of salt. Whoever passes over the salt gets his feet cut. But you will say, 'Oh, how nice these waters are.' Everything will turn to water and you will pass through the water and you will arrive at the gates of a palace. At the entrance of the palace stands a lion and a sheep. In the sheep's plate there will be bones and in the lion's plate, straw. You will have to put the bones in the lion's plate and the straw in the sheep's plate. Go into the palace and you will see there forty lions. If their eyes are open, it is a sign that they are sleeping. And if their eyes are closed, it means that they are awake. Go into the kitchen and you will find there forty pots of food. You must taste one tablespoon from each pot. After that you will get to the queen's door. This door is made of bells. When anyone opens it, the bells ring and wake up the lions. I will give you two packages of cotton so you can plug up the bells and afterwards open up the door. You will see the queen sleeping on her bed. Next to her bed is a tree. On this tree are the leaves you are looking for. You must fill up one sack with these leaves and then you must go up to the queen and exchange her ring for yours. On your way back, you must do all these actions again but in reverse."

The man thanked the third brother, took the items that he needed, and started out on his way. He acted according to the directions he had received. After seven days, he returned with the sack filled with the healing leaves and the queen's ring on his finger.

The young man arrived at the bakery and kebob store of his brothers-in-law. When they saw the sack they asked, "What is in this sack?" The young man told them the whole story. And the brothers-in-law invited him to stay the night with them. The young man agreed. "But before I go to sleep," he said, "allow me to sign your backs." The two of them agreed and the youngest brother-in-law signed their backs and went to sleep.

During his sleep, the brothers-in-law tied his hands and legs and poured a potion into his eyes so that he could not see. They put him into the sack and left him in the room. Then they returned to the palace to bring the king the sack of leaves. When the young man awoke, he found himself blinded and didn't know what to do. But on a tree, outside the room, a little bird chirped, "If this young man had any *seikhl*, he would squeeze the leaves dropped on the floor and he would be cured." Because this young man understood the language of animals, he took a few of the leaves that he had noticed earlier were on the floor and squeezed them on his eyes. He realized then that his vision was restored.

In the meantime, the king was also cured and he promoted his sons-in-law to become his assistants. At the same time, he threw out his youngest daughter.

After a very difficult way, the third young man came to his wife and told her, "I have brought the leaves." His wife laughed at him saying, "My brothers-in-law brought the leaves before you."

In the meantime, the queen, who had been keeping watch over the tree with the healing leaves, woke up from her sleep. She realized that her ring was gone and that there was food missing from the pots, as well as leaves missing from the tree. She immediately ordered all her servants to search the whole world for the person who took her ring and the leaves. After they looked in many different places, they finally arrived at the place where the king lived with his family. When she heard how the king had been cured of his blindness, she immediately threatened to destroy the whole city if they didn't reveal to her how it happened. Many people came to her and told her many different stories in order to save the city. But the queen understood that everybody was lying and she ordered that they be taken away.

Then the two sons-in-law of the king came and they showed her the leaves. "Tell me how you got them?" asked the queen. The two men said, "We found a forest and we picked the leaves from the tree." And the queen ordered that they be beaten for lying.

When it was the turn of the third young man, he told her how he arrived at the tree and how he managed to pick the leaves while she was asleep. The queen was still not convinced and she asked for some additional proof. It was then that the young man showed her her own ring. The queen asked, "Where are the leaves?" The young man told her all the bad things that had happened to him caused by his brothers-in-law. The queen asked for another proof of this. And the young man told her, "See the backs of my brothers-in-law where I have put my seal and my mark." The queen ordered that the two men be brought before her and, in truth, there were these marks on the backs of each of these men.

The queen said to the young man, "Half of my kingdom and half of my wealth is yours." The king threw out his two sons-in-law and he brought his third son-in-law and his wife to live in the palace. Everybody lived happily ever after for all the days of their lives.

End of Story Note

IFA 10,125 from *A Tale for Each Month 1974–75*, Story #6, collected by Ofra Elias as told to her by her mother Rakhel, Iraqi Kurdistan (Noy). **Tale Type: AT 551** (The Sons on a Quest for a Wonderful Remedy for their Father). As happens in this tale type, the youngest succeeds with the help of someone and various magic objects. There are many parallels in the Israel Folktale Archives from Morocco, Tunisia, Yemen, Persian Kurdistan, Iraq, Afghanistan, and India.

Motifs: D1500.1.4 (Magic healing leaves); D2161.3 (Magic cure of physical defect); H1151.4 (Task: Stealing ring from finger); H1010 (Impossible tasks).

Because the storyteller was a woman, the editor, Dov Noy, states in his annotations of the tales: "The examination of the opening of this version proves that there is a deviation from the story type: the story does not open with the king and three of his sons but with the three daughters of the king who are married to the three sons-in-law. It is possible to suppose that the adherence to the story tradition, the richness of unnatural motifs, and the conflicts in the essence of the story, in opposition to the deviation in its beginning and ending, come from the over-consciousness of the storytelling mother to her daughter-audience. In the beginning the mother wants to 'catch her ear' and to raise her interest and her identification with what is told. That is how the king's sons are turned into daughters even though they don't have any role in the plot. This is also how the more compromising and realistic direction of the story is understood towards the end of the story" (*A Tale for Each Month 1974–75*, 161–162). Depending on who is telling the story, the protagonist may be changed from male to female or, as is more likely, to go in reverse, since there have probably been more male storytellers in a community than female, at least in public places.

The magic object of leaves or flowers or fruit that heal blindness or revive from death can be found in a number of other folktales, such as "The Life-Giving Flower" and "The Healing Fruit," both in my *Tales of Elijah the Prophet*, and the Yemenite story "The Mute Princess" and a parallel story to this one, "The Wonderful Healing Leaves," both found in *Elijah's Violin* (Schwartz). Also see "Can Fate Be Changed?" in this collection.

—PS

40

The King's Three Questions

There was once a good king who loved the Jews. But he had a wicked minister who hated the Jews and demanded that the king expel all the Jews from the land. However, the king explained that he had no reason to expel them. But the minister advised him: "Invite a representative of the Jews and tell him you have three questions that you would like to ask the Jews. And whoever will know the answers should come to you and answer. And if they don't answer within one month, the Jews will have to leave the country immediately."

The king did as his minister advised. The king invited a representative of the Jews to come to the palace and said to him, "I have three questions. Find someone among you who can bring me the answers to these questions. And if he will know the answers, then good. But if not, then all the Jews will have to leave the country."

All the Jews gathered in the synagogue and announced a general fast, with prayer and *tzedakah*. But they were very afraid to go to the king. Everyone was crying about this terrible expulsion that was about to happen to them.

Among them was a very simple Jew. He was not very wise and he volunteered to go to the king. Since there was no one else who had the courage to go to the king, they agreed that he should try. After thirty days, the man came before the king and the king asked the three questions. "One, when will the end of the world be? Two, where is the center of the world? Three, what have I buried in my courtyard?"

The man stood there and didn't know what to answer. All of a sudden he saw a bird fly, and he said to the king, "There is this bird here who flies every day to the mountain of rock and that you can see there from afar. Every time he passes by the mountain of rock, he scratches some more of the rock. And when the bird will finish scratching the whole mountain of rock, then it will be the end of the world."

"And how do you know?" asked the king.

"If you wish, we would wait until the mountain disappears so we can see for ourselves if it will be the end of the world or not."

"I am satisfied," answered the king. "And where is the center of the world?"

"Here, in this place where we are standing," answered the man.

"And how do you know?" asked the king.

"If you do not believe me, you can measure it and then we will argue," answered the Jew.

"I am satisfied with this answer too," replied the king.

"And what have I buried in my courtyard?" asked the king.

Now the simple Jew did not know what to answer. He became scared and filled with despair, so he began to whisper to himself, "Oi va voy, I am buried here, just like a dog."

When the king heard what he had whispered, he shouted, "True! I had a very important dog that I cared about and he died. So I buried him in my courtyard." Hearing these three answers, the king gave the Jews their rights to remain in the land.

So the simple Jew was sent home with great honors and all the Jews were saved from the terrible threat of expulsion. As for the evil minister, he stayed in the palace, but his head was bowed from shame.

End of Story Note

IFA 275 from *Seven Folktales*, Story #5, collected by Miriam Yeshiva from Peninnah Me'ir, from Rumania (Noy).

Tale types: AT 922 (The Shepherd Substituting for the Priest Answers the King's Questions); AT 1641 III (The Covered Dish).

Motifs: H512 (Guessing with life as wager); H541.1 (Riddles propounded on pain of death); K1956 (Sham wise man); N688 (What is in the dish: "poor Crab"); H681.3.1 (Where is the center of the earth?); H701.1 (How many seconds in eternity? . . .); H584 (Other riddling answers).

This story combines two international popular tale types in which a simple but clever shepherd answers the king's riddle questions and succeeds by accident. The origin of the story may have been seventh-century Egypt, according to the folklorist Walter Anderson. What is most interesting in the story are the questions asked. In many Jewish versions there are other similarly enigmatic riddles that are found as international motifs, such as "How many seconds in eternity?" H701.1 "How many seconds in eternity? A bird carries a grain of sand from a mountain each century; when the whole mountain is gone, the first second of eternity has passed."; H681.3.1 "Where is the center of the earth? And Rabbi Yehoshua ben Hananya puts up his finger and says to the wise men of Athens, 'Here, and who will say that this is not so? Bring ropes and measure it.'"

The third question in the story comes from the second tale type. The origin of this question is from India and possibly China and is very common in the oral tradition in Europe and Asia. It is connected to the tale type AT 1641 III and motif N688 with the question "What is in the dish?" or in this version "What have I buried in my courtyard?" The despairing hero answers with the name of an animal, usually a name he gives himself, but with this chance remark, he happens to guess the answer correctly. So with the question, "What is in the dish?" the character responds in one story, "Poor crab." Of course, that is exactly what is in the covered dish. Sometimes the response, said while talking to himself, is "Here you are buried, fox." This is similar to what happens in this variant. The motif is found in Rumanian, Hungarian, and Slavic versions.

One of the earliest of questions and it is found in Jewish legends (*Sanhedrin* 39A) is "How many stars in the heavens?" Other popular questions are "What much am I worth?", "How much water is in the sea?", "What am I thinking?", "What have I never seen?", "How will the Messiah come?", "What does God's face look like?" These last two questions reflect a religious character and come from earlier Jewish sources. Some Jewish folk stories include riddles based on the Bible or legend.

There is a German tale, found also in Grimm, which is a variant of this tale. See "Kunz and His Shepherd" in *Ma'aseh Book* (Gaster), which includes the three questions "Who can tell me how far the heavens are from the earth? Who can tell me where the sun rises? Who can tell me what the king is thinking?".

For a more humorous version of this story, see "The Wicked Murdim" in *The Wandering Beggar or the Adventures of Simple Shmerel* (Solomon). This is a humorous tall tale parallel to the Purim story with a reverse motif. In this story, it is the clever Jew-hating prime minister, wanting to find a way to rid the kingdom of Jews, who sets up a contest to see if a Jew can ask him a question to which he would not know an answer. This is a reversal of the usual sequence where the king asks the questions of the Jews. If the prime minister knows the answer, then the Jews will have to leave the country. If not, then they can stay. On his wanderings, our naive Simple Shmerel had been seeking the meaning of the Hebrew phrase "Aineny Yodaya," which literally means "I don't know." And when he hears the challenge of asking such a wise man any question, he asks the prime minister what the Hebrew phrase means. When the prime minister responds with the correct answer, "I don't know," the king, thinking he doesn't know the answer, punishes him and, thus, must allow the Jews to remain in the kingdom. Shmerel is really a hero. A play on words helps to bring about the happy ending. For a story that incorporates wordplay, see "The Fulfilled Dream" in this collection.

For more stories about riddles, see "The Jewish Weaver's Wisdom" and "The Indian King and the Jewish Shepherd," and "The Yemenite King and His Jewish Advisor" in this collection.

—PS

41

The Emir, the Jewish Advisor,
and the Sheep

The Emir of Bukhara had a wise Jewish advisor. Because his love for this advisor was so great, the Emir promoted him above all his other ministers and advisors. Is it any surprise that the others were jealous of this Jewish advisor and so they waited very patiently for the day when they could devise some way to make him fail at something so he would lose favor in the Emir's eye.

One day, when the Emir was feeling especially in a good mood, the other advisors decided on a scheme against the Jewish advisor. So what did they do? They all went to the Emir, and as they bent their knees to bow, as was the custom, they began to speak. "Long live the Emir! We would like to try and test your wise advisor in order to know if his wisdom is as great as it is said. And if he fails in this test he will die."

"And if not," responded the Emir, "you will die." And the Emir continued, "But you should know that there are many ears listening to you right now. And you must know that the wisdom of my advisor will stand up to any test and you will certainly all lose."

The ministers again bowed and the advisor entered. The head of the ministers turned to him and said, "I have one problem to put before you which you must solve, dear advisor. If you succeed in solving this enigma according to the contract we will sign between us, it will be noted that your wisdom is greater than ours and that the high opinion the Emir holds about you is correct. But if not, then your fate will be decided by the Emir."

"And what is this perplexity? I am ready to hear it," asked the Jewish advisor.

The minister answered him, "We have brought a sheep that weighs twenty pounds and in forty days, when we will come back, we will weigh this sheep in front of the Emir and in front of you, and we want that his weight should be exactly the same weight as it is today, without any additions or subtractions to his weight—not even one gram. His wool should be combed and shiny as it is today and you will feed him and water him for the whole forty days according to what will be written in the contract. Do you think you can fulfill this mission?"

And the Jewish advisor called for the contract and signed it, putting a copy in his pocket. He quickly turned away from the ministers so they couldn't see his expression, but, in his heart, he was very scared for the fate that awaited him. What if he didn't succeed in this mission, because he knew that it was a conspiracy arranged by these jealous ministers. With a broken heart and a broken spirit, he left the castle. But the other ministers stayed with the Emir and continued sitting and laughing, believing in their hearts that this would, once and for all, restore the power to their hands.

The Jewish advisor had one daughter and she was beautiful and very wise. Every day the daughter would prepare food for her father and wait for him to come back from the palace. She would also prepare a towel, his slippers, and a pot of hot water for him to wash his hands and feet. After the advisor would put on his slippers, he would sit in his favorite chair and drink cup after cup of green tea and, with great pleasure, tell his daughter all the news from the palace, what he saw there and what he heard there, and even about the jealousy of the other ministers and about all their trickery. But this time, when the advisor returned from the Emir's palace, the daughter felt that this time there was something different. Her father did not smile and he was not as he usually was on every other day. So she approached him and asked him, "Father, why is your face so sad? And why does it look like you have a shadow across your face? Did something bad happen? I have never seen you in this mood before."

He hid his face from his daughter as tears ran down his cheeks. He didn't wash his hands and his feet and he didn't drink the green tea that he loved so much. The daughter thought to herself, "Did they actually succeed, those that hate my father?" She wiped her father's face very gently and she talked to him very soothingly, "Dear father, you know that I have no one else in my life. Please tell me what has happened so that maybe I can help you."

The father spoke with a broken heart and with many sighs. "My dear daughter. Don't ask me what is in my heart. Why should I make you sad with my problems? After thirty years of service as a loyal advisor to the father of the Emir and to the Emir now himself, your father was asked to find a solution to a riddle that all the ministers gave me. How could you find a solution to this puzzling problem so you could help me?"

But the daughter kept insisting. "I know, Father, how deep your worry is. But don't hide it from me. Many elders say that sometimes the wisdom of a young person can be even greater than the wisdom of an older person. Please tell me what they asked of you, and maybe, with God's help, we can find a solution to this problem."

The father looked at his daughter for a long time. When he realized that she was certain about what she said, he told her about the problem he would have to solve: that the weight of the sheep must not go up or down, even by one gram, after forty days of feeding and watering. He also told his daughter that this was all according to the conditions set in a contract that he had signed.

When the daughter heard the mission, she broke out into laughter and told her father to wash and to drink his tea. "And that's all, father? I will tell you what to do. After all, everything is very very simple."

What his daughter said had a great effect on his mood as if the breath of life was given to a dead man. It was so sweet. He got up from his chair, hugged and kissed his daughter with all his heart because he knew that whatever his daughter said would be and she would not disappoint her father.

In the meantime, the sheep was brought to the advisor's house and the Emir's servant was ordered to tie it up in the garden of the front yard. At that point, the daughter said to the father, "Go, father, go to the *shuk*, the market, and buy us a wolf."

The father fulfilled his daughter's request without hesitation and came home with a wolf. When the time came to feed the sheep, as was written in the contract, the daughter brought the wolf in front of the sheep. The sheep ate, but, as it was eating, it was shaking with fear that the wolf might attack it and eat it. The sheep alternately looked at the straw and the wolf. After the sheep had finished its food, it ran with fear into its cage. Afterwards, when they weighed the sheep, they found that its weight did not change. And that's how the advisor and his daughter fed the sheep every day. When the father showed surprise, the wise daughter explained to her father, "At the time of the sheep's feeding, its enemy would be standing before it, and this would be so that the sheep eating would shake so much that the food would be digested very fast and therefore the weight of the sheep would remain the same." After forty days, when they weighed the sheep, they found that its weight did not go up or down, not even one gram. And so, too, its wool was combed and clean and shiny, as it should be.

The advisor hugged his daughter and showered her with many kisses. At the appointed time, the advisor brought the sheep to the Emir's palace. All the ministers were sitting there waiting for him. The advisor only came in with the sheep and they saw the sheep with its combed wool and it was if they all saw a ghost or death. And their embarrassment grew when the sheep was weighed and it was found that the sheep weighed exactly the same as forty days earlier. The Emir opened his mouth with great joy and with thanks to God. And then he turned to them and said, "I have let you goad my advisor in order to make him foolish. He has proven that his wisdom is greater than your wisdom. And because you did not listen to me, your fate will now be the fate that you would have done to him. And therefore I order you all to be hung by a strong rope so to be seen that no one should try to denounce people who are inno- cent even if their religion is different than yours, because everyone is created in God's image and every man has to respect and value his neighbors."

When the Emir and the Jewish advisor were alone, the Emir turned to him and said, "Your treatment of the sheep was amazing and the way you succeeded was above every expectation. Please tell me the truth, who is the person who told you what to do and how to do it. At the time that the other ministers spoke to you, forty days ago, about the sheep and its weight, I saw how your face and mood darkened. It seemed as though your whole soul was in torment. At that time you did not know the solution to your problem."

The Jewish advisor answered, "May the Emir live forever. There is no one wiser than you. I must tell you the truth. I have a daughter, an only daughter, who is wise and smart above any imagination. She advised me about the treatment for the sheep."

"If you have such a wise daughter," said the Emir, "isn't it right that she be my wife and you be my in-law. Go bring her to me." The advisor did not say anything. And the Emir asked him, "Why are you hesitating?"

And the advisor said, "Long live the Emir. But I must tell you that, even though I raised my daughter from the time her mother died, I do not know what is in her heart. Send messengers to her and they will bring her to you."

The Emir turned and sent two runners to the advisor's house in order to bring his daughter to the castle. But she resisted coming with them and said, "Ask in my name, please, if the Emir will fulfill my request and then I will fulfill his request."

"And what is your request?" asked the messengers.

"My request is that the Emir should spread gold coins along the whole way from his castle to the gate of my house so that I may step on them on my way to him. All the coins that stick to my feet will be distributed to the poor."

The messengers ran quickly back to the palace to tell the Emir about her request. Immediately he gave a command to open up the doors of his treasures and sprinkle the gold coins along the road leading from his palace to the gates of the advisor's house. The coins only covered part of the way. So the Emir ordered that the treasures of his father's be brought, but those coins only covered another part of the way. And so the Emir turned to the Jewish advisor for advice about what to do. He explained to the Emir, "Even though I do not know what to do, my daughter will know. But what is in her heart I do not know."

And so the Emir sent messengers to the Advisor's daughter and this is what she explained to them. "First of all, you must all collect all the gold coins that you have already spread out in the streets. Afterwards the Emir must command that these gold coins must be made into four horseshoes. Then these horseshoes must be put on the horse that I will ride when I come to him."

The messengers ran back to the Emir and told him what the young woman had said. And the Emir sat absolutely shocked by the wisdom of this young woman and said to himself, "This is the woman that God has given to me."

Immediately he ordered that all the gold coins be collected and that the young woman's request be carried out. This is the way the advisor's daughter arrived at the Emir's palace, on the horse with the golden horseshoes. The Emir welcomed her and invited her to sit down next to him. After that he ordered that the golden horseshoes be broken up and handed out to the poor as the young woman had requested.

After a few days, the Emir celebrated his wedding with the advisor's daughter in a royal ceremony. But on the wedding night, as he was entering their chamber, the Emir announced to his wife in direct words, "Tomorrow morning I am going out with your father and with a whole unit of soldiers for a journey of seven years. I am leaving you to take my place. When I return to my castle, I want you to fulfill three tasks. The first is this: In this bag, which is closed and sealed with my personal seal, there is now one thousand gold coins. When I return, I want there to be two thousand gold coins. The second task is this: You should give birth to a son even though I will not come to you before I leave. And the third is this: Your female horse should give birth to a pony without my male horse coming near it. When you fulfill my demands, I will see when I return my son riding the pony and holding in his hand the sealed sack with the two thousand gold coins."

The next day, the Emir left the palace riding on his stallion on his way to the great journey and with him the advisor and the whole unit of soldiers.

After she weighed her thoughts, the young woman made her decisions. She gathered together forty beautiful tall young women and commanded that her officers teach them the basics of war, how to use a bow and arrow, how to ride fast on horses—and also how to play cards. And these young women were trained day after day, from the early morning hours until the late evening hours. After three months, they had learned well and knew all of the skills of a soldier. Then they got all dressed as male soldiers. And they also knew how to play cards.

When the Emir's wife saw that she could trust these women, she got them all together and told them, "In another three days we are going out to a distant and dangerous place. You must be ready even for war. If I fall into the hands of the enemy, you must do everything possible in your power to free me." And the three days passed and on the fourth day every young woman got on a steed. Each one was dressed in a soldier's uniform, outfitted with a bow and arrow and everything else that a soldier needs. They looked like soldiers in every way. The Emir's wife, dressed as a general, rode before them.

When the Emir's wife saw, from a distance, her husband's camp with all the tents of his soldiers in a great field, she ordered all her women-soldiers to put up their tents on the side of the mountain where they could not be seen. After a short rest and a meal, the Emir's wife chose six soldiers and sent them one after another to look around the area. Then she took six other soldiers with her to visit the Emir's camp. But before she left she ordered her next-in-command to guard the camp. When the seven riders, the Emir's wife and her six soldiers, arrived at her husband's camp, the faces of the soldiers clearly showed their surprise to see such tall and attractive riders. After the riders had passed by, they quickly ran to the advisor and told him what they had seen. While the soldiers were describing to the advisor the beauty of the soldiers, suddenly one of the soldiers called out in a loud excited voice, "Here they are coming back again."

When the advisor's daughter saw that the Emir was coming out of his tent to see for himself the beauty of these soldiers, she quickly got down from her horse, stood at attention, and saluted in front of him. The other riders followed her example. The Emir invited them into his tent and during the conversation he asked, "Where do you come from, from what kingdom?" And the general answered, "We have come from a very distant land and it's only by chance that we passed by this camp."

After an hour of pleasant conversation, the women got up on their horses ready to go back to their camp, but the Emir stopped them and asked them to stay and to be guests at his camp, at least for one night. "Then you may go on your way tomorrow."

But the general promised him that they would return the next day with an even greater number of soldiers and then they would be his guest at dinner.

After the soldiers had left, the Emir expressed his surprise at their attractiveness and height to his advisor and they continued to talk about these guest soldiers. But the advisor said to him, "In my opinion these soldiers are women and not men." In order to confirm what he thought, the advisor told the Emir, "For the evening meal, the Emir order *dooshpera* to be served. And when they eat this, it will prove that they are women, because women especially love this food."

The next day, before they left their camp, the Emir's wife said to her women-soldiers, "This evening we are going to eat at the Emir's camp. You do what I do. If I eat, you eat. If I drink, you drink."

When the soldiers arrived at the Emir's camp, the Emir received them graciously, and he hosted them in his dining hall camp where there was a great table. The first course which was served in an enormous plate were these *dooshpera*. And the Emir said, "Welcome guests. Please begin eating." In the meantime, the chef entered the dining hall and announced, "The second course of *dooshpera* will be ready in only a few minutes."

The general of the guest soldiers took one *dooshpera* and began to chew it. And while the general was still chewing, the chef came in with another great plate filled with *dooshpera*. And all this time the Emir was trying to get the guests to eat more. Again the general took another *dooshpera*, but this time she stuck it on her spear. And all the other guest soldiers did the same. The Emir was shocked. The general then turned to the Emir and with a bit of sarcasm and said, "What! Are we all women that you should serve us *dooshpera*!" And all the other people at the table began to laugh heartily. Immediately the Emir ordered that other food be served. And within a few minutes the table was filled with all the delicious food and they all ate and drank as much as they wanted because they were indeed hungry and thirsty.

The general sat next to the Emir and drank a lot with him. And then the Emir suggested that they should play cards after the meal and that the loser would fulfill any request that the winner had. The general agreed and, at the end of the meal, the Emir and the general sat down to play cards. At the same time, the other guest soldiers also played with their hosts. When the game between the Emir and the general ended, the Emir had lost. Then the general asked him, "According to the conditions we have set between us, my request is that your seal be given to me for one night. Tomorrow night I will return it to you." The Emir fulfilled the general's request immediately. The guests thanked their hosts and with good wishes rode back to their camp.

As soon as the women soldiers returned to their camp, the Emir's wife opened up the sealed bag, put in another thousand gold coins, and closed the bag with the Emir's seal. So now the bag contained two thousand gold coins as the Emir had asked. The first task was accomplished.

The next day, before evening, the women riders rode to the Emir's camp and the general returned the seal to the Emir. Again the Emir invited all the riders for another great meal. And again afterwards they played a card game with the same condition as the night before. And again the general won. And this time she asked for the Emir's horse for one night. The Emir was forced to lend the general his special and favorite horse. The Emir's horse was brought to the general and they rode back to the camp. That night the Emir's stallion was brought together with the general's female horse. The next night the Emir's horse was returned, cleaned, and brushed.

On the third night, the Emir held a great banquet and everything was as before. But this time, the general let the Emir beat "him" in the game and then asked him, "What is it you want?" The Emir answered, "I want you." The general was shocked. "How is that possible for I am a man, just like you. However," the general continued, "I have a beautiful sister in my camp who is younger than I am. I will bring her to you tomorrow evening." And the Emir agreed to this and they left each other with thanks and other good wishes.

As she entered her tent, the general gathered all her soldiers together and told them, "Tomorrow evening I will stay at the Emir's camp, but as a woman. And there is no doubt that he will not let me leave his tent, even after three days. If you see that I have not returned by the fourth day, you must immediately attack and kill his soldiers. You must kill them all, even the Emir. But if I come back, you must all be ready to leave the camp, even if it is night, in order to go back to our country." The soldiers listened to what she said and vowed to follow her orders. She then took off her uniform and put on some beautiful clothes and made herself attractive and desirable, as any woman would who was to be brought before the Emir. Together with six accompanying soldiers she went to the Emir.

When this group arrived at the gates of the camp, the Emir came out to receive them very graciously and to bring them into his tent. He again prepared a great banquet for this small group. All the guests ate and drank until they were drunk. And the Emir spent the whole night in the company of this "sister of the general," who, as we know, was really his wife.

When morning came, the guests wanted to leave the camp. But the Emir did not let them go. Only after three days did the guests succeed in convincing the Emir by saying, "Your Majesty, there was an agreement between you and our general. When he won, he returned everything to you after one day, whether it was your seal or your horse. But you, your Highness, have broken your promise and you have not returned his sister to him, even after three days. If you really want her, give her to us as we are responsible for her. Tomorrow we will send her along with our general and then you and our general may make up any kind of agreement between yourselves."

What the guests said sounded logical to the Emir and he immediately ordered that the young woman be sent back with many gifts. He even accompanied them for part of the way as befits the head of a kingdom. Then he returned back to his own camp.

Early the next day, the Emir sent one of his soldiers to the camp, which was on the side of the mountain, in order to bring the young woman back to him. But the messengers came back empty-handed explaining, "I did not see any camp, only empty desert around. I did not see one living soul in the place."

The Emir's wife had returned with her soldiers to her palace. At the end of nine months she gave birth to a son. The female horse gave birth to a pony and in the sack was two thousand gold coins sealed with the Emir's own seal. So all three tasks were completed successfully.

At the end of seven years, the Emir sent a messenger to his wife. "On such and such a day, I am coming back with my advisor and my unit of soldiers to my city. Come out to receive me."

But, truthfully, in the Emir's heart was the memory of the beautiful young woman who had been in his tent for three nights.

When the Emir entered his city with all his soldiers, he received a royal welcome. At the head of all who welcomed him was his wife who had taken his place. She was riding on her horse, and next to her was her son who was riding on the pony. In his hand was the sack of money. When the Emir saw the child, he immediately took out his sword to cut off his head, but his wife held her son to her and yelled out, "First ask, then you may do as you wish." And so the Emir put his sword back in his sheath and his wife explained. "I have a woman's reason and I will go away for one moment. But then I will tell you everything."

Her soldiers were all ready and waiting, but hidden from the Emir's eyes. They were dressed in their soldier's uniforms and she herself quickly put on her general's uniform. They then slowly approached the Emir and bowed in front of him. The soldiers saw them and they immediately began to shout, "Look here are those beautiful soldiers that we saw in our camp!" When the Emir heard this, he immediately understood his wife's trickery, but it also proved to him who she was. The Emir raised his son into his arms and kissed him with all his heart and the three of them together entered the palace.

After a few days, the Emir held a great banquet for all his ministers and gave many gifts to those who were with him. His happiness knew no bounds. The Emir promoted the Jewish advisor to become his second in command for he was the father of his wife. To his wife, he said, "From now on you will be queen of the land. The royal crown will be put on your head for you have found favor in my eyes for your beauty and for your wisdom. I will never do or proclaim anything without coming to you first for advice. I will always learn from your wisdom. I will always receive your advice from your wise heart for it is written, 'A person should listen to wise advice.'" *Shomaya l'eytza hakhama.*

And so it was! And so it will always be!

End of Story Note

IFA 8464 from *A Tale for Each Month 1968–69*, Story #3, collected by Moshe Barukhof from Elijahu Mani Aharanof, from Bukhara (Cheichel-Hechal).

Tale Types: AT 875 (The Clever Peasant Girl); AT 891 (The Man Who Deserts his Wife and Sets Her the Task of Bearing Him a Child); AT 1528*D (Contest in Cleverness between Jew and Gentile; Jew Wins); AT 876 (The Clever Maiden and the Suitors); AT 884B (The Girl as Soldier).

Motifs: H1072 (Task: Give sheep good care but do not let it fatten); K1814 (Disguised as a courtesan, wife makes love to her husband); J1111.4 (Clever peasant daughter); H561.1 (Clever peasant girl asked riddles by king); H373 (Bride test: performance of tasks); H1010 (Impossible tasks); H561.1.1.1 (Clever daughter construes enigmatic sayings); H1050 (Paradoxical tasks); J1545.4 (The exiled wife's dearest possession); K1837 (Disguise of woman in man's clothes); H1385.4 (Quest for vanished husband); H1578 (Test of sex: to discover person masking as of other sex).

With parallels in the Israel Folktale Archives from Persia, Tunisia, Morocco, Libya, Egypt, Turkey, Syria, Israel (Bedouin), Yemen, and Afghanistan, this international tale type can be found all over the world.

The opening of this story is similar to a number of other Jewish folktales where the king has both Jewish and non-Jewish advisors. But due to the jealousy of the Jewish advisor, the other advisors devise a way to have the king test the Jewish advisor's wisdom. In every Jewish version, it is the Jewish advisor, or his wiser daughter, who wins the king's favor in the end.

The task of feeding a sheep for forty days and returning it at the exact same weight at the end of that time comes from *A Thousand and One Nights* with the same solution as in this story.

There are many Jewish folktales where a sheep figures either as a "character" (see "The Agunah, the Rabbi, and the 'Sheep'" in my *Tales of Elijah the Prophet*) or in some way as an element in the story, such as in this story and in "The King, Bahlul, and the Clever Maiden," also in this collection. Sheep were important domestic animals in ancient Israel and they are a familiar symbol for the Jewish People being cared for by God, the shepherd. They also have symbolic importance at Passover for two reasons: there was the sacrifice of the lamb (the paschal lamb) as the Israelites were about to leave Egypt; and lambs are associated with this spring holiday also because they are born at this season and serve as a symbol of redemption and rebirth.

Another intriguing theme, in this story, is that of the young woman who disguises herself as a man in order to succeed in performing certain impossible tasks required of her to prove her wisdom. It is a key element in several other Jewish folktales, such as "Elijah's Violin" and "The Pirate Princess" (a variant of Reb Nachman's story) in *Elijah's Violin* (Schwartz), in IFA 8160 ("The Two Lovers"), and my version of Reb Nachman's story "The Emperor's Daughter and the King's Son" in this collection. However, in "Caliph Harun Al-Rashid" (also in this collection), the young woman who is required to fulfill the same tasks does disguise herself, but as a daughter of the Sheik, not as a man.

—*PS*

42

Princess Zohara and Prince Ali

Once upon a time, long ago, there was a king and he had an only daughter named Zohara. Of all the children that were born to him, she was the only one who remained alive. The king loved his only daughter very much and he built a glass palace for her. He brought maids and female servants and young girls to entertain her. One morning, Zohara got up and looked out the window and saw that snow had fallen during the night. Just then a seller of coal passed by and she saw that some of his coal kept falling from his wagon onto the snow. After that, in the same path, she saw a young boy who held a slaughtered chicken and she saw that some of the drops of blood fell onto the snow. And the seeing of these things, the snow and the coal and the blood, caused a great sigh to come from the heart of Zohara.

She called out to one of the young girls who was with her and said to her, "Look, look how beautiful the coal and the blood are on the snow. How I would love to have a prince whose eyes and whose hair would be dark as coal and whose skin of his face would be as pink and as delicate as blood, and white teeth as white as snow. Does there exist as beautiful a man as this?" And the young girl replied to the princess, "Prince Ali is as beautiful as that."

"Oh please, help me," cried the princess. "Tell me where I can find him." And the young girl sighed and answered, "This is a very difficult thing. Prince Ali demands of his future wife many many difficult conditions. And no princess has succeeded in fulfilling all of them. But you can try. Perhaps you might write him a letter."

And the Princess Zohara wrote a letter to Prince Ali and in it she described how beautiful she was, what was so wonderful and rare in her father's kingdom, and that she would like to meet him. And Prince Ali answered her that if the princess wanted to meet him, she must fulfill the following demands: "To wear out three pairs of iron shoes; to be sold three times as a servant in the slave market; to cure a person who has a sickness of the mind; the revive a person from his grave; to hear a crackling noise as though her bones were breaking apart; and to see one who has become yellow like a mat."

So what did the Princess Zohara do? She took a basket filled with food for the way, golden coins from her father, and said goodbye to her father and to her maidens and went on her way. She walked around in the forest and climbed up mountains and passed through rivers and went down into valleys until, on the horizon, she saw a small village and then the first of her pair of clogs was torn and worn out.

At the end of the day Zohara arrived at a small hut. In the hut was an old poor woman. The woman's face showed that she was not a friendly, not a generous, and not a hospitable woman. When Zohara asked to stay for one night in the hut, the old woman refused, saying, "My hut is narrow, just like a doghouse, where a dog's tail is even outside." So what did Zohara do? She took out a gold coin and gave it to the woman. All of a sudden the hut became "larger" and there was enough room for Zohara.

Before the old woman fell asleep, Zohara said to her, "Tomorrow sell me in the slave market and you can keep the money for yourself that you receive for me." The next day, the old woman sold Zohara and the master who bought her took her to his home. On the door to his house, Zohara noticed a sign of mourning. Zohara went inside and immediately went to work. All of sudden, she heard the two servants arguing between themselves and one said to the other, "Today I will not serve her. I'm afraid. You go." "No, no, why don't we send the new maid. Let her struggle with her."

Zohara interrupted them and said, "Who is it that you don't want to serve and who are you afraid of?" "The daughter of our master is crazy," the older maid explained, "and she is always giving us death threats so that we are afraid to serve her."

"I will serve her the food," Zohara announced. "You both probably throw the food and run away. This is something you are forbidden to do.

I will serve her the food very slowly and in slow portions and you will see that everything will be all right." Day after day, Zohara would go up to the room of the daughter, and talk to her very gently until the young woman was calmed and stopped thrashing around.

One day, Zohara opened a window that was closed in the room of the master's daughter. What did she see? A group of very strange people who were cooking and boiling something. One of them yelled to his friend, "It's already been a year that we have been cooking this magic potion and there's no use for it. The young girl could get better." And Zohara understood that these very strange people were cooking some sort of magic spell and, with it, they were making this poor young girl crazy. Toward the end of the day, Zohara went up to them and said, "I would ask for one coal of fire because tonight my young lady mistress is going to get married. And from all the dancing and laughing and carrying on I'm afraid that all the candles will blow out." "What?" asked one of the men. "We have been wasting time and money and energy and nerve in order to make that young girl crazy, and she is about to get married?" And immediately they spilled out the whole vat filled with the magic spell and left and abandoned the place.

Zohara returned to her master's house and went up to the young girl's room and found her as she was about to leave the room. "No, no," called the princess to the young girl. "First, let's prepare your father. Don't go to him by surprise without first letting him know that you are restored to health." The young girl stopped Zohara's words with a question, "Where was I all this time? What have I done? Who kidnapped me from my parents?" And Zohara answered her, "You didn't do anything bad and no one kidnapped you. There was a group of witches that made some sort of evil spell that drove you crazy, but now you are whole and healthy. I am going to talk with your father to tell him all that had happened to you." Zohara went down to talk with the master and asked him, "What would you do if I brought you your daughter whole and healthy just like all the other young women in the kingdom?" Replied the desperate and sad father, "I would give my whole life for my daughter." "Right now," answered Zohara, "your daughter is healthy. Tomorrow I will bring her and you will see this for yourself."

The next day, Zohara brought the young woman to her parents. And her father's happiness is impossible to describe until he said to Zohara,

"You are worthy of marrying my only son." "No," Zohara refused and asked, "Please give me, sir, a certificate signed by you that I have healed your daughter of an evil spell and a sickness of the mind. Then afterwards, please release me and send me from here." The master gave Zohara everything she requested and said goodbye to her.

The princess put on her feet a second pair of iron clogs and began to wander on the road, and she passed through rivers and went up mountains and down into valleys. She went into places where even camels and horses would not succeed in walking. Finally she arrived at the hut of the old woman. This time, again, the old woman refused to receive her. Zohara, again, took out a gold coin and the old woman agreed to host her. Before she fell asleep, Zohara said to her, "Tomorrow sell me in the slave market and the money you receive for me you will take for yourself." The next day, the old woman sold Zohara and the new master took her to his home.

In this house there was also a sign of mourning. Zohara went inside with the master and inside the house she found many many women crying and keening. She asked the meaning for the crying and wailing and someone explained to her, "The son of our master died a year ago and the father has sworn that the crying and mourning will never stop in this house." In the evening one of the maids passed out a drink to all the people in the house and, after drinking it, everyone fell asleep as if they were dead. Zohara was suspicious of the drink and the second evening, when the maid handed out the drink, Zohara pretended as if she were drinking from her glass, but, instead, she really poured the drink down her nightgown. Afterwards she pretended to be asleep.

In the middle of the night, that same maid got up, got on her broom, and rode it outside. Zohara crept outside and ran after her until they got to the cemetery. There she hid behind one of the gravestones and watched. The maid took her necklace and swept it across the grave and the grave opened. From within the grave out came a beautiful young man. From his mouth came the cry, "No, I prefer to die and to be in this grave rather than to marry you." "You will get sick of this grave," cried the maid to him. "In the end, you will marry me." "No, never," yelled the young man. And the maid bucked at him and he fell back into the grave's pit. The maid closed the grave and went back into the house.

When the maid returned to the house, Zohara was already lying down on her mat as if nothing had happened. The next day, Zohara went up to her master in order to talk with him and asked him, "What would you do if I were to bring you your son alive and healthy?" And the master answered her, "Why are you wounding my heart? Why are you talking of painful things and of things that are not of this world? My son died a year ago." "No, sir," yelled Zohara, "your son is not dead. And you must help him. Listen carefully to what I tell you. First of all, take the necklace from the maid and get her away from here."

"Girl," yelled the master in surprise, "I don't understand you. What are you talking about? My son is dead. Dead! Dead! Don't you understand?" "Never mind, Master," and Zohara repeated what she had said. "Your son will return tomorrow, or the next day, as if he had been in a distant land and returned from there." So Zohara went herself to the maid, who was sleeping at that time, and stole the necklace. Afterwards, Zohara went to her master and said to him, "Send that maid from here." The master did as Zohara advised and sent the maid to a different city. In the middle of the night, Zohara got up and went to the cemetery. She swept the necklace on the grave, and it opened and the young man came out. "No, no," his cries were heard. "I choose to die . . ." Zohara stopped him and said, "You do not have to die. God has saved you and you will go back to your father in peace." The young man called out when he heard these words, "Blessed be the one who has returned me my soul. Who are you? Where are you from?"

"I have come to save you. I will bring you back to your father's house. That is what will gladden his heart." His father did not believe the sight in front of his eyes. "Oh, my daughter," he called out to Zohara in happiness. "You have brought a new light to my house. What can I do for you?"

"First you must kill the evil maid," answered Zohara. The master agreed. "Immediately I will bring about a death warrant for her. But what can I do for you because you have saved my son? You will marry him," said the father. "No, no sir, my reward will be that you give me a letter that states that I have revived your son and then send me away," replied Zohara. The master gave Zohara the letter that she requested and released her.

Zohara put on the third of iron clogs because the second pair had been totally worn out. And again the princess wore out her clogs by wandering on her feet, and went up mountains, and went through rivers, and went down into valleys, and wandered through forests until she arrived once again at the old woman's hut. Again her clogs were worn out and this time the old woman received Zohara without any conditions or payment. The next day, she sold Zohara in the marketplace, as she had done the previous two times. And Zohara's new master put Zohara on a white camel and brought her to a palace whose doors were made out of solid silver and the round knockers were made out of gold. The lady of the house received Zohara very happily and told her, "For so many years I have waited for you." And Zohara was surprised.

Zohara began her work. And then a miracle happened. Cut roses with tightly closed buds all of a sudden opened by themselves. "My lady, my lady," called Zohara, "look, the roses are opening by themselves." "Ah," cried the lady of the house, "they only open when my brother visits me. He does this once a year." The lady of the house ordered Zohara to wear a white dress and golden shoes and said to her, "I will put a stone under the rug. When you bring out the coffee, trip on the stone and spill the coffee on my brother." Zohara did this and the lady of the house got up and slapped her. The young man interrupted and said, "My sister, that is not nice. Don't hit her. I will go home and change my clothes." After he left, the two woman laughed at the success of their plan.

The next day, during the cleaning of the house, Zohara looked and saw that the roses were opening again. Again Zohara was amazed and called out, "My lady, is your brother coming today again, for you said that he only comes but once a year?" The lady hurried and put Zohara in a bag of nuts, painted her face the color of yellow, like a mask, and laid her down in her bed. And thus the two pretended as if Zohara were sick from being shamed by the incident that happened the day before. A short time later, the beautiful handsome prince arrived. "What a surprise you prepared for me, dear brother, for only yesterday you were here. I am used to you only visiting me once a year. What happened?" asked the lady.

"My dear sister," explained the prince to her, "I came to ask about the health of the young servant. I thought to myself that she probably got scared and even sick because of the incident that happened yesterday." The lady pretended to be shocked, "How can you ask only about some lowly servant?" "My dear good sister, you have made a terrible mistake," answered the prince. "She is not lowly at all. The opposite is true. She is as high and as gentle as a princess." "She is truly very sick," announced the lady to her brother. "Would you like to see her?" The prince went into Zohara's room. The lady winked at her. Zohara made a movement and the nuts shook until the young man cried out, "My sister, what have you done to her? Her bones are falling apart." "Why is that important? So she'll die. She soils her clothes," answered the sister. The prince left the house with tears in his eyes. The next day, Zohara began to clean the house, and again, wonder of wonders, once again the roses opened. "My brother likes you," called the lady. "Now I will take care of things." What did she do?

She took Zohara, made her beautiful, and put a royal crown on her head and a royal cape on her shoulders. Then she took the three pairs of worn-out iron clogs and tied them on her back. On the clogs she placed the two letters that proved that she had cured a crazy girl and revived someone dead from the grave. And when the handsome prince, who was none other than Prince Ali, saw Zohara in her beautiful outfit with the three pairs of worn-out iron clogs and the certificates, he knew that his conditions had been fulfilled. He almost fainted when he realized that Zohara had to go through such long and drawn-out tortures. He immediately took her to his parents' house and married her.

Zohara and Ali lived with happiness and wealth and saw in their lives many blessings and successes.

It was good for them and it should also be good for us.

End of Story Note

IFA 5528 from *71 Folktales from Libya*, Story #63, collected by Simkha Shamaka from a woman from Tripoli, Libya (Noy).
Tale Types: AT 874 (The Proud King Is Won); AT 425 IV (Search for Husband).
Motifs: H1125 (Task: traveling till iron shoes are worn out); H1233.1.1 (Old woman helps on quest); H1114 (Task: climbing glass mountain); Q482.1 (Princess serves as menial); H1010 (Impossible tasks); J1111 (Clever girl).

This story has many similar motifs to IFA 10,094. In these stories there are strong, vivid folklore images: black coal and red blood on white snow; the impossible tasks of wearing out three pairs of iron shoes, to hear crackling noise as though the bones were breaking apart, to see one who has become yellow like a mat, etc. Sounds and color intermingle with the narrative. Everything seems the opposite of what should occur, such as when the princess must do menial work as a servant as part of her task. Other things occur that are "magical," such as cut roses with tightly closed buds opening up suddenly when Prince Ali is about to arrive. Like the metaphor of the closed buds, this story includes penetrating outer layers that lead us to inner secrets.

While there is no tale type of a clever princess (only "The Clever Peasant Girl"—AT 875), this is certainly the story of a very clever and courageous young woman.

The end-line blessing is one of the traditional story endings from the Middle East.

—PS

43

The Tiger and the
Son of the Woodcutter

A man and his wife were going into the forest to bring wood in order to prepare for the winter that was approaching. The couple had one small boy and they didn't know where to leave him. So what did they do? They took him with them and they began to chop trees. Because they were so occupied with their work, they didn't pay attention to the young boy who began to explore different paths and wander away from them. And when he wanted to find his parents again, he couldn't see them. He could no longer hear them chopping trees. He looked and he looked but he was lost deep in the woods.

Now when the parents were finished cutting all their wood, they came to the place where they had left their child but they didn't find him. They called out his name, but he didn't answer. They looked for him everywhere, but they still didn't find him. They called the villagers to help search the woods, but the boy was nowhere to be found. And when they were tired of looking, all the people returned to their homes. And the poor parents, too, returned to their home, but without their child—and with great sadness in their hearts.

Meanwhile the child walked down one path and then another. On the way he met a lonely tiger. The tiger was happy to meet the young boy and took the boy with him to his cave.

In the morning, every day, the tiger would go out from his cave and bring food for the boy. He would prepare different kinds of food for him. And that is how the boy lived with the tiger, in the cave, without knowing another person or another animal. His only companion was the tiger, who raised him.

When the boy grew up, he began to think about himself and where he was. And one day, when the tiger got up and left the cave to go hunting for food, the now-grown young man got up and left the cave and went to the nearby village. There he asked the villagers about his parents. While he was telling his story, he also praised the tiger who did so much good for him.

The people of the village remembered the boy who had been lost in the forest and, immediately, they went to tell his parents about their son. The parents came to see the young man. Recognizing him instantly, they were filled with happiness. "You are our son," they exclaimed. The parents related to their son everything that had happened since that sad day so long ago in the forest. Then they asked him, "But what happened to you, my son? Where were you all these years? Who took care of you?"

And the son told them about the many years that had passed and how he had lived with the tiger in the cave. But he couldn't remember how he got to the cave. However, he assured his parents that the tiger had been very good to him and treated him with great tenderness.

Listening to his son's tale, the father, nevertheless, judged the tiger harshly and he thought to himself, "This tiger must have stolen my son. Since he has caused me great suffering and great grief all these many many years, I will get revenge on him. That tiger must die."

What did the father do? He took his rifle and asked his son, "Take me to the tiger's cave." And the two of them went and found the cave and the tiger in it.

And when the tiger saw "his" son, after not having seen him for many days and afraid that harm had come to him, he was very happy that the boy had returned to him. But, at that minute, the boy's father pointed the rifle and a bullet entered the head of the tiger.

The boy looked at his tiger father, the one who had raised him, and who was now drowning in his blood. And then the son looked at his human father and said, "A vicious animal is the tiger, but even more vicious is man." And the young man fell on the ground and wept.

End of Story Note

IFA 1193 from *Druse Folktales*, story #24, recorded by Salman Falah from memory.

Tale Type: AT 178 (Faithful Animal Rashly Killed).

The beginning of this animal tale is the motif (B531) where an animal, in this case a tiger, gives food and raises a human child. It is the reverse of nature because normally we think of a tiger as a vicious man-attacking animal, yet here the tiger is a nurturing caretaker of the child. The story continues and is similar to the tale type AT 154, part III: "An ungrateful man puts his dogs onto the fox [tiger] that was good to him."

The ending of the story is similar to the tale type AT 160: "Grateful Animals; Ungrateful Man."

Motifs: B331 (Faithful animal rashly killed); W154.8 (Grateful animals: ungrateful man).

However, the tragic ending points up a pessimistic relationship toward man rather than animals. The story belongs to the genre of animal story, which accounts for a number of stories in the Israel Folktale Archives collected from Yemen, Iraq, Israeli Arabic, Tunisia, and Russia.

For more about Druse, see note to "The Twelve Sons of the Emir" in this collection.

—PS

44

The Bequest

There was once a very rich man and he lived in a beautiful house filled with many possessions. Anything he wanted, he would always find in his house. His riches were very very great; he had gold and silver and many valuable treasures. And in addition to all his riches and beauty that he had in his house, he also had three sons. They were all hero soldiers: good, honest, and faithful to their father. They always did what their father asked and they always showed him the respect that he deserved.

All the people in the country respected this man and respected his high position. They also loved him because he was always concerned about everyone; he always took care of his fellow citizens.

One day, the father held a banquet for his sons and his entire family. After they had all eaten, and everyone's heart felt good from wine, the father got up and said, "My sons, will a man live forever? And if he goes to the next world, what will happen to all of his possessions that he accumulated during the years of his life on his earth? Therefore, my sons, I have called you here today for you to hear what I have left in my will. Days come and go and I will leave you all my wealth. As to how it should be divided, I ask that you please divide it according to your conscience. Remember that you two older brothers are of one father and one mother. And although the youngest among you is the son of a different mother, a woman I married after the death of your mother, he is the same as you. Remember that all my possessions are a gift from our Creator in Heaven. I didn't get them through thievery or in any unlawful way, but rather I only got them through a straight and righteous way. Righteousness and honesty have always ruled me all the days of my life.

So, my sons, go the same way that I have found and remember that your soul within you belongs to Hashem. Our part in the world is to work harder for the one goal, that righteousness and honesty should rule and to help in saving our fellow man.

"And now my sons, my death will come soon. And here is what I want you to do for me. Upon my death, put me on the back of my camel and it will lead you, without stopping on the way, until it will get to a place very far from here, a distance of three days and three nights. And when the camel reaches that place, it will stop there and, in that place, you will bury me. For three nights you must watch over my grave. Divide the nights in order and each one of you will guard for one night. And remember, when anyone approaches you, greet them with 'Hello, grandfather.' Then all will be well." After the father finished his words, he blessed his sons with all the blessings. Then everyone returned to their homes.

When the father died, the sons did not forget what he had said and, indeed, found everything ready; the coffin that was covered with gold, the inside covered with cloth, and the best camel in the herd, which belonged to their father.

They placed their father's body on the back of the camel and they began to ride behind it for the long journey. On the way, they began to talk about the will and what he had left them, their legacy. The older son said to his brother, "This youngest boy, even though he is our brother and the son of our father, his mother is not our mother and he endangers our position. He could even ask for the greatest part of father's legacy since he is the son of our father's old age and his mother is still alive. The law will only permit us to take half of the legacy. The other half will be given to him and his mother. Therefore let us give him wine every evening in order to make him drunk at the time that he has to guard on the third night. On the day after, we will have our revenge on him."

The youngest brother was very clever and he did not drink the wine. And because he heard what they had said, he said to them, "My brothers, I am the youngest among us. Therefore, I will give you all your honor and I am ready and willing to guard the grave all three nights so that you may eat and drink and rest. After all, you are older and get more tired than I do."

The oldest brother said, "No, we will do what our father ordered.

Each of us will guard one night just as our father requested." And what the oldest brother said was accepted.

When the camel arrived at the specific place, the brothers went and dug the grave and buried their father in it. When they finished the burial, they were very tired. And night came. The first tour of guarding began. The oldest brother put on his sword and went to stand guard over the grave. The other two brothers began their preparations to sleep. At midnight, the oldest brother saw something as if someone was coming closer to him. He immediately got up, took out his sword and stood ready for whoever was coming. All of sudden, he saw a great big animal, like a tiger, getting closer to the grave. It looked as if it were ready to attack. The older brother let the animal get closer until it was ten meters from him. He then turned to the tiger and said, "Hello grandfather." "Hello," answered the animal. "If you had not begun by saying 'hello,' I would have probably torn your head off."

As the animal was talking, the oldest son took out his sword and stabbed the animal. The animal said, "Stab me again." But the oldest brother refused, saying, "I will not stab you again because it is known that if you stab an animal twice, it gets healed. And then it will attack the stabber and eat him." After an hour, the animal died. The oldest son cut off the animal's head and put it in his sack. He then moved the body of the animal further away from the grave, dug a pit, and buried it. The oldest brother came back from his guarding and prepared breakfast for his brothers because that was the custom. When he finished his preparations, it was already dawn. The brothers got up from their sleep and found everything ready for breakfast; coffee, small rolls, and hot coals ready to cook their breakfast. When they finished eating, they took the camel for a walk. Then the three of them sat down and recalled different occurrences in their lives and memories from the time when their father was alive. That's how they sat, remembering many different memories until the evening.

When night came, they went back to the grave and the second son tied his sword to his waist and went to guard. At midnight, a big animal came before him. The animal was even more huge than the first one. The son who was guarding didn't know what to do. He lost all sense of what to do. Then he remembered what his father had told him, and he found courage in his heart and in his soul. He turned to the animal and said,

"Hello, grandfather." And the animal said, "Hello to you. And if you hadn't begun by saying 'hello,' I would have drunken your blood." What the animal said made the second son very angry and he took out his sword very quickly and cut off the head of the animal. After that he buried the body a little distance away and he put the head in his sack. By then it was dawn so he returned to prepare the customary breakfast.

In the morning, the brothers rose and ate all that they wanted. Again they took the camel that their father loved so much for a walk. When they returned from the walk, the two older brothers said to the youngest brother, "We have done our duty. Now it is the last night before us. You must do what we have done. Make sure the breakfast is ready and after breakfast we will pack up to leave. Don't forget what our father told us."

The first hours of guarding did not pass easily for the youngest brother. And when the stars came out and lit up the sky, the evening felt a little better. He began to recall his private memories so that he would not forget them so quickly and to fill his soul with memories. As he was remembering his father, he kept wondering to himself, "How wonderful life was when a father lived on the land in this world. All the days of my childhood I did not lack for anything. Everything was given to me because my father loved and cared for me and made sure that no evil would come to me." In this way the youngest brother sat, lost in his thoughts. The campfire was warm. All of sudden, something got close to the fire, stopped, and breathed into it. Immediately the fire went out.

The youngest son understood immediately what had happened and he got up and said, "You, King who ruled over all existence, bring back the fire that has disappeared or I will not know what my sin is or what my crime is. And, without fire, how can I prepare the food for my brothers that I am required to prepare in the morning. You do your will, my King, but please bring back the fire."

And a hidden voice answered, "Leave the place and go far away because only there will you find the fire. The only way to succeed and to return to your brothers is to take the right precautions."

And the brother put his sword in his belt and went out into the great forest. Where he was going he didn't know. But he went in the direction where his legs took him. All of sudden, a little distance away, he saw a little spark of fire and he began to run toward it. However, when he got closer to the spark, he understood that this was not fire but a figure whose legs were on the ground and whose head was in the sky. What did he do? He decided to get closer to this figure and to ask for charity and pity from it. He went up to it and touched its legs and began to plead, "O sir, O King, please make time go backwards again and return the night to me." The figure answered, "My son, I would be willing to help you if I could but I am responsible for this day only. I have no permission to make the night longer. Our laws do not permit it, but here, behind that mountain, lives the person who is responsible for the night. Go there to him, in the same way you have come to me, and you will get what your heart desires." And the youngest brother bowed before the figure responsible for the day and turned toward the person responsible for the night.

And when he came before him, he said, "Thank God, for He has pity and does miracles for people, and He puts the stars and the moon in his kingdom of night because all the world is great." And the leader of the night heard this, got up and asked the young man, "What is it that you want at this time?" "I ask you, Your Great Highness who rules over all the armies of heaven, please return the night to its beginning because, if the dawn comes, my soul is in danger because I have not yet succeeded in obtaining my goals. Please have pity on me for the dead and for those who are alive as well."

"You have a very good heart, my son," answered the leader of the night. "You also knew how to approach me and, because of that, I will return the night to its beginning. Go back on your way and don't be afraid and God will help you succeed on your way." The youngest brother thanked the leader of the night and continued to look for the fire, for only with it could he go back to his brothers and fulfill his debt to them. And that is how the young boy, valley after valley, went up mountain after mountain, went again down valley after valley, until his eyes saw a very small light inside a cave that was in the side of one of the mountains. He said to himself, "When I get there, I will ask those who are in the cave for only a few coals and then I will return to my brothers." When he arrived at the cave, he saw twelve men and they were all in a deep sleep. On the fire was a great pot and in there meat was cooking. It was unfortunate because the campfire was found inside the cave and in order to get to it he had to step over the twelve people. And so the young boy began to step over the sleeping men so as to get to the fire. So he took a few of the hot coals and, even a small piece of meat, but he had to go out of the cave in the same way, by stepping over the twelve men. Then he stumbled over the legs of one of them and fell down. The sleeping people suddenly jumped up and wanted to kill the intruder. Finally they calmed down and said to the boy, "Indeed you are a thief, but a very good thief. Would you like to join us? We are prepared to go now to the king's castle in the neighboring city to steal all of his treasure."

The young man answered with a smile, "I am willing to join you because if I refuse, you will kill me." But, he thought to himself, "If I join you, there's a chance that I can be saved and free myself." So the thieves packed up their tools and they went on their way to the castle.

They arrived at the castle wall and they set up a ladder. Then they turned and said to the young man, "You will have the honor of going first." The young man climbed the ladder without fright, jumped over the wall, and landed on the roof of the castle. There he stood, took out his sword, and waited for the thieves. When the first of the thieves got to the other side of the wall, the young man cut off his head. That's what he did with all the other thieves too. When he saw the twelve thieves lying on the ground, he came down from the roof of the castle, climbing to the highest courtyard, and from there he found the way down. When he began to go down, he decided "I must do some sort of a heroic deed that will be remembered in my brothers' hearts for a long time."

So what did he do? He opened the first door that he saw on his way, and without thinking, he went in. There he saw the king and the queen sleeping. So what did he do? He tied their hair together and then took their clothes that were lying about and changed sides, putting the queen's clothes on the king's side and the king's clothes on the queen's side of the bed. That is what he did with all the people who were living in the castle.

When he got to the first floor, he heard the sound of a harp from one of the rooms. So what did he do? He opened up the door quietly. And who did he see in the room? The king's daughter sitting sadly and plucking at her harp. And when the king's daughter saw a strange person standing in the room, she got very frightened. But he calmed her down and said, "I love you at first sight. But why are you awake at this time of night when it is so late?"

And the princess answered him with a question, "Everything is enclosed and locked here and I am sitting inside the palace. How did you come here?" The young boy told the king's daughter all that had happened, how he had arrived at the palace, how he killed all the thieves, and how he had tied up all the hair. "And all these things will prove my story," he said, "because even the king and queen are tied together by their hair." And he smiled. Then he asked the king's daughter to keep his secret. "I must go now to my brothers," he told her, "because everything happened because of the fire. If you have fire, give it to me and I will be grateful to you all the days of my life."

The king's daughter gave him fire and the young man left her saying, "Don't tell anyone that I was here because, if I have the possibility, I'll visit you again." The youngest brother went out of the palace gates and it was still the same night when he got to the place where his brothers were sleeping. Then he prepared the morning meal for them. When morning light came, the brothers awoke and they ate, and they didn't know anything of what had happened to their youngest brother during the long night. After breakfast, the three brothers made ready to leave the place where their father was buried. They put all their belongings on the camel, and they began their return to the royal city.

When they got to the gates of the city, they were stopped by the king's guards. Then they were invited to the great banquet that was being held in the king's palace, because this was the king's order. "Every stranger that comes into my city will be invited to a meal because I want to thank God that I was saved from death this night."

The brothers were happy to hear about the announcement. They said to each other, "We can eat today all that we want, without paying for it, at the king's palace. And then we can continue on our way." When the brothers arrived at the palace, the king's daughter recognized the youngest brother and she told her father, "That is the man who has saved us from the thieves."

The king ordered that the three brothers be brought to him and to be received with great honor. At the end of the meal, the brothers asked permission to be on their way. But the king stopped them by saying, "You must remain here until tomorrow."

In the evening, when all the people in the palace went to sleep, the king asked them, "Each of you must tell us your story about what has happened to you during the past few days." And each brother, in turn, told his story. The oldest brother told how he had cut off the head of the animal and how this proved how brave his heart was. Then he showed the king the head of the animal that he had kept in his sack.

The second brother also told his story. "And this also proves what a hero I am and how brave my heart is." And he too showed the king the head of the even bigger animal that was in his sack.

Then the youngest brother told his story, which was much longer. He told about his meeting with the leader of the day and the leader of the night and about the pity that the leader of the night had for him and brought the night back to its beginning in order to make it longer. He also told how he killed the twelve thieves and how he tied the hairs of the king and queen, and of everyone else in the palace. He didn't hide anything about his meeting of the king's daughter and he admitted that the minute he saw her he fell in love with her. He also revealed that there was a promise of love between them that was made during that night.

The king was very happy when he heard the story of the young man and thanked him for killing the twelve thieves. Then he turned to all those who were present and said, "I now proclaim and announce in my whole country that from this day forward that everything that is in my palace belongs to this young man. He will stay here in this palace and my daughter whom he loves will marry him, if she gives her consent. His place will be as a prince in this country. And you, his two brothers, you may live anywhere you like in my kingdom. If you stay in my country you will have a good life until the end of your days."

After a few days, the two elder brothers decided to return to their father's house. Before they left, the youngest brother said to them, "Brothers, I have so much now, so accept my share of our father's wealth."

The three brothers embraced and the older two left the palace with honor and in peace.

End of Story Note

IFA 6237 from *A Tale for Each Month 1964*, Story #2, collected by Jacob Zohar from his father Shalom from Yemen (Kagan).
Tale Types: AT 530 Part I (Reward for the Vigil); AT 304 Part II (Killing of Giants).
Motifs: G346 (Devastating monster); H1471 (Watch for devastating monster. Youngest alone successful); H1462 (Vigil for dead father); L10 (Victorious youngest son); L131 (Hearth abode of unpromising hero); B315 (Animal helpful): B155.3 (Camel deciding burial place).

In this complex story, most of the story's subject has a universal character and there are, indeed, a number of variants from many countries. However, in the first part of the story, there are Jewish elements of a righteous Jewish father bequeathing a spiritual inheritance. The idea of an ethical will stems from the time of Abraham in the Bible. In Genesis 18:19, God says of Abraham: "For I have known him, to the end that he may command his children and his household after him, that they may keep the way of the Lord, to do righteousness and justice; . . ." Giving these injunctions, whether in writing or orally given, form the Jewish ethical will (*tzvua'ah*). In such a will, the parent leaves not only the material inheritance, but a legacy of moral lessons, wisdom, a right way to live. The Hebrew word for inheritance, *yerushah*, connotes the material legacy that can be spent at the heir's discretion. However, the Jewish legacy is better referred to as a heritage, *morishah*, specifically Torah, which is inalienable and must be handed down from generation to generation. As it is written, "The Torah that Moses commanded us is the heritage of the Congregation of Jacob" (Deuteronomy 33:4).

Also, in this story, at the end of his instructions about his burial, the father blesses his sons, just as Jacob blessed his children and grandchildren before his death. In Genesis 49:28–30 it is written: "28 . . . and this is it that their father [Jacob] spoke unto them and blessed them; everyone according to his blessing he blessed them. 29. And he charged them, and said unto them: 'I am to be gathered unto my people; bury me with my father in the cave that is in the field of Ephron the Hittite,

30. in the cave that is in the field of Machpelah, . . .'" And Joseph did everything as he was charged by his father.

The single theme of the three sons guarding a place is similar to "The Three Brothers," an Elijah the Prophet story, in my *Jewish Stories One Generation Tells Another*. In this story, each brother is tested and only the youngest knows how to appreciate his "gift" granted by Elijah. There is no sibling rivalry as there is in this story of three brothers. There are even some parallels in the biblical story of Joseph and his brothers. And of course, in folklore and in the Bible, it is always the youngest who is the most unpromising, but who proves to be the most clever and always wins the reward in the end.

—PS

45

The Queen and the Forty Robbers

There was once a widowed queen and she had many children. Her oldest daughter had married and lived across the courtyard of the palace. The other children, mostly girls, lived in the palace and together they ruled the kingdom.

One day, forty robbers came and they decided to break into the queen's palace and steal all her possessions. From her window, the queen saw the strangers riding and getting closer to her city. She was very frightened and called out, "What will I do? How do I know what they will do?" Immediately she went and opened one of the rooms in the palace and brought all her daughters to stay together in that room. The queen then got dressed, put on her perfume and make-up, and prepared a beautiful table, a banquet. When the robbers came to break down the door of the palace, the widowed queen opened the door wide, dressed in her magnificent clothes and jewels and giving off a beautiful fragrance of perfume. The head of the robbers came in and she received him in a very welcome manner with a gracious smile. "Welcome. It is a very long time that I have waited for you. Do you not know that a woman as I am has been widowed for many years. I have been living without a husband and I have been waiting for you. How is it that you remembered to come to me?"

The robber was shocked for a moment, but then he realized that the queen's doors were opened before him. And if that were indeed true, then she waited for him. He realized that all this money is there to be given to him so why should he rob? A whole kingdom is waiting for him. He turned to his people and ordered, "Go away. I will speak with the queen myself."

The two were left in the house alone—the queen and the robber. Before they began the feast, they sat to talk awhile. The queen said to him, "Now we will be able to get married soon. I will give birth to a son and he will grow up to great things. Do you know how much I want a son? The best teachers will instruct him and he will grow up to be talented and very educated." And that's how the two of them sat together and talked. Then the queen continued, "And after he will grow up, he will be very wise and knowledgeable. But according to law, he will probably go out to war. If that happens, what will happen to us? What will we do? Our son will go the way of many others. How will this be different from other people?"

The queen paused for a moment, then resumed talking, "If he goes to war and he dies, what will we do? He would have been our only son. And he would have been wise and knowledgeable, more than all the others."

And the robber asked, "What is your meaning in asking 'What will we do?'"

The queen replied, "How will we cry for him? It would be terrible for this young man. His mother would have lost him as many other mothers have lost sons. We will cry for him the same way that other families cry for their lost sons."

And the queen said to him, "His name will be called out in the entire kingdom to show that he was such a successful son, that he was powerful and wise. We should cry for him the way other sons are cried for. I will show you how to cry for a son like this."

Immediately the queen got up from her place, opened up her windows wide, and began to cry in a great voice, "Ali, Ali, my son, how I have raised you for many years. I have put your wishes before mine. Ali, Ali, come back my son, my heart, my soul. Come with all your armies. Come back with all your power." And afterward she turned to the robber, "That is how you mourn and cry for our future son."

Now the queen was very wise for the name, Ali, was actually the name of her son-in-law who lived with her daughter close to the palace. The window opened directly toward the house of her daughter and son-in-law.

When Ali heard the cries of his mother-in-law, he got very alarmed. He turned to his wife and said, "Your mother is crying out 'Ali, Ali.'"

Something must have happened at the palace. I must go quickly to her. And what's more, she is asking me to come with my whole army."

So Ali gathered his whole army together and quickly went to the palace. When he arrived, the queen said to him, "Here is the robber. Catch that thief that came into my house and wanted to steal all my possessions. Take him to jail."

The robber said, "But we have not eaten yet. We have not even been married yet. And already a son has been born and his name is Ali and he has died in the war. But here he has arrived already with his army." And still puzzled by the outcome of his misadventure, the robber was led off to the jail.

We should all learn well from the queen's wisdom.

End of Story Note

IFA 10,294 from *A Tale for Each Month 1974–75*, Story #19, collected by Eti Serok from Rahel Mizrahi, from Sephardi Israel (Noy).

Tale Types: AT 956D (How the Girl Saves Herself When She Discovers a Robber under her Bed); AT 958 (The Shepherd Youth in the Robbers' Power); AT 227 (Geese Ask for Respite for Prayer); AT 122C (The Sheep Persuades the Wolf to Sing); elements of AT 1430A (Foolish Plans for the Unborn Child) and AT 1450 (Clever Elsie); AT 954 (The Forty Thieves).

Motifs: K551.5 (Girl calls for help); J2060.1 (Foolish plans for the unborn child); J2063 (Distress over imagined troubles of unborn child); J2198 (Bewailing a calamity that has not occurred); Z71.2 (Formulistic number: Forty).

There are thirteen parallels of this story in the Israel Folktale Archives from Morocco, Iraq, Yemen, Israel-Sephardi, and Persia. Here we have a wise and intelligent queen who uses her cleverness to trick robbers. From the beginning, her "welcome" and the reversal of what might be expected as her reaction keeps the tension in the story for us. This story belongs to the type of story where the weak one succeeds by causing the stronger to become part of the "plan" to reveal his scheme or to trick him into helping the rescuers to come. There are also sound psychological lessons to be learned from the queen's clever plan.

The title of this story conjures up a connection with the well-known *The Arabian Nights* story, "Ali Baba and the Forty Thieves" in two clues: the name of the queen's son, Ali; and the number forty. There are also six versions of the Ali Baba story in the IFA from Morocco and Yemen. In this story, the teller actually focused on the thieves' leader rather than all forty thieves as a collective hero. Also, in the Near East, the number forty represents a number meaning a great number between ten and 100. It also can refer to a long time that is not specified, such as, the days of the flood (Genesis 7:17) and the number of years that the children of Israel would wander through the wilderness (Numbers 14:33). The number seventy in the Torah is another formulaic number which means many many years. In the reference to the bullocks, which totaled seventy, (Numbers 29:12–38) this number corresponded to the seventy nations of the world. Other instances referring to the seventy known languages of those times or the seventy names of God mean that there are voluminous languages and names of God. The numbers are symbolic and not actually limited to forty or seventy.

—PS

46

Ashmedai's Magic Flute

There was once a king who was blessed with plenty of sheep and cattle. He also had a shepherd who would go out every day with the sheep to the pasture. One of the days the shepherd saw a surprising sight: dogs—and these dogs were running after the son of the king of the demons. The shepherd immediately ran and saved the demon from the teeth of the dogs. The grateful demon-son said to him. "You have saved me from the dogs that were going to eat me. And I will pay you back by taking you to my father Ashmedai, who is the king of the demons. My father will look at you for three days without doing anything. On the third day he will ask you, 'What would you like in return for doing this good deed of saving my son?' You will ask and you will receive anything your soul and heart desire."

So the shepherd and Ashmedai's son went on their way. On their way they met one of the Ashmedai's relatives who was asleep. On her finger was an expensive ring. The shepherd liked the ring and wanted to steal it, but the demon-son said to him, "Don't steal this ring because its thief will die after three days." But the shepherd scoffed at what he had said and stole the ring.

They continued on their way until they arrived at Ashmedai's palace. And Ashmedai looked at the shepherd for three days. On the third day he asked the shepherd, "What would you like in return for doing such a wonderful thing for my son?"

"I ask," answered the shepherd, "for a shepherd's hat that is invisible. I would also ask for a magic tablecloth that will fill up with food every time I spread it out. And I would ask for a magic sack that will be

306

full of gold anytime I open it. I will also ask for a stick that has a power in it to open any door, no matter if it's locked with many locks—and a magic flute that, whoever plays it, can call all the demons and ghosts to help him when he needs help."

Ashmedai fulfilled the shepherd's requests and sent him on his way. The shepherd returned very happily to his house, taking with him the wonderful gifts.

However, before he could even tell his wife and son what had happened to him, the prophecy of Ashmedai's son came true, and the shepherd fell to the ground and died.

His widow and his son were very sad and they remained poor because they didn't know the power of the gifts, and, naturally, didn't know how to use the objects to help them. But they kept these objects and put them away. After a time, the young son also became a shepherd like his father.

One day when the young son was about to go out to take care of his sheep, he asked his mother to give him a cloth in order to sit on it when he eats his meal on the field. The mother gave him Ashmedai's cloth that was folded up in the room. When the shepherd spread out the cloth, he saw that it was filled with all different kinds of good food. The son was surprised at what happened, but he sat down and ate with a great appetite.

When the son returned home, he told everything to his mother. The next day, before he went out to the fields, he said, "Mama, the sun is very strong, please give me a hat." And his mother gave him the hat that his father had brought back with him, which was Ashmedai's gift.

The son only had to put the hat on his head when he automatically turned invisible and his mother couldn't see him. But when he took off the hat, he immediately became visible again. "This must be a miraculous hat," laughed the boy. And then he asked his mother, "Go give me the flute that father brought home, so I can play it to the sheep in the field." When the boy went out to the field, he played the flute for the sheep, but all of a sudden all these demons and monsters and giants and ghosts appeared. They all bowed before him and asked him what he wanted. They even put him on a royal throne and put a golden crown on his head, saying, "You are our king and for the king there is no need for sheep. Let us all eat the sheep." They said it and they did it. When they had finished their meal, the boy played his flute again, and they all disappeared. And now the boy became once again a poor shepherd, but without sheep. What could he tell the king?

So what did he do? He tied himself up in ropes and screamed, "Thieves caught me! Thieves took everything from me, all my sheep!" The king heard about this terrible robbery and he was angry but he didn't punish the young shepherd.

Some days passed, and one day, the young boy asked his mother for his sack in order to put all his savings into it. The mother gave him the sack that his father had brought. All he had to do was put in his very few coins, but as soon as he opened the sack, it was filled with coins, gold coins. The boy went and bought a great big store and sold all kinds of food and clothes without charging the poor people very much because he had so much. All the other residents of the town left all the other stores and other merchants and only bought at this young man's store.

The merchants got very angry and they went to complain before the king. They said, "This young man is selling all his merchandise so cheaply that it has gotten to the point that no one will buy any of our merchandise." The king believed what they said and decided to throw the boy out. He turned to his beautiful daughter who knew the magic and the whispers of the demons. And she agreed to help him, saying, "Leave it to me. I will take care of getting him out."

That evening the princess invited the young man to a party. And at the height of the happiness of the party, she ordered her servants to throw the young man out of the third floor window. But the young man blew on his flute, and the demons and all the ghosts waited for him on the ground to make certain that he would land safely without any injury.

The next day, the young man went to the palace, but the iron gates were locked. He knocked on them with his magic stick, and they immediately swung open. He arrived at the princess's room and knocked on it with his stick, and the door opened and he entered the room. The princess ordered her servants to throw him out of the window from an even higher place in the palace. But again, the demons and ghosts were there to help him so that he landed safely on the ground.

The next day the young man again returned to the palace. He wore on his head the magic hat so that he would be invisible. He arrived and no one could see him, not even the princess. All of a sudden, he took off his hat, and the king's daughter was surprised to see him. She ordered her servants to throw him out of a fifth-floor window. But again when she looked out of the window, she saw him get up from the ground in full health and happily laughing up at her.

The next day the young man arrived at the palace with a sack of money. This time the princess ordered her servants to throw him out of the sixth-floor window. But this time, too, he returned home without injury. And again the next day he came back to the palace with his tablecloth in his hand. He spread out the tablecloth in her room and ate everything that his heart desired. The princess got very angry and ordered that he be thrown out of the seventh-floor window. But when he landed, he just broke out with laughter because he did not feel anything when he landed.

On the following day, he came to the palace and played on his magic flute and immediately all the demons appeared and put a golden crown on his head and they placed him on a throne. Then they blew on their horns and they led him and everybody else into the palace. When the king heard the voices of the demons and their trumpets, he ran to the roof of the palace and announced, "I will give anything the young man asks for."

"Give me your daughter to marry," demanded the young man. The king wanted to refuse, but his daughter said to him, "Send me to him and this time I will take care of him."

The princess went to the young man and showed him respect and she gave him much wine to drink. When he became drunk, he didn't know the difference between his right and his left. She asked him, "What is the secret of such amazing feats?"

And because he was under the influence of the wine, the young man told her his secrets and told her about the magic flute of Ashmedai and about all the other magic possessions he owned.

The king's daughter collected all his magic possessions and turned the flute around and the entire demon army went away. Afterward, she tied up the young man in ropes and she called for her gigantic servant and told him to throw the young man into the river. But the young man woke up from his drunkeness and, on his way, he realized that the flute was still near him. He leaned over and blew on the flute and the demons came and carried him away to the forest.

In the forest he saw two big apple trees. One had red apples and the other had green apples. The young man hid behind one of the trees and he saw a man passing in the forest eating one of the red apples. Immediately two horns that reached up to the sky grew out of the man's head. And afterward he ate a green apple, and the horns disappeared. The young man filled a basket with the red apples and a few of the green apples. Then he got dressed up as an apple merchant and went to the market. He sold the king and all his ministers a red apple. And when they tasted the apples, everybody grew long horns that reached up to the sky. They all became scared and alarmed and surprised. They called all the wise doctors in the land, but none of them knew how to get rid of the horns.

In the meantime, the king's beautiful daughter ate one of the red apples, and she too had horns growing out of her head. Then the young man disguised himself again, but this time as a doctor. When he arrived at the palace, he promised to cure everybody on the condition that the king's daughter should be his wife. And when the king agreed, and all of them agreed, he gave them the green apples to eat. Just as suddenly the horns disappeared.

Then the young man revealed his identity and the beautiful princess married him and the young couple lived happily ever. And they never lacked for anything.

End of Story Note

IFA 6053 from *Min Ha-Mabua*, Story #7, collected by Rivka Ashkenazi from her father Sasson, from Iranian Kurdistan (Marcus).

Tale type: AT 566 (The Three Magic Objects and the Wonderful Fruits).

Motifs: D812 (Magic object received from supernatural being); **N821** (Help from little man); **D5** (Enchanted person); **D1470.1** (Magic wishing object. Object causes wishes to be fulfilled); **D1451** (Inexhaustible purse furnishes money); **D1475.1** (Magic soldier-producing horn); **D992.1** (Magic horns grow on person's forehead); **D1375.1** (Magic objects cause horns to grow on person); **D1375.2** (Magic object removes horns from person); **D895** (Magic object returned in payment for removal of magic horns); **Q94** (Reward for cure).

This is a very popular international tale type found in numerous countries of the world, including Sweden, Finland, Holland, Ireland, Scotland, Rumania, Hungary, Poland, Italy, Greece, Turkey, India, Chile, Argentina, America, Israel-Arabic, and Yemen. A version of this tale type is also found in Grimm.

There is a story from Iraq (IFA 1928) that also includes three wondrous objects with magical characteristics, which behave very differently: a traveling magic cloak; an enchanted hat that makes the wearer invisible; and a brass ring, which fulfills any request asked of it by its owner. The young hero must answer three riddles in order to prove his worthiness for the princess's hand in marriage. For versions of this story, see "The Clever Young Man" in my *Jewish Stories One Generation Tells Another* and "The Magic Flute of Asmodeus" in *Elijah's Violin* (Schwartz).

Ashmedai (also known as Asmodeus) is the king of the demons, according to talmudic *aggadah*. Ashmedai is first mentioned in the Apocrypha (Book of Tobit) and in talmudic legends he is also the antagonist of King Solomon. Ashmedai is mischievous, powerful, devious, and clever, and possesses magic powers. For more stories of Ashmedai, see *Lilith's Cave* (Schwartz).

—PS

47

The King, Bahlul,
and the Clever Maiden

One day the king said to Bahlul, his brother, "Here is one toman. Go out and bring me something woven and unwoven, a cooked food that is not cooked, and bring the toman back to me."

Bahlul realized that his brother's request was some kind of scheming plan so he decided to run away from the palace. He just began to wander from place to place. On his way a man joined him and Bahlul said to the man, "Let us take a shortcut." This man thought that Bahlul might have been crazy so he didn't pay much attention to him.

On their way the two of them saw a farmer planting seeds in his field. Bahlul turned to the farmer and asked, "Tell me, farmer, do you eat everything that you plant or will you eat it in the future?" The man was surprised at what Bahlul asked, but again he was quiet.

And the two of them came to the side of a river and Bahlul said to his companion, "Let us build a bridge over the river." And the man said to himself, "This man is certainly acting strange."

And on their way they saw a funeral procession. And Bahlul turned to the coffin and asked, "Are you really dead or is there still some life in you?" And his companion laughed to hear what Bahlul had said, but again didn't pay attention to those words.

Then when they finally were about to go separate ways, Bahlul said to the man, "Beware of going into your house without knocking on the door." The man just smiled at Bahlul, but in his heart he really laughed at him and thought he was truly out of his mind.

When the man arrived at his home, he did not knock on the door, but just opened the door and went inside. At that same moment, his daughter was washing herself. Hearing the door open, she hurriedly rushed into the next room, but in her hurry she hit her forehead on the doorpost and was hurt. At that moment, the man realized that Bahlul was a wise man, after all.

When her father sat down to eat, he told his daughter about the foolish words of his fellow walker. But his wise daughter said to him, "Dear father, but you did not get the full meaning of his words. What he said was wise and thoughtful. For instance, two people walking together will definitely shorten the way and make it as though it were a shortcut. The farmer who owes money for the seeds he is planting has already eaten what he will reap from his land. And if one man carries the other on his back while they are passing over a river it is as though they are building a bridge. And if a dead person leaves children after him, it is as if he continues to live."

Afterward the wise daughter sent her servant to Bahlul with thirty meatballs, seven eggs, a roasted pigeon, a shriveled-up chicken, and a plate of pilaf. On her way, the woman servant ate two of the meatballs, one egg, one wing of the pigeon, a thigh of the chicken, and a bit of the rice at the bottom of the pilaf dish. Bahlul immediately took what the daughter had sent him and said to the servant, "Thank your lady for me and ask her, Are there only twenty-eight days in the month? And only six days in the week? And if your big one has been torn off and your small one has not grown a wing? Are there stars that are missing in the sky? And if there's a cloud, is it torn?"

Bahlul's questions intrigued the wise young woman and then she understood that her servant had put her hand in the food that she had sent with her. And so she scolded the servant and invited Bahlul to her home.

When he arrived, she asked him, "What brings you to our town?"

"I am running away from the king," answered Bahlul. "He gave me one toman and demanded that I bring him something woven and unwoven, a cooked dish that is not cooked, and to bring the toman back to him."

The young woman said to him, "Give me the money and I will bring you what he asked."

And so what did the wise young woman do? She gave the coin to her servant and sent her to an animal merchant and instructed her to say, "Send me a good sheep and you will have this toman as your pledge. And if the sheep stays with me and I like the sheep, I will pay you the price for the sheep. But if not, then you must return the toman to me and I will return the sheep to you."

When the sheep arrived, the young woman cut a little piece of wool from its stomach, and cut one of its testicles. She sewed up the place that she had cut so that the sheep merchant would not notice it. Half of the wool she had cut she rolled up into a tablecloth, and the other half she spun. The testicle she cut into two pieces and only half of it she cooked. Then she returned the sheep to the merchant in order to receive back the toman in return. All this Bahlul saw and he also understood that he had the answer for the king. In return for all she did for him, the young woman asked only for one red apple, in other words, a beautiful young man.

Bahlul returned to the king and gave him what was woven and not woven, and the cooked dish that was not cooked, and gave him back the toman that had been returned. The king was surprised because he did not think that Bahlul could do such a clever and wise thing. Bahlul then revealed to the king the secret of his success and the wisdom of the woman.

One day the king dressed up in peasant clothes and went with Bahlul to meet the wise young woman in order to see for himself her goodness and her character. When they arrived, they knocked on the door. But when the young woman opened the door, she lingered in the doorway. Afterward he asked her for a cup of water to quench his thirst. But she brought water in which there were pieces of straw. The king asked her why she lingered in the doorway and the meaning of the straw floating in the water. And the young woman answered him and said, "My meaning is clear. I lingered at the door in order to prevent the two of you from sitting down too quickly after such a tiring long walk and getting your legs entangled. And I put the pieces of straw floating in the water so that you would not drink the water all at one time and too fast. Because if you did, you would have had a stomachache and you might have caught cold."

The king was surprised at the cleverness and the beauty of this young woman and he became very attracted to her. In fact, he fell in love with her. Then Bahlul stood up and said to the young woman, "Here is your red apple. Now I have returned the payment in kind."

I was there and drank a *l'khayim* to their happiness.

End of Story Note

IFA 1625 from *With Elders Is Wisdom*, Story #5, collected by Hanina Mizrahi from memory, from Iran.
Tale Types: AT 875DI*c (IFA) (King asks vizier to buy a sheep, to roast and to boil it, to weave a carpet from its wool, and to return it alive. The clever daughter castrates the sheep, roasts and boils the testicles, and weaves a carpet from the sheep's wool.); AT 875A (Girl's riddling answer betrays a theft); AT 875B (The Clever Girl and the King).
Motifs: H586.3 (One traveler to another: Let us carry each other and shorten the way); H586 (Riddling remarks of traveling companion interpreted by girl at end of journey); J1111 (Clever girl); H561.1.1.1 (Clever daughter construes enigmatic sayings); H580 (Enigmatic statements).

In folktales there are recurrent tasks, riddles, and questions that intrigued the folk in many countries. Certainly one of the reasons we have these repeated riddles, some in rhyme, in addition to other numerous mnemonic inventions, is to help those tellers who told in the oral tradition remember the tales. Variants of this tale include IFA 3475 (Wisdom of Life), IFA 11,459 (He Who Has Found a Wife, Has Found a Great Good), as well as in Ibn Zabara's *The Book of Delight* and "The Wise Village Maiden" in *Mimekor Yisrael*, Vol. 3 (Bin Gorion). The variants come from Persia, Yemen, and Iraq.

This is a folktale with a number of enigmatic riddles that are deciphered by a clever young woman. The tasks then are successfully accomplished by her, thus winning the "red apple," a symbolic term for the loved one. The tale opens with the king challenging his brother to perform certain tasks. What follows are some puzzling remarks made by Bahlul to a man he meets on the road. These are similar to the enigmatic remarks a chamberlain makes to a peasant in the story "The Dream Interpreter" in my *Jewish Stories One Generation Tells Another* and that Elijah tells to the doctor in "The Secret of the Shammash" in my *Eight Tales for Eight Nights*. See also "Caliph Harun Al-Rashid" in this collection.

For other stories involving clever women who accomplish difficult enigmatic tasks, see "Princess Zohara and Prince Ali," "The Camel's

Wife," and "The Yemenite King and His Jewish Advisor" in this collection.

The ending line is a formulaic ending to bring the listeners out of the story and back to real time. This ritual closing signals the end of the story for the audience.

—PS

48

What Made Rabbi Yitzhak
Change His Behavior

The followers of Rabbi Levi Yitzhak of Berditshev asked their rabbi:
"Rabbi, why don't you do the mitzvah of *chesed shel emet*? After all,
this is the last good thing you can do for a dead person and yet you don't
always accompany Jews on their last journeys after they die?"

And Rabbi Levi Yitzhak answered them, "It is not my way to
accompany rich people on their last journeys after they die because I
don't want their descendents to say that the rabbi only gives respect to
our father or grandfather because he was a very rich man. And I don't
accompany poor dead people to the cemetery because then the debt
collectors and the money collectors and others would say I only
accompanied them to the grave because they couldn't support their
families respectfully. And since the Jews are either rich or poor in our
town, I never have the chance to do this mitzvah of accompanying the
dead."

However, when Rabbi Yosef Halprin, who was a very rich man with
a lot of wealth and possessions, died, Rabbi Levi Yitzhak put aside all his
work and study and joined the people to accompany the coffin to the
funeral. Since this was not his usual way, the people who knew him were
amazed and asked the rabbi the reason why he had made such an exception. Rabbi Levi Yitzhak explained, "I have an extraordinary respect for
what this man had done and this is what is making me change my
behavior. In order that you will understand better why I accompanied
this coffin and changed my usual actions, I must tell you three stories
about this man and his goodness.

The first story is about a Jew who sold his grain and produce to stores and to bakeries. And one time, he lost the amount of 200 rubles, which he had to give to one of his suppliers. His heart was heavy about this loss. And so he announced in public that this money was lost. This was made known to Rabbi Yosef Halprin, the head rabbi of the city. Then the rabbi told the merchant that he himself had found the money. The merchant was very happy that his money was found and Rabbi Yosef Halprin returned the 200 rubles. After some hours, when the merchant returned to the bakery, he found the lost money, which had been put by mistake on top of a sack of flour. He ran back to the rabbi and wanted to return the 200 rubles to him, but the rabbi refused to accept them. The two of them came to my *Beit Din* and Rabbi Yosef claimed, "I gave him the money the first time I heard about his problems and, if this grain merchant doesn't want it, he should go and secretly give it out to people who need money."

The second story is about a young new teacher who was very poor and a father of a very big family. He had studied for years at the yeshiva but he didn't find any kind of work to support himself in the town where he was born. So this teacher decided to try his luck in a different town. Before he left, he said to his wife, "Don't worry, my wife, you will not want for anything. The head of the town, Rabbi Yosef Halprin, promised me that he will support you with the amount of twenty rubles every month. The wife believed the husband even though she knew that the husband had not talked to the rabbi and had only said this to her to calm her down. But he knew she was an *eshet chayil* and that she would get along. So the teacher packed up his belongings, his *tallit* and *tfillin*, and some food for the way, and left to go to the nearest town where Jews lived. In this place, the Jews were farmers and he hoped that he would be able to collect an amount of money great enough in order to support his household. After a few weeks passed without any money coming in, his wife went to the office of Rabbi Yosef and said to him, "Rabbi, you promised my husband to give me twenty rubles every month until he finishes his time as teacher in the next town. And since he left, I have not received anything from you."

Even though this matter was not known to him, the Rabbi didn't hesitate and he gave the woman twenty rubles and promised to send her, with the help of God, twenty rubles every month. Even though Rabbi Yosef kept up his promise or rather his "agreement" between him and the teacher, he knew very well that the husband had left his wife and children alone. At the time of Pesach, when the season of teaching was over, the teacher returned to his home and, in his hand, there was a great amount of money that he had received from the fathers of his students. He also had presents for his wife and his children, whom he thought had a difficult life while he was away for those six months. When he arrived at his house, he saw to his amazement that his wife and his children were dressed nicely and the house was clean and bright and the table was set with the best foods. "How is it possible to support the family in such a grand manner while I was away. I didn't even leave you with any money, not even one ruble in the house."

The wife answered, "Didn't you tell me that the Rabbi Yosef promised you support of twenty rubles for each month that you would not be home? He sent me this amount every month according to your agreement that you had between you."

The teacher went directly to the rabbi in order to return the 120 rubles, but the rabbi would not accept even one ruble. This time he also claimed that the money did not belong to him because he had given it up a half a year ago.

And when the two of them came to my *Beit Din*, the rabbi also explained that he should give it secretly to *tzedakah*, the same way he had declared in the first instance.

And now a third tale about Rabbi Halprin. One cloth merchant, one of the more important *balabatim* in the city, lost almost all of his possessions and declared bankruptcy. With a heavy heart, he decided to go to the head of the city, Rabbi Yosef, and ask for a loan of several hundred rubles so he could repay his debts. The rabbi asked him, "Who will be your co-signer for this loan in case you do not repay it?" And the borrower answered, "*HaKodosh Baruchu*, God Himself will be the co-signer. With His help, I will repay all the money that you have lent to me." And Rabbi Yosef said, "I will accept your co-signer and I trust in God because I believe that He will help you in returning this amount of money." So Rabbi Yosef took out the hundred ruble bills and gave them to the cloth merchant. And when it came time for the debt to be due, it was already in the hands of the cloth merchant, even more than the loan. And he came to Rabbi Yosef to return his loan and add his thank you and his blessings. But this time the head of the town refused to accept even one ruble and claimed that he gave up this money and it would be better if it went to the people who really needed it.

And when Rabbi Yitzchak finished these three stories about Rabbi Yosef Halprin, he added, "Don't these stories tell us about this wonderful Jew. He came before me in three law decisions. And these show what a true person and good Jew he was. I would make an exception to my behavior for such a person and I would fulfill the mitzvah of *chesed shel emet*."

End of Story Note

IFA 7612 from *A Tale for Each Month 1967*, Story #3, collected by Zalman Baharav from Azriel Broshi of White Russia (Cheichel-Hechal). There is a variant, "The Three Deeds of Yehezkil the Merchant" (IFA 681).

This story, classified as a Religious Tale, includes all the stories of the International tale type 759 (God's justice vindicated) where the good deeds of the righteous are repaid, but specifically the tale type is AT 759*D (IFA) (Three cases of generosity).

Motifs: V252.1 (Virgin Mary returns borrowed money and reveals cheat) and J1559.1 (A present or a retaining fee).

There are four versions of the Jewish oikotype recorded in IFA and over forty versions of AT 759 from Morocco, Libya, Egypt, Turkey, Syria, Persia, Iraq, Afghanistan, Rumania, Poland, Lithuania, and Russia.

The stories include the performance of the mitzvah of hidden charity by a leader of the community who, when he dies, receives a beautiful funeral although he had been considered a miser in life. The leader had supported a Jew's family when this Jew became poor and even before he went out to look for work in other cities, usually promising his family the leader's support *without* speaking to the leader about this beforehand. In the end, the tale type is connected with AT 940* (The Forgiven Debt) and AT 849* (The cross as a guarantee). However, instead of the Christian symbol of the cross as security, in the Jewish versions it is God (*HaKodosh Baruchu*) who appears as the guarantor (motif J1559.2).

Rabbi Levi Yitzhak of Berdichev (died in 1809) appears as a hero in frame stories in other parallel stories, e. g. IFA 2910.

See the note to "Two Friends" in this collection which is also a Rabbi Levi Yitzhak story.

—*PS*

49

The Indian King
and the Jewish Shepherd

Once there was an Indian King who was not very clever. And he was also very jealous. However, his advisor was very educated and, in fact, he was really the one who ruled the matters of state with wisdom and faith. One day the jealous king said to his advisor, "Bring before me the teacher who taught you wisdom and knowledge so that he can answer the questions I want to ask him. If you don't bring your teacher here within a week, you will die."

Feeling very depressed, the advisor returned to his house, went into his chamber, and cried bitter tears. He had had a very wise teacher, but that was so long ago. Even if his teacher were still alive, who would know where he lived now. And the advisor sat and didn't know what to do in order to satisfy the king's request.

The advisor had one daughter who was very beautiful and very wise. Her father loved her very much. When she saw her father's face and saw how distressed he was, she understood that he had a great worry in his heart. She asked him to tell her what was troubling him.

And the advisor told his daughter about the demands of the king. She smiled and said, "Don't worry, father. Not too long ago I happened to talk with our shepherd, a Jew named Sasson. And I found out that he is a very wise man. I'm sure that this shepherd can successfully fulfill the place of your teacher. And when he comes before this foolish king, he will be able to answer all of his questions."

The advisor agreed to this plan and called Sasson, the shepherd, and told him everything. "Of course," promised the advisor, "if you pass the test, I will give you many blessings and gold."

"First, give me appropriate clothes and I will go before the king," answered Sasson.

The advisor dressed Sasson in new clothes and the Jew went to the palace. When the king asked him if he had been the advisor's teacher, Sasson answered, "Yes, I was his teacher."

And the king sat him down before him and said, "I will speak to you in a sign language. You must also answer me in sign." And the Jew agreed.

First the king showed the Jew one finger. And the Jew answered by holding up two fingers.

And then the king held up three fingers. And the Jew answered by holding up four fingers.

Then the king made a circle with his right hand. The Jew also made a circle in the air with his right hand, but in the opposite direction, ending with the thumb pointed downward.

The king was very happy with the wise answers of the teacher and ordered that he be given 5000 rupees.

When the advisor heard what happened, the ministers all said, "It is no wonder that our advisor is so wise because his teacher is so wise." And then they asked the king, "What was the meaning of all these hand movements that you did with the teacher?"

And the king answered, "Very simple. I showed the teacher one finger, meaning that I had one belief in one God. And the teacher answered with two fingers, meaning that there is one God and one King. Then I showed the teacher three fingers. My meaning was that without three, God, King, and the advisor, the country would not exist. The teacher answered my question very well by holding up four fingers, because he added the whole kingdom itself. In the end, I showed him the symbol of the circle. In other words, it is the king's wish for other conquests to take all the world in his arms. And the teacher made the same movement, but in the opposite direction, with the down side, showing me that at the end of all conquests, the conqueror must eventually go down to hell. Therefore, I knew that the advisor's teacher is indeed wise and he earned his prize."

Then the advisor went home and was very happy and lighthearted. He related all of the events to his daughter. And she reminded him of his promise to reward Sasson and thank him for his service. And the advisor made a great banquet and he invited Sasson the shepherd as his guest. The advisor asked him, "What were the meanings of the signs that you and the king made?"

"It's all very simple," answered the Jew. "The king showed me one finger because the king wanted one sheep from me. I answered him with two fingers because I was even willing to give him two sheep. When the king showed me three fingers, I saw that it was not enough for him to take two. So then I promised him four. The most important thing is that he should be happy. But then when he made a circle, in other words, he wanted all my herd, I made him a circle in the opposite direction, meaning that whoever takes a lot will not have anything left because he will have to die and be buried in the ground just like everyone else."

The advisor laughed and everyone in his house laughed. And as a thank you for Sasson for all that he had done in saving him from a great tragedy, he gave him 2000 rupees. And ever since then, Sasson, the Jewish shepherd, has lived in wealth and with great respect all the days of his life.

End of Story Note

IFA 4418 from *A Tale for Each Month 1962*, Story #6, collected by Zvi Moshe Haimovits from Sasson Yitzhak, from India (Noy).
Tale Type: AT 924B (Sign language misunderstood).
Motifs: J1804 (A conversation in sign language mutually misunderstood); H541.1 (Riddles propounded on pain of death); H607 (Discussion by symbols).

This is an international type of story where the signer, who uses gesture with which to communicate in a debate, is a shepherd. In this variant of the discussion by sign language, there is no religious confrontation, as is often the case in stories involving a priest and a Jew, who is usually a naive but clever chicken dealer. In these versions (AT 924 and AT 924A), Jews are forced to debate with the Jew-hating king/priest/ advisor and win or else they will be expelled from the kingdom.

There are many Jewish variants in the IFA from Iraq, Tunisia, Yemen, Turkey, Egypt, Kafkaz, and Afghanistan. See "A Dispute in Sign Language" (IFA 505) in *Folktales of Israel* (Noy). Also in another of my versions of this story, the clever signer is the Sephardic trickster character, Joha, who wants to teach an arrogant scholar a lesson by debating him in sign language. Here too there is no religious argument. See "Going Along with Joha" in my *Chosen Tales*.

For stories with other kinds of challenging riddling debates, see also "The Jewish Weaver's Wisdom" and "The King's Three Questions" in this collection.

—PS

50

The Horse That Got Stuck in the Mud

Once there was a king who loved tales, tales that were long and didn't have an ending. Once the king ordered that a proclamation be made: Anyone who can tell the king a story that does not have an ending, will receive a great golden prize.

And many storytellers came from all the corners of the country and they told long long stories that continued for days and weeks and months—but in the end, they ended, even though they were long.

The king didn't award any prizes to any of them, because he was looking for a story without an ending.

One day a poor Jew came to the king. This young man, Hershel, was clever and shrewd. He told the king, "I have a story for you that you will not have to listen to for so many long weeks, but it does not have an ending." And Hershel began to tell his story.

"Dear sir, in a faraway land, there was once a king who went out to hunt. He rode alone in the forest. Then his horse got into some deep mud and got stuck."

And here Hershel stopped his story and did not continue the telling.

The king asked him, "Well? So what happened to the king in the forest?"

So Hershel answered, "The king's horse got out his front legs but then his hind legs got stuck in the mud." And again the Jew was quiet.

"So?" the king asked the Jew. "What happened then to the king?"

"Nothing. When the horse got out its front legs from the mud, his back legs got stuck deeper in the mud."

"So then what happened next?" asked the king.

327

"Nothing. Nothing happened in the forest with the king and the horse. The horse got its front legs out of the mud, but its back legs were stuck. And when he got his back legs out of the mud, then his front legs got deeper in the mud. And therefore this story has no ending because the mud in the forest was very deep. And the king with his horse, they kept getting deeper and deeper in the mud. And the horse couldn't get out of the mud."

And Hershel got the promised prize.

End of Story Notes

IFA 2969 in *The Kept Promise*, Story #2, recorded by Berl Rabach from memory, from Galicia.

This story is within the category of a Formula Tale and under the subheading of Cumulative Tales in *The Types of the Folktale* (Aarne and Thompson).

Tale Type: AT 2017 (The Crow on the Tarred Bridge).

Motif: Z39.3 (The crow on the tarred bridge): Z11 (Endless tale); Z20 (Cumulative tales).

There are many variants of this story found in Finland, Lithuania, and Hungary in which the animal has different parts of the body alternately stick in tar or mud or some other sticky material.

There is some similarity between this story and *The Arabian Nights*. In *The Arabian Nights*, the young woman telling tales with an incomplete ending has to keep the king in suspense and stimulate his desire to hear the end so she can save her life. However, this story has a type of inner story that is without an end in order for the clever young man to win the reward.

May you, my readers, ever be in love with stories, long and short, and may your stories all have happy endings—and beginnings.

—*PS*

Glossary

Unless otherwise noted, the following expressions are mostly Hebrew. Nearly all of them are used in Yiddish as well as Hebrew, but a Yiddish pronunciation is indicated with (Y). Ashkenazic pronunciation is indicated by (A), Sephardic pronunciation by (S). Vowel combinations: ei = long a; ai = long i.

Aggadah Those sections of Talmud and Midrash containing homiletic expositions of Bible, stories, legends, folklore, anecdotes, maxims; *Aggadah* is found throughout the Talmud, intermingling with *halakha* (law), and deals with the spirit, rather than the letter, of the law.

Agura (Agurot, plural) Iraqi-Kurdistan coin

Aliyah Ascent; going up to live in the land of Israel

Balabatim (plural) Heads of the household or important heads of the synagogue or city

Beit Din Rabbinical court

Beit Knesset Synagogue

Besht Acronym for the Baal Shem Tov, the founder of **Hasidism**

Bimah An elevated place or platform in the synagogue where the rabbi and cantor stand and where the Torah is read

Bris (A) "Covenant"; circumcision ritual of boy child on his eighth day when the child's name is officially given and he enters into the Covenant of Abraham

Challah A special white bread, usually braided, for Sabbath and holiday meals

Chesed Shel Emet "Act of true kindness," giving last respects to the dead by accompanying the deceased to the grave

Chuppah Jewish wedding canopy

Chutzpah Unmitigated impudence

Daven (Y) To pray; chanting of prayers

Dervish A member of any of various Mohammedan ascetic orders in Turkey and Persia

Dinar (**dinari,** plural) A coin used in the Near East

Dooshpera Thin pieces of dough that are shaped in triangles and filled with meat and fried onions (Bukharian food)

Elijah the Prophet The prophet who lived in the Kingdom of Israel in the ninth century; folklore hero who excels in the domain of miracles; often appears in dreams where he reveals mysteries or resolves difficult problems or questions

Eretz Yisrael The Land of Israel

Erev Evening

Eshet chayil Woman of valor

Farbrengen (Y) A hasidic gathering, usually with singing, dancing and storytelling

Gaon Head of an Academy, Great teacher

HaKodosh Baruchu "The Holy One, Blessed Be He"

Hamantaschen A triangular shaped pastry filled with poppy seed or other fruit fillings eaten at Purim; said to be shaped like the villain Haman's hat

Hashem "The Name"; metonym referring to the name of God

Hasid (**Hasidim,** plural) "A pious one." A follower of Hasidism

Hasidism The Jewish religious sect founded by Israel ben Eliezer, also known as the Baal Shem Tov (the Master of the Good Name), in the eighteenth century. The emphasis is on faith and joy in prayer through song, story, and dance.

Havdalah "Distinction"; the ceremony that marks the end of the Sabbaths and Festivals and separates the holy day from the weekday

Kiddush Sanctification; blessing recited over wine

L'khayim "To Life," the traditional Jewish toast

Maggid "Teller"; a traveling rabbi who teaches Judaism through stories

Midrash (**Midrashim,** plural) A method of interpreting Scripture to bring out lessons through stories or homilies; a particular genre of rabbinic literature. A midrash, sometimes in the form of a story or folktale, explains or "fills in the spaces between the words" of Torah text.

Mishloakh manot Giving a dish of at least two different foods to neighbors and charity to the needy at Purim

Mitzvah (mitzvot, plural) A good deed; a commandment or precept

Morisha "Heritage"

Moshol A parable; specifically the illustrative story within the frame of the opening question and connective moral at end

Motzei Shabbos Saturday night after the Sabbath ends

Nimshal The commentary that supplies the moral of the fable

Oikotype A local tale-type extant in a specific ethno-cultural area

Pesach Spring holiday of Passover celebrating the Jews' freedom from slavery in Egypt

Pilaf A Persian/Indian dish of rice and meat

Pookh Eye paint

Purim "Lots"; a holiday that commemorates the Jews' victory over the evil Persian prime minister Haman. The defeat of the enemy was accomplished through the wisdom of Esther and Mordecai. This is a holiday of joyous celebration when the Scroll of Esther is read, people dress in costume, give charity, and exchange gifts of pastries (especially **hamantaschen**), candies, and fruit.

Rebbe (Y) Rabbi, teacher, or learned man

Ruble Russian/Galician coin

Rupee Indian and Afghanistan coin

Sandak The one who holds the boy child during the **bris**

Seikhl Common sense

Shabbos (A); **Shabbat** (S) Sabbath; the Jewish Sabbath begins on Friday evening at sundown and continues until sundown on Saturday; it is a day of rest spent in prayer, study, and meals while refraining from work.

Shalom "Peace"—also used as a greeting

Shammas The caretaker of the synagogue

Shekhinah "Presence"; the feminine aspect of God. The *shekhinah* is often described as having wings that shelter the Jewish people.

Shivah "Seven"; Refers to the seven days of mourning following burial.

Shuk Marketplace

Shul (Y) Synagogue

Shum Garlic

Shum Davar Literally, "Nothing"—an expression

Simkha Happy occasion or celebration, such as a wedding

Tallit (S); **Tallis** (A) A four-cornered prayer shawl with fringes worn during morning, Sabbath, and festival services.

Talmud Chakham Torah scholar

Tfillin Phylacteries. They consist of two black leather boxes containing parchment inscribed with Bible verses and connected to leather straps. One is worn on the left arm and the other on the forehead during morning prayers, except on Sabbath and festivals.

Toman Iranian coin.

Torah The first five books of the Bible, called the Five Books of Moses. The Torah is read aloud in the synagogue on Mondays, Thursdays, Sabbath, and festivals, as long as a quorum is present. Torah can also mean the entire body of Jewish teaching and sacred literature.

Tzedakah Justice; charity

Tzvua'a Will; also an Ethical Will

Vayyikra Leviticus; the third book of the Torah

Yahrzeit Anniversary of a person's death

Yerusha "Inheritance"

Yerushalayim Jerusalem

Zion A name for Jerusalem as a spiritual symbol

Z'miros (A) Joyful songs sung primarily during and after Sabbath and Festival meals

Bibliography

The Israel Folktale Archives (IFA), founded in 1956 by Dov Noy, has collected over 20,000 folktales from informants in the various ethnic communities in Israel. These tales are published in the IFA Publication Series, with over thirty-five volumes published by the Haifa Municipality Ethnological Museum and Folklore Archives. Each tale is assigned an IFA number and is kept in the archives.

Aarne, A., and S. Thompson. (1964). *The Types of the Folktale: A Classification and Bibliography.* 2nd rev. ed. Helsinki: Academia Scientarum Fennica.

Ausubel, Nathan. (1948). *A Treasury of Jewish Folklore.* New York: Crown.

Ben-Amos, Dan, and Jerome R. Mintz, trans. and eds. (1970). *In Praise of the Baal Shem Tov.* (*Shivhei ha-Besht*). Bloomington, IN: Indiana University Press.

Ben Yehezkel, Mordechai. (1928–1929). *Sefer Ha-Ma'assiyot.* (Hebrew). 4 vols. Tel Aviv: Dvir Co., Ltd., 1925–1929; 2nd enlarged edition, 6 vols. Tel Aviv: Dvir Co., Ltd., 1960.

Bialik, H. N., and Y. H. Ravnitzky, eds. (1992). *The Book of Legends* (*Sefer Ha-Aggadah*). Trans. by William G. Braude. New York: Schocken Books.

Bin Gorion, M. J. (1976). *Mimekor Yisrael.* 3 vols. Bloomington, IN: Indiana University Press.

Bloch, Chaim. (1920). *Gemeinde der Chassidim.* (German). Vienna.

Buber, Martin. (1947). *Tales of the Hasidim: Early Masters.* New York: Schocken Books.

Bushnaq, Inea. (1986). *Arab Folktales.* New York: Pantheon Books.

Calvino, Italo. (1980). *Italian Folktales.* New York: Pantheon Books.

Cardonne, M. (1770). *Melanges de Literature Orientale.* 2 vols. Paris.

Cheichel-Hechal, Edna, ed. (1968). *A Tale for Each Month 1967.* (Hebrew). Haifa: IFA Publication Society.

————. (1970). *A Tale for Each Month 1968–1969.* (Hebrew). Haifa: IFA Publication Society.

————. (1973). *A Tale for Each Month 1972.* (Hebrew). Haifa: IFA Publication Society.

Cone, Molly. (1965). *Who Knows Ten.* New York: Union of American Hebrew Congregations.

Courlander, Harold, and Wolf Leslan. (1950). *The Fire on the Mountain and Other Ethiopian Stories.* New York: Henry Holt.

Derenbourgue, J., ed. (1881). *Kalila VeDimna.* (Deux Versions hebraiques du livre Kalilah et Dimnah). Paris.

Eisenstein, J. D., ed. (1915). *Otzar Midrashim* (Treasury of Midrashim). (Hebrew). 2 vols. New York.

Falah, Salman, and Aliza Shenhar. (1978). *Druse Folktales.* (Hebrew) Haifa: IFA Publication Society.

Farhi, Y. S. (1870). *Oseh Pele.* (Hebrew). 3 vols. Livorno. (Also Leghorn, 1902.)

Frankel, Ellen. (1989). *The Classic Tales: 4,000 Years of Jewish Lore.* Northvale, NJ: Jason Aronson.

Gaster, Moses. (1924). *The Exempla of the Rabbis.* Leipzig. (Also New York: Ktav, 1968.)

————. (1934). *The Maaseh Book of Jewish Tales and Legends.* 2 vols. Philadelphia: Jewish Publication Society.

Gaster, Theodor H. (1969). *Myth, Legend, and Custom in the Old Testament.* New York: Harper & Row.

Gittes, Katharine S. (1991). *Framing the Canterbury Tales: Chaucer and the Medieval Frame Narrative Tradition.* Westport, CT: Greenwood Press.

Goiten, S. D. (1973). *From the Land of Sheba: Tales of the Jews of Yemen.* New York: Schocken Books.

Green, Arthur. (1981). *Tormented Master: A Life of Rabbi Nahman of Bratslav*. New York: Schocken Books.

Hadas, Moses, trans. (1966). *Fables of the Jewish Aesop: From the Fox Fables of Hanakdan*. New York: Columbia University Press.

Hanakdan, B. (1921). *Mishlei Shualim (Fox Fables)*. (Hebrew). Ed. by L. Goldschmidt. Berlin: Erich Reiss. (Also Jersualem: A. M. Habermann, 1946.)

Harlow, Jules, ed. (1972). *Lessons from Our Living Past*. New York: Behrman House.

Heinemann, Benno. (1978). *The Maggid of Dubno and his Parables*. New York: Feldheim Publishers.

Ibn Zabara, J. (1912). *The Book of Delight (Sefer Sha'ashuim)*. Trans. by I. Abrahams. Philadelphia: Jewish Publication Society.

Irvin, Bonnie D. "What's in a Frame? The Medieval Textualization of Traditional Storytelling" in *Oral Tradition*, Vol. 10/1 (1995).

Jason, Heda. (1965). "Types of Jewish-Oriental Oral Tales" in *Fabula: Journal of Folktale Studies* VII, 115–224. Berlin: Walter de Gruyter & Co.

———. (1975). *Types of Oral Tales in Israel, Part 2*. Jerusalem: Israel Ethnographic Society.

Jellinek, A., ed. (1853–1877). *Beit Hamidrash*. (Hebrew). 6 vols. Leipzig and Vienna. (2nd ed. Jerusalem: Bamberger and Wahrmann, 1938.)

Kagan, Ziporah, ed. (1964). *A Tale for Each Month 1963*. (Hebrew). Haifa: IFA Publication Series.

———. (1965). *A Tale for Each Month 1964*. (Hebrew). Haifa: IFA Publication Series.

Kaplan, Rabbi Aryeh, trans. (1983). *Rabbi Nachman's Stories*. Brooklyn, NY: Breslov Research Institute.

Lane, E. W., trans. (1839–1841). *Arabian Nights' Entertainments*. (Rev. ed. *Tales from the Thousand and One Nights*. Trans. by N. J. Dawood. Harmondsworth, Great Britain: Penguin Books, 1955.)

Legrand d'Aussy. (1829). *Fabliaux inedits*. 5 vols.

Levin, Meyer. (1975). *Classic Hasidic Tales*. New York: Penguin Books.

Lonzano, Menahem di. (1853) Ma'arikh. Leipzig.

Marcus, Eleazer, ed. (1966). *Min Ha-Mabua*. (From the Fountainhead). (Hebrew). Haifa: IFA Publication Society.

Meshalim Shel Shlomo (Parables of King Solomon). (Hebrew). In *Beit Hamidrash* 4:145–152.

Mizrahi, Hanina, ed. (1967). *With Elders Is Wisdom*. (Hebrew). Collected by H. Mizrahi. Haifa: IFA Publication Society.

Nahman of Bratislav. (1881). *Sippure Ma'assiyot*. Warsaw. (Also Lemberg, 1902.)

Neugroschel, Joachim. (1987). *Great Tales of Jewish Fantasy and the Occult*. Woodstock, NY: The Overlook Press.

Neuman (Noy), Dov. (1954). *Motif-Index of Talmudic-Midrashic Literature*. Dissertation. Bloomington, IN: Indiana University Press.

Newman, Louis I. (1987). *The Hasidic Anthology: Tales and Teachings of the Hasidim*. Northvale, NJ: Jason Aronson.

Niflaoth ha-Maggid Koznitz. (Yiddish). (1911). Piotrkov: A. J. Kleiman.

Noy, Dov. (1961). "The First Thousand Folktales in the Israel Folklore Archives: in *Fabula* 4:99–110.

———. (1961). *Folktales of Israel*. Chicago: University of Chicago Press.

———, ed. (1963). *Seven Folktales*. Collected by Miriam Yeshiva. Haifa: IFA Publication Society.

———, ed. (1963). *A Tale for Each Month 1962*. (Hebrew). Collected by A. Elbaz and S. Elbaz. Haifa: IFA Publication Society.

———, ed. (1966). *Moroccan Jewish Folktales*. New York: Herzl Press.

———, ed. (1966). *A Tale for Each Month 1965*. (Hebrew). Haifa: IFA Publication Society.

———, ed. (1967). *71 Folktales from Libya*. (Hebrew). Haifa: IFA Publication Society.

———, ed. (1967). *A Tale for Each Month 1966*. (Hebrew). Haifa: IFA Publication Society.

———, ed. (1971). *A Tale for Each Month 1970*. (Hebrew). Haifa: IFA Publication Society.

———, ed. (1972). *A Tale for Each Month 1971*. (Hebrew). Jerusalem: IFA Publication Society.

———, ed. (1976). *Faithful Guardians*. (Hebrew). Collected by Zvi Moshe Haimovits. Haifa: IFA Publication Society.

———, ed. (1976). *The Golden Feather*. (Hebrew). Collected by Moshe Attias. Haifa: IFA Publication Society.

———, ed. (1978). *A Tale for Each Month 1974–1975*. (Hebrew). Jerusalem: IFA Publication Society.

————, ed. (1979). *A Tale for Each Month 1978.* (Hebrew). Haifa: IFA Publication Society.

Patai, Raphael. (1988). *Gates to the Old City.* Northvale, NJ: Jason Aronson.

Perry, B. E. (1952). *Aesopica.* Chicago, IL: University of Chicago Press.

Petirat Rabbenu ha-kadosh mi-Belz. (Hebrew). Lemberg, 1894.

Rabach, Berl. (1975). *The Kept Promise: Six Folktales from Galicia.* (Hebrew). Annotated by Otto Schnitzler. Haifa: IFA Publication Society.

Rodkinson-Frumkin, M. L. (1865). *'Adat Tzaddikim.* Lemberg.

Rush, Barbara, and Eliezer Marcus. (1980). *Seventy and One Tales for the Jewish Year: Folk Tales for the Festivals.* New York: American Zionist Youth Foundation.

Sadeh, Pinhas. (1989). *Jewish Folktales.* Trans. from the Hebrew by Hillel Halkin. New York: Doubleday.

Schram, Peninnah. (1987). *Jewish Stories One Generation Tells Another.* Northvale, NJ: Jason Aronson.

————, and Steven M. Rosman. (1990). *Eight Tales for Eight Nights: Stories for Chanukah.* Northvale, NJ: Jason Aronson.

————. (1991). *Tales of Elijah the Prophet.* Northvale, NJ: Jason Aronson.

————, ed. (1995). *Chosen Tales: Stories Told by Jewish Storytellers.* Northvale, NJ: Jason Aronson.

————, and Gerard Edery. (1999). *The Minstrel and the Storyteller: Stories and Songs of the Jewish People* (CD). New York: Sefarad Records.

Schwartz, Howard. (1988). *Miriam's Tambourine: Jewish Folktales from Around the World.* New York: Oxford University Press.

————. (1991). *Lilith's Cave: Jewish Tales of the Supernatural.* New York: Oxford University Press.

————. (1994). *Elijah's Violin & Other Jewish Fairy Tales.* New York: Oxford University Press.

————. (1996). *Next Year in Jerusalem: 3000 Years of Jewish Stories.* New York: Viking.

————. (1998). *Reimagining the Bible: The Storytelling of the Rabbis.* New York: Oxford University Press.

————, ed. (1991). *Gates to the New City: A Treasury of Modern Jewish Tales.* Northvale, NJ: Jason Aronson.

————, and Barbara Rush. (1999). *A Coat for the Moon.* Philadelphia: Jewish Publication Society.

Schwarzbaum, Haim. (1968). *Studies in Jewish and World Folklore.* Berlin: Walter De Gruyter & Co.

Sefer Hanokh. (1542). Venice.

Simon, Solomon. (1942). *The Wandering Beggar.* New York: Behrman House.

Teller, Hanoch. (1985). *Souled! Stories of Striving and Yearning* (Book 2). New York: New York City Publishing Company.

————. *Soul Survivors.* (1985). New York: New York Publishing Co.

Thompson, S. (1966). *Motif-Index of Folk Literature.* 6 vols. Rev. ed. Bloomington, IN and London: Indiana University Press.

Timpanelli, Gioia. (1998). *Sometimes the Soul: Two Novellas of Sicily.* New York: W. W. Norton & Company.

Valden, Aharon. (n.d.). *Kehal Hasidim.* (Hebrew). Warsaw.

Weinreich, Beatrice Silverman. (1988). *Yiddish Folktales.* Translated by Leonard Wolf. New York: Pantheon Books.

Wiesel, Elie. (1972). *Souls on Fire: Portraits and Legends of Hasidic Masters.* New York: Random House.

Wistinetski, Y. H., ed. (1538). *Sefer Hasidim.* (Hebrew). Bologna.

Yalkut Sippurim Umidrashim. (Hebrew). (1923). Warsaw.

Yassif, Eli. (1999). *The Hebrew Folktale: History, Genre, Meaning.* Translated from Hebrew by Jacqueline S. Teitelbaum. Bloomington, IN: Indiana University Press.

Yushzon, B., ed. (1976). *Me'otzranu Hayashan.* (Hebrew). Sifriyat Maariv.

Zipes, Jack. (1991). *Arabian Nights: The Marvels and Wonders of The Thousand and One Nights.* New York: Signet Classic/Penguin Books.

————, ed. (1991). *Spells of Enchantment: The Wondrous Fairy Tales of Western Culture.* New York: Viking.

————, ed. (2000). *The Oxford Companion to Fairy Tales.* New York: Oxford University Press.

Index

Abraham, 299
Abraham ben Samuel Ibn Hasdai
    of Barcelona, 11
Aesop, 14, 76
Aharanof, Elijahu Mani, 278
Akiva, R., 14, 21, 76
Al-Aldeni, R. Dovid, 52
Al-Harizi, Judah, 10
Al-Rashid, Caliph Harun, 230–
    243, 279
Alfonsi, Petrus, 12, 67
Ali, Prince, 280–286
Anderson, Walter, 265
Ansky, S., 87
Apuleius, 5
Arabian Nights, The, 1, 7–8, 35
Arabic culture, 9–10
Ari *See* Luria, R. Isaac
Asher, Mordecai, 223
Ashkenazi, Rivka, 311
Ashmedai, 306–310
Attias, Moshe, 131
Ausubel, 164

Baal HaNes *See* Meir, Rabbi
Baal Shem Tov, 17–20, 46, 82–
    87, 110, 115–118, 229,
    252–256
Baba, Ali, 304
Baer, R. Dov, 256
Baharav, Zalman, 229, 322
Bahlul, 312–316
Barukhof, Moshe, 278
Basile, Giambattista, 6–7
Bathsheba, 113–114
Beggers, 164
Behar, Dinah, 178
Benjamin, Walter, 210
Benjamin the Righteous, 188
Besht *See* Baal Shem Tov
Bialik, Chaim Nachman, 155
Bloch, Chaim, 56
Boccaccio, Giovanni, 5–6, 12
Bort, Moshe, 223
Boxed tales, 11
Bresnick-Perry, Roslyn, 47, 100,
    142, 207, 215

Broshi, Azriel, 322
Buber, Martin, 87
Bukhara, Emir of, 267–277
Burton, Richard, 13
Bushnaq, Inea, 210

Calvino, Italo, 210
Chaim, R., 81
Charity, 163
Chaucer, Geoffrey, 6
Cheicel-Hechal, Edna, 3, 159
Clawson, W. H., 3
Cohen, David, 174
Cohen, Elana Zohar, 188
Cohen, Flora, 188
Cohen, Ziona, 159

Dani'eli, Yonatan, 123
David, King, 88–90, 112–114
De France, Marie, 14, 76
De Leon, Moses, 15, 21
Dervish, 190–206
Dreams, 159–160, 179, 181, 223
Druse, Israeli, 210–211, 290
Dubno, Maggid of, 148–155 *See Also* Kranz, R. Yaakov

Eingeschachtelt, 2, 20–21
Elias, Ofra, 262
Eliezer, R., 52
Elijah the Prophet, 60, 159, 225–229, 300
Epstein, Morris, 8, 12

Fables, 14–15, 76, 155
Faigele, Rachel, 81
Falah, Salman, 210, 290

Fate, 179–181
Forty, The number, 304–305
Friendship, 62–68

Gabai, Sima, 242
Gabay, Abraham, 136
Galland, Antoine, 7
Gaon from Berditshev, 143
Gaster, Theodor H., 52–53
Gid'on, David, 35
Ginzberg, 52
Gittes, Katherine S., 3
Goldman, William, 24
Grimm Brothers, 7
Guggenheim, 78–79

Hanakdan, Berechiah ben Natronai, 14, 76–77
Haimovits, Moshe, 174, 326
Halprin, R. Yosef, 318–321
Haman, 161–162
Hanuka, Efraim, 251
Harlo, Jules, 155
Hasidism, 17
   oral tradition of, 56
   purpose of stories in, 18
   tales, 256
Hassan II, King, 160
Hatam, Queen, 190–193, 204–206
Healing leaves, 257–262
Hillel, 13
Hoca, Nasreddin, 90
Hodja, Nasruddin, 99

Ibn al-Fatih Ahmad ibn Husayni, 9
Ibn Zabara, Joseph, 10, 14, 76–77

Isaac ben Solomon Ibn Sahulah, 13
Israel, R., 17 *See Also* Baal Shem Tov
Israel ben Eliezer *See* Baal Shem Tov
Israel Folktale Archives (IFA), 3

Jacob, 299
Jacob Ben Eleazar, 11, 77
Joel, R., 11, 77
Joha, 164
John of Capua, 11–12, 77
Joseph, 224, 299–300
Justice, 175–178

Kabbalah, 16–17
    Lurianic, 16
Kaplan, R. Aryeh, 19, 46
Kasem, Abu, 33, 35
Kleiman, A. J., 118
Kosnitz, Maggid of, 110, 117
Kozenitz, Maggid of *See* Kosnitz, Maggid of
Kramer, Chaim, 46
Kranz, R. Jacob, 15, 164 *See Also* Dubno, Maggid of

Laba, Shelomo, 136
Leftwich, Joseph, 87
Levi, Akabab, 207
Lublin, Seer of, 110
Luria, R. Isaac, 16
Lying, 212–215

Maimonides, 9, 163
Makamat, 9–11, 13
Manchester, Dora Markman, 34

Manchester, Cantor Samuel E., 113
Mashlad, Menasheh, 248
Mendelssohn, Moses, 78–81
Me'ir, Peninnah, 265
Meir, R., 14, 76, 157–159
Messiras Nefesh, 67–68
Mintz, Jerone, 17
Mizrahi, Abraham Mordekhay, 159
Mizrahi, Hanina, 99, 207, 215, 316
Mizrahi, Rahel, 304
Money, 171–173
Moshol, 155

Nachman of Bratslav, R., 19–20, 24, 46–48, 54, 279
Nathan, R., 46
Nathan the Prophet, 113–114
Neugroschel, Joachim, 87
Nimshal, 155
Noy, Dov, 2, 19, 23, 51–52, 123, 131, 181, 211, 223–224, 262

Oikotype, 51, 142, 229
Ostropolier, Hershele, 164

Parable, 15, 60, 77, 113–114, 155, 164
    Jewish, 15, 155
    need for, 151–154
Pardes, 21–22, 25
Parrot, 47
Pearls, 2
Peretz, Isaac L., 68, 87
Perrault, Charles, 7

Pitre, Giuseppe, 47
Plagashvili, Semion, 229
Purim, 161–163

Rabakh, Berl, 329
Rabi, Moshe, 51
Riddles, 10–11, 60–61, 242,
    249–251, 265–266, 316
Rodkinson-Frumkin, M. L., 110,
    256
Rokeah of Belz, Joshua ben
    Shalom, 106–110
Romulus, 14, 76
Rush, Barbara, 155
Rushdie, Salman, 24

Sanzer Rav, 81
Sasson, the shepherd, 323–325
Schacter, R. Zalman, 51
Scheinfarber, Hinda, 31, 147
Schnitzler, Otto, 123
Schnorrers, 164
Schwartz, Cherie Karo, 53
Schwartz, Howard, 4, 19, 99, 110,
    155, 181, 256
Sela, Hadara, 31, 147
Serok, Eti, 304
Seventy, The number, 304–305
Shabsi, R., 115–117
Shamaka, Simkha, 287
Shamur, Sasson, 170
Shemesh, Aviva, 142
Shmelke of Nikolsburg, R., 87
Simeon bar Yohai, R., 15–16
Skills, 171–173
Sofer, Adon, 242
Solomon, King, 15, 57–61, 72,
    76, 89–90, 113, 311

Sosenski, Wolf, 178
Statya, Josef, 51
Stories-within-stories, 1–2, 5, 7,
    11, 14–15, 19–21, 24–25,
    114
    of the Middle Ages in Spain, 9
Story
    animal, 69–75, 178, 290
    chain, 3–4, 14
    cumulative, 4, 131, 207, 329
    frame, 2–4, 6–7, 9–13, 46, 67,
        77, 113, 188
    Jewish, 8–9, 21–24
    need for, 151–154
    and oral tradition, 24–25, 48
Straparola, Giovan Francesco, 6–7

Talmud, 7–8, 21, 52
Teller, Hanoch, 56, 81
Timpanelli, Gioia, 47
Truth, 175–178
Tye, King, 191–206

Ungratefulness, 244–247
Uriah the Hittite, 113–114

Valden, Aharon, 110
Von Noyshaf, Yacov, 161

Walker, Barbara K., 90
Weinreich, Beatrice, 87
Wiesel, Elie, 81
Will, Ethical, 299

Yassif, Eli, 4, 215
Yehoshua ben Hananya, R., 265
Yehoshua, Ben-Zion, 105
Yehoshua-Raz, Refael, 105

Yeshiva, Miriam, 163, 265
Yitzhak ben David, 111
Yitzhak of Berditshev, R. Levi,
    147, 318, 320–322
Yitzhak, Sasson, 326
Yushzon, B., 81

Zehariah, 165–169
Zemer-Tov, Jacob, 181
Zipes, Jack, 13
Zohar, 16–17, 21
Zohar, Jacob, 299
Zohara, Princess, 280–286

About the Author

Peninnah Schram, an internationally known storyteller, author, and recording artist, is Associate Professor of Speech and Drama at Yeshiva University's Stern College and Azrieli Graduate School. As a storyteller, she is known for her elegant and dynamic way of telling stories. Her books include *Jewish Stories One Generation Tells Another* and *Tales of Elijah the Prophet*. She has recorded six folktales on the CD *The Minstrel and the Storyteller: Stories and Songs of the Jewish People*, performed with singer/guitarist Gerard Edery. She is a recipient of the prestigious Covenant Award for Outstanding Jewish Educators from The Covenant Foundation and The Circle of Excellence Award from the National Storytelling Network. She lives in New York City.